Doing Battle

OTHER BOOKS BY PAUL FUSSELL

Theory of Prosody in Eighteenth-Century England

Poetic Meter and Poetic Form

The Rhetorical World of Augustan Humanism:
Ethics and Imagery from Swift to Burke

Samuel Johnson and the Life of Writing

The Great War and Modern Memory

Abroad: British Literary Traveling Between the Wars

The Boy Scout Handbook and Other Observations

Class: A Guide through the American Status System

Thank God for the Atom Bomb and Other Essays

Wartime: Understanding and Behavior in the Second World War

BAD: or, The Dumbing of America

The Anti-Egotist: Kingsley Amis, Man of Letters

EDITOR

English Augustan Poetry

The Ordeal of Alfred M. Hale

Siegfried Sassoon's Long Journey

The Norton Book of Travel

The Norton Book of Modern War

CO-EDITOR

Eighteenth-Century English Literature

Doing Battle

THE MAKING OF A SKEPTIC

PAUL FUSSELL

LITTLE, BROWN AND COMPANY

BOSTON NEW YORK TORONTO LONDON

First Edition

Copyright acknowledgments appear on p. 300

Library of Congress Cataloging-in-Publication Data

Fussell, Paul
    Doing Battle : the making of a skeptic / by Paul
Fussell. — 1st ed.
    p. cm.
    Includes index.
    ISBN 0-316-29717-8
    1. Fussell, Paul. 2. English teachers — United States —Biography.
    3. Critics — United States — Biography. I. Title.
PE64.F85A3 1996
820.9 — dc20   96-3451

10 9 8 7 6 5 4 3 2 1

HAD

Published simultaneously in Canada
by Little, Brown & Company (Canada) Limited

Printed in the United States of America

*

To the Memory of
Three Teachers at Pomona College
Who Encouraged Me,

Joseph Warner Angell
Charles Shiveley Holmes
Frederick Ludwig Mulhauser

*

TO THE READER

Late in the afternoon of March 15, 1945, in a small woods in south-eastern France, Boy Fussell, aged twenty, was ill treated by members of the German Wehrmacht. His attackers have never been identified and brought to justice. How a young person so innocent was damaged this way and what happened as a result is the subject of this book.

ACKNOWLEDGMENTS

I am happy to acknowledge help from Caroline Beatty, Ted Dow, Donald Fanger, Betty Fussell, Edwin Sill Fussell, Samuel Wilson Fussell, Toby Harke, George Justice, Florence Fussell Lind, Lawrence T. Lorimer, Donald M. Pattison, John Scanlan, James H. Silberman, John F. Votaw, and Andrew Woods. Carl Nichols, M.D., onetime second lieutenant, 410th Infantry, has jogged some of my wartime memories, and I am grateful for his comradely assistance. Carl Dawson's book *November 1948* has stimulated many of these memories. Richard M. Stannard's *Infantry: An Oral History of a WWII American Infantry Battalion* has helped me recover details of Company F, 410th Infantry, in 1944 and 1945. The "Delinquent Elegies" in Donald W. Baker's book *Unposted Letters* have brought back my own images of dead army youngsters. Although about quite a different war and its effect upon a different young man, W. D. Ehrhart's *Vietnam-Perkasie: A Combat Marine Memoir* has been an inspiring model of clear-sightedness and artistic energy. And I have been heartened by the interest and sympathy of Roy Livengood, historian of the Ninety-first Infantry Division in the Second World War.

I must thank the administrators of the Morgan Lectureship at Dickinson College for the opportunity to present some of this material to faculty, students, and friends of the college. I have recycled parts of the essay "My War," which first appeared in *Harper's*, January 1982, as well as bits from my book *Thank God for the Atom Bomb and Other Essays*. But my deepest debt is to Harriette, my wife. Her love has sustained me throughout.

Doing Battle

— I —

$\mathcal{A}$LSACE, THE GERMANIZED eastern province of France with borders on Germany and Switzerland, has a few large cities like Strasbourg, Nancy, and Colmar, but for the most part it is a land of farms and small towns, a poor place, where in 1944 and 1945 the inhabitants (most of dubious loyalty to the Allied cause) eked out a hard living in picturesque but primitive houses and barns, set in the midst of steaming manure piles. The most impoverished people slept with their animals to keep warm and wore wooden shoes to negotiate the mixture of mud and cow dung that was underfoot during winter and early spring. There was a small town every few miles, and the one I was in on March 12, 1945, was named Obermodern. I was a twenty-year-old second lieutenant, the leader of a rifle platoon in Company F of the 410th Infantry, 103rd Division.

In one officers' bull session at the company command post, the dining room of a house whose family had long before fled the shells that frequently landed in the town, someone commented on the number of American tanks in the vicinity and wondered if an attack was being prepared. Trying to persuade myself, I scoffed at the idea, arguing that we'd never attack again in our sector. Why would we? After all, Patton to our north was outflanking the Siegfried Line, and anything we did in Alsace would be a foolish waste of energy.

Then, melodrama: the company commander entered, just back from a briefing at battalion headquarters. His face was solemn, notable because his accustomed relation to higher authority, while essentially respectful, had in it an element of play. (His normal reaction to any silly order emanating from battalion was "Fuck 'em'!") He was bringing back the news that Operation "Undertone" was about to begin, which meant that the whole Seventh Army would go on the attack on March 15. The 103rd Division would be in the lead, and our second battalion — that is, us — had been elected to make the main effort in the initial breakthrough. We were to seize by 9:00 A.M. the town of Gundershoffen, a few miles ahead, and establish there a bridgehead over a small river running through the town, thus securing passage for an armored column that was to pass through us and link up with the Third Army. The theory was that this would envelop numerous German units. After this dire briefing, we four platoon leaders set to work spreading the word among our men, issuing our own orders, checking equipment, and accumulating ammunition and K rations. And trying to keep our own anxieties from showing.

My sergeants received the news with their usual composure. Indeed, it was their skill at controlling emotion that, among other things, had earned them their stripes in the first place. Platoon Sergeant Edward K. Hudson busied himself concealing his fear beneath an elaborately busy act of "checking" on the three squads' material preparedness for attack. At this stage (we'd been in combat four months) we all assumed that no moral, psychological, or spiritual preparation would be necessary. The three squad leaders were excellent young men but all notably different. Sergeant Nelson, from somewhere in Scandinavian America, had a tipped-up nose and looked rather like an elf when he smiled, which was often. He was bright and loyal and courageous. Sergeant Partin, from somewhere in the South, was less bright, but he was solid and entirely trustworthy. Sergeant Engle, another Southerner, now and then constituted a problem, for he was the smartest of all of them. Back in training, Hudson had suggested that I bust him to private for impertinence, and I had. When we went overseas he regained his rank, although he was still given to impudence and sly resistance. But he knew his stuff and could manage his men.

The night before the attack, Hudson and I for the first time slept together, for we were very seldom in a house with a double bed. Fully clothed, we occupied an immense *lit matrimonial* in the house serving as our platoon headquarters and went to sleep immediately, escaping into lucky oblivion from the menaces promised in the morning. At 3:00 A.M. we got up, strapped on our equipment, and joined the rest of F Company in a small abandoned local café for a real breakfast. The company on this occasion included the cooks, whom we'd not seen for months. They had come up during the night with their stoves and pots and pans, and they regaled us with a heartening hot breakfast: biscuits, shit-on-a-shingle, real coffee with canned milk. Noted but made light of were the condemned-men implications of all this.

H-Hour is 6:30. By that time we've marched two or three miles in darkness and arrived at the edge of a woods on a hill overlooking a shallow valley with a narrow river. As the light comes up, I suddenly recognize the place I'm standing as the setting-off point of two failed night patrols I've led my platoon on. Not a happy augury of success now. At 6:30, seven hundred guns open up behind us, laying down a fifteen-minute barrage in front and also informing the Germans that we are about to attack. As the barrage ends, we notice a tiny figure zigzagging back from the battlefield-to-be. It proves to be a combat engineer, who has been out there some time in the dark, getting ready to ignite the smoke pots, which are now belching a blinding, choking white chemical smoke designed to conceal us as we attack.

As we get ready to move forward, because of the trees I can see only three or four men of my platoon, disposed along the front of the woods at ten-yard intervals. They look toward me with white faces. Although I think I am no more scared than usual, this time my mouth is dry and it seems hard to get my breath. I hear a whistle blast behind and step forward, shouting in a loud, would-be firm voice, "Let's go!" We step off and soon we are running downhill. We don't think of the mines we might be stepping on, and luckily we don't meet any. But the adjacent units have a less happy experience: they run into a field filled with wooden Schu-mines, and many feet and lower legs are blown off. One man in Company G to our left lost his foot that day, and later he noted a home truth familiar to us all: "Sooner or later you're going to get it in combat. You can't roll the dice every day and not get waxed."

The smoke, which almost blinded us and made us cough and curse, I now realized was to conceal exactly where we were crossing the river. I don't remember how we did it. A single footbridge, emplaced in the night by the engineers? Long logs thrown across the banks? Whatever, we got across and, still running, were soon in the midst of a small town our artillery had just destroyed, leaving flocks of audibly angry poultry and many Germans, freshly killed. We kept going and, breathing hard now and gesturing toward the rear the German prisoners who came up to us, crying, cringing, gibbering — the artillery had done its unimaginably cruel work — we reached the top of a low hill overlooking a compact woods. The Germans had by now got their artillery firing, and shells landed among us. Being lazy and inept, we did not immediately dig in but lay out in the open for an hour, cowering from the shells and wondering what to do.

Finally the order came down to cross an eight-foot-high road embankment and assemble on the other side, away from the enemy. We did this by platoons. By this time the road was a machine-gun target, and as each man plunged frantically across, he occasioned a burst. I was not terribly scared by the artillery shells, which clearly weren't being observed but only fired mechanically according to some prearranged plan. What terrified me was the obviously observed machine-gun fire I'd have to race crossing the road. The two scouts and Hudson had gone first and got across safely, and I sent the others over one by one, remaining behind until I should have to go over myself. Noticing my hesitancy, a sharp-eyed lieutenant colonel warned me to get myself together or I'd be in a lot of trouble. Thus rebuked, I took a deep breath, climbed up the embankment, scuttered across the asphalt where the machine-gun bullets were striking off sparks, and tumbled, unhit, down the embankment on the other side. The lieutenant colonel had accurately diagnosed the cause of my delay — sheer unofficer-like terror.

We now had the embankment between us and the Germans in the woods, which we were going to have to clear. It was already well past the 9:00 deadline for arriving at the bridgehead town. In fact, it was now three in the afternoon and the orders from battalion to get moving became increasingly impatient, shrill, and, finally, insulting. In the absence of reconnaissance, which might have suggested a more clever tactical solution, the quickest way to take the woods, it was clear, was by sudden direct assault. That day we had two heavy machine guns with the company, directed by Second Lieutenant Raymond Biedrzycki (pronounced *Bedricki*), a phlegmatic former sergeant recently field commissioned. On a whistle signal from F Company commander, these were suddenly lifted to the top of the embankment and began traversing fire along the near edge of the woods, while we, bayonets fixed, climbed up and over, cursing and yelling and firing at the woods as we ran. It was very like going over the top in the Great War, an effect enhanced by the two water-cooled machine guns on their heavy tripods firing continuously over our heads. They were Model 1917, exactly the same as in the First World War. From this frontal attack on a prepared German position, I expected a ghastly carnage of the Great War type, but nearing the woods and looking back over the field we'd just crossed, expecting to see there the bodies of the dead and wounded, I saw nothing but an occasional gas mask and folded raincoat, discarded in the rush.

We were doing fine until we entered the woods. Then, rifle and machine-gun fire began immediately. Many of us were hit before we could throw ourselves down. Shouted orders could not be heard over the noise, and paralyzed by the machine-gun fire an inch above our heads (you could feel the heat of the bullets), we could only hope that someone else was applying some means of relief. Hudson and I, a foot apart, were bellowing at each other in our frustration, anger, and fear. While pressing every inch of me into the ground as tightly as possible, I managed a look to the left, to see one of my men, a stout blond youth, suddenly rise and, kneeling, level his rifle at the machine gun. There was a savage burst of fire, and out of the back of his field jacket, just where, on the other side, his heart would be, flew little clouds of dust, cloth, blood, and human tissue. He was a new replacement whose name I'd not yet learned. Looking to the right, I saw a similar scene: Sergeant Engle stood up to return fire, and the machine gun caught him right in the mouth. He dropped to his knees, and, looking toward Hudson and me, spit out his blood and teeth onto the green forest floor. Thank God, at that point one of my men, quite un-ordered-to, slipped around with a grenade, flanked the machine gun, and destroyed it together with its teenaged operator. Sergeant Engle we could do nothing to help, for we were obeying the order "Leave the wounded to be cared for by the medics and press on." (Magically, he survived, to become, after years of facial reconstruction, an Episcopal minister.)

In shock as we all were — this was by far the worst combat we'd faced so far — we moved forward in the woods, encountering trenches and dugouts the Germans had been preparing for months. Most of them now wanted to surrender, and as we shouted, "Kommen Sie heraus, Hände hoch!" they dragged themselves out, weeping and hoping not to be killed in anger. Many were. Now and then one of our men, annoyed at too much German delay in vacating a position, would throw in a live grenade, saying things like "Here. Divide that among you." Once we began rampaging inside the forest, the conflict turned decidedly unfair. One man recalls, "We did all the shooting. They did all the dying." We must have killed thirty or forty and captured more than that. Some of the captured, we found, were wearing GI woolen trousers, seized from some overrun U.S. quartermaster warehouse, doubtless in the Bulge. It was a tradition of the line that Germans caught with American clothing or equipment be treated harshly. We made these poor scared souls remove their trousers, kicking them severely in their butts to make our point clear.

When we reached the farther side of the woods, we began reorganizing to continue the attack, although it was now well past four o'clock. Along this far edge of the woods there were some large earth-and-log bunkers, once the dormitories of the defending troops. Together with Sergeant Hudson and Lieutenant Biedrzycki, I sat on top of one to plan our next move. Suddenly, off to the left, at the forward edge of the woods, a deafening *crack!* Then, five seconds later, another, closer. And then, another, still closer. Something like a tank or self-propelled gun was firing systematically across the edge of the woods, and my men were leaping into whatever cover they could find. Many threw themselves into the entrance of the bunker the three of us were on top of, but many couldn't make it: there were cries and shouts, and one man screamed, "They blew my legs off! They blew my legs off!" Hudson, Biedrzycki, and I did not take cover, and the reason is curious. I stayed put because, virtually accused once of cowardice, I didn't want to be seen being ostentatiously prudent a second time. The other two followed my lead in remaining in the open, I imagine because I was the senior and they thought they should follow my lead. Now, curiously, I was thoroughly brave. As the shells came closer and closer, the three of us lay flat: by then there was nothing else to do, for the time to take cover had quite run out. Then, an unspeakably loud metallic *clang!* right overhead. It was the loudest sound I'd ever heard. I was temporarily deaf, and in the sudden silence I drifted for an instant back to my serene beginning.

The Pasadena I was born into, in 1924, thoroughly deserved its reputation as a highly privileged "suburb" — the word had not yet taken on pejorative overtones. It was a dull, safe, trim little city of some sixty thousand where those who commuted to the tougher Los Angeles eleven miles away returned in the evenings to raise families in gentility and peace.

Southern California was not yet synonymous with shallowness, compulsory "leisure," show business, and sleaze. For many it was a serious place, and Pasadena especially seemed a moral oasis in the midst of the surrounding drink, sex, drugs, and gambling. The tone was that of Midwestern uprightness, and the rules were plain: do not smoke, or drink, or swear, or gamble; attend church; pay your bills immediately; work hard; tell no lies; succeed — and never buy anything on the installment plan. Pasadena, says social historian Kevin Starr,

> *once upon a time constituted a state of mind. Here the genteel tradition grafted itself onto Southern California circumstances. Pasadena embodied the certainties and pursuits of the white Protestant upper middle classes: education, refinement, a cautiously progressive point of view on social and political issues, all of it modified but not enervated by the sunshine of Southern California. Thus Pasadenans played tennis and golf and spent time at country clubs but they also read books and cared intensely about literature and serious theater.*

Like Arizona and other salubrious places in the Southwest, California had earned among Eastern physicians a reputation as a warm, dry environment beneficial to tuberculosis patients. In the pre-antibiotic days when I was young, it was still a haunt of TB sufferers. In the early 1920s a number of local physicians established The

Preventorium, an institution for needy tubercular boys from the East. Some hotels — like the Hotel Green — seemed populated entirely by patients, wheeled out on balconies to relish the warm sun and air or pushed slowly around the grounds. Peace and quiet dominated: the number of electric automobiles silently tooling around the streets with old ladies at their joysticks must have set a record for similar towns.

It was a place of some wealth and patrician social responsibility. The streets were immaculate. Because of the benign weather, street crosswalks stayed brightly white for years, and pedestrians had always the right-of-way when crossing. The public schools were superb, a model for the nation, and the city government (run by a city manager, not a mayor) was incorruptible, performing its functions in a tasteful Italian Renaissance domed city hall. The police and fire departments were known for their discipline and efficiency. Churches abounded, and Sunday was spent attending them. There was an impressive public library with eight branches, situated so that no resident would live more than a mile from one. The national yearly per capita average of library books borrowed was four. In Pasadena, it was twelve. Well before the Volstead Act in 1919, Pasadena had made up its mind on the liquor question and prohibited saloons within the city limits. But for all these amenities, an opera house would have been unthinkable: this was a philistine city, and despite its attractiveness, profoundly un-European in its self-satisfied puritanism.

If not entirely Anglo-Saxon, the population seemed distinctly Caucasian. There was, to be sure, a "colored" district, but one never passed through it, nor through the places where the "Mexicans" were said to live. The few Japanese were silent, industrious gardeners working meticulously around upper-middle-class premises. Anyone dropped into Pasadena for the first time might have been tempted to designate it Luckyville, for it seemed to have reached the condition all American places aspired to in the 1920s and 1930s: it was beautiful, peaceful, harmonious, comfortable. If Los Angeles was, sadly, an example of the Real, Pasadena came close to representing the Ideal.

It was tuberculosis that caused my father, Paul Fussell (I am officially Jr.), to be born in Pasadena in the first place. Without that, he would have been a native of Wallingford, Pennsylvania, a suburb of Philadelphia, and would probably have become a member of the Pennsylvania bar. His mother, Sara Haswell, had married Edwin Neal Fussell, the son of a local physician. Edwin was variously a typesetter, a traveling cigar merchant, and a post-office inspector. He and Sara had had one son, Edwin Briggs Fussell, before a doctor diagnosed the young father's tuberculosis and advised an immediate move to a warmer climate. At great sacrifice but hopefully, the Fussell family moved to Pasadena, where Sara's husband soon died. But not before a second son, my father, was born. Sara Fussell, early widowed and with no income to speak of, brought up her two boys on the minuscule salary of a grade school teacher, augmented, in due course, by the small ad hoc earnings of her boys. My father, for example, sold aluminum kitchen ware door-to-door. His brother grew fonder of drinking, smoking, and swearing than Pasadena and his mother approved of, and after high school he took off for Seattle, where he embarked on a lifelong career as an editorial writer for the Seattle *Post-Intelligencer*. Unlike his brother, who stayed in Pasadena and looked after his mother, E. B. Fussell became a fervent Democrat and conservationist, throwing himself into the populist battle against the "lumber interests."

In those days very few young people continued their education past high school, and in those days a high school education, in a well-to-do place like Pasadena, was effective preparation for a life not only of worldly success but of judgment. For example, Edmund Burke's *On Conciliation with the Colonies*, not the easiest work of thought and rhetoric for adolescents, was widely taught in high schools. And discussed and debated. Today it's seldom read even in "universities." When I was a boy my father was my only relative who'd graduated not just from a university (California, 1917), but from a law school as well (Boldt Hall). In those places he distinguished himself as a notable hard worker and puritan — his chastity and sobriety were the wonder of his friends — and he was conspicuous as a debater and quick thinker. Not long ago, I was told by one of his former law partners, Secretary of State Warren Christopher, that my father possessed "the quickest mind of any man I've known."

Their law firm was O'Melveny & Myers in Los Angeles, and my father devoted himself to corporation law. When he was born in 1895, California had been a state of the Union for only forty-five years — aristocratic Spanish families were still to be met with — and there was a great deal of incorporating to be done, of such new enterprises as the real estate business and soon the film industry, and later, the aircraft-building companies. And always, of course, oil.

He rose rapidly in the law and was soon financially stable. Then comfortable. Then rich — one reason, together with the benignity of Pasadena, that Paul Fussell Jr. was so easily insulated from the real world. Raised by a hyperstrict mother, my father did not drink or smoke, nor did he gamble or swear. Indeed, I heard him swear only once. When I was in junior high school I committed some misdemeanor with a bean blower, as I recall. When he heard of it, he grew red and permitted a "Damn" to escape his lips, an offense never to be repeated. When Santa Anita "Park" was built, he strenuously objected to the pari-mutuel activity there. When he had to attend parties where drinking was going on, he stuck resolutely to ginger ale. Although he finally had to tolerate his children's cigarettes, he never smoked at all, barring some preposterous experiments with a pipe when he was a boy ordnance officer in the First World War. What he did do was work, to support his mother and his own family. You did that sort of thing then, especially if you came from Pennsylvania church stock, both Presbyterian and Quaker.

The intellectual and social superiority of Father's family to Mother's was always assumed. It had produced, we were told, a flock of teachers and physicians, and one distant relative, William Shepherd, was said to have been in the boat when Washington crossed the Delaware to harass the British at the Battle of Trenton in 1776. The Fussell family claimed artistic distinction as well. It was proud that a great-uncle of mine, Charles L. Fussell, had been a student of Thomas Eakins at the Pennsylvania Academy of the Fine Arts.

Because they were less given to such social bragging and self-satisfaction, I knew less about Mother's side of the family than Father's. Wilhma Wilson Sill was born in 1894 in Bloomington, Illinois. If one of my grandfathers was a casualty of tuberculosis, the other was a casualty of mass production. Mother's father, William David Sill, was early employed as a carriage trimmer: that meant that with his own hands he put the fringe on top of surreys and installed the upholstery. The rise of the automobile industry ruined that trade, and father, mother, and beautiful blonde girl-child moved all the way west to new possibilities in Pasadena. Here, her father performed a series of odd jobs like house painting and carpentry while she attended high school and, for a short while, the University of California at Berkeley. (Her college ukulele, a conventional fixture in those raccoon-coat days, became one of my toys.) She knew my father at high school and college, and their acquaintance ended in marriage and the birth of three children: Edwin in 1922, two years later Paul Jr., and Florence in 1926.

Mother's parents were extremely modest and kind. Her mother we kids denominated Marblenanna for her practice of giving us marbles when we visited. (Father's mother was Chickinanna: she, like so many others in those days, raised chickens.) Grandfather Sill, tall and slender with a white mustache, projected the dignity of a quietly decent, very private working man. I never saw him wearing anything but a three-piece salt-and-pepper suit. (The idea of him dressed in anything like "leisure wear" is quite unthinkable.) We children loved both the elder Sills in a way we never could the punctilious, didactic, constantly fault-finding Chickinanna. In the conventional style of mothers-in-law, she took every opportunity to demean and humiliate the alien woman who had had the impertinence to marry her son. Regardless, we liked visiting Chickinanna because of the cuckoo clock in her living room, from which the little bird appeared regularly to flap its wooden wings and to "cuckoo" the time. Every night, the clock was wound up by pulling to the top two cast-iron weights shaped like elongated pinecones. In the style of the period was a conviction of my mother's sustained by her mother-in-law, namely, the persuasion that she was distinctly subordinate to her husband and properly devoted not to matters of moment but to details of feeding, laundry, and minor discipline, with an occasional revel at a women's club. Mother always asserted that she stemmed from Irish stock, partly, I suspect, to annoy Anglophile Father.

My earliest and most innocent memories are of our first house, a small bungalow on Pasadena's Waldo Avenue, a modest street on the Los Angeles side of town and thus fine for commuting. This house had not had the benefit, unlike our later ones, of thoroughly snobbish zoning ordinances, and nearby were laundries, commercial garages, and auto-parts and repair businesses. Snapshot evidence indicates how vigorously under the sidewalk peppertrees Ed and I played out with tricycles and wagons a mimic version of Southern California automobile culture. There's little evidence that we ever played with our sister.

In this house, still in a crib, I conceived a similarity in form, if not function, between a size D flashlight battery and a jar of Vaseline. There, in the backyard, I once witnessed the silent movement, in and out of each other's coils, of a nest of black snakes. Not yet acquainted with the lore of snakes, I wasn't at all afraid of them. They looked to me as harmless as a basket of kittens. But there was one frightening moment in my earliest years. A black maid had lit the gas oven carelessly, and the resulting explosion had burned off her eyebrows and lashes without causing further damage. Her appearance scared me, and I had to be comforted and assured that she was really all right.

From overheard gossip we children were able to understand that a "depression" was underway, but we didn't know enough economics or sociology to wonder at our father's choosing, just now, to build a costly, luxurious upper-middle-class house on the other, and much better, side of town, where instead of auto-repair shops, one found Cal Tech and the Huntington Library. This new house was an eloquent registration of Father's sentimental Anglophilia. Where did a young Californian pick up such a thing? Partly in law school, of course, as he spent lonely nights over *Blackstone's Commentaries* and mastered Coke upon Littleton. But partly also from the several months he spent at Trinity College, Cambridge, after the First World War had ended with thousands of idle American soldiers in Europe and little shipping to bring them home. Many were put to studious waiting, at Oxford, Cambridge, and the Sorbonne, a novel experience of learned civility few forgot. Ever after, Father displayed in his oak-paneled "den" a print of the Great Court of Trinity and carved wood plaques displaying the "arms," in bright red and white, of that college and of the university. Not to be outdone in the social-class competition, Mother displayed in the hall her own family's "coat of arms," attained from a mail-order company. It featured a shield, with crossed weapons, ribbons, and a helmet on top, and below, the motto *Tam Fidus, Quam Fixus,* satirically translated by my brother as the motto of an early repairman, "I am Fidus who fixes."

Not surprisingly, this first house Father had built for his family aped a compact British manor house, as understood in Southern California. Outside, it featured dark brown beams against light brown stucco with a shingled porte cochere, diamond-paned leaded windows, and servants' quarters — that is, a maid's room with bath. The lot was not large enough for such authentic touches as sheep to keep the grass cut or a fake ruined Gothic tower in the distance, but we did have such luxuries as a stagnant water-lily pool in the backyard, together with a sundial on a fluted concrete pedestal. In its quiet and secure "British" way, the house made an anti-California statement, nestled as it was between two more conventional "Spanish"-style houses with white plaster facades, colored tiles, and terra-cotta roofs.

While father was an "attorney" — he seldom referred to himself as a lawyer — our neighbors in the Spanish-style houses were, on the one side, a society dentist and, on the other, the owner of a flourishing lumberyard. We got along well with the no-nonsense lumberyard man, but the dentist was not in great favor with our teetotal family, for he gave stylish and noisy cocktail parties in his large screened porch in back, and the smell of gin was often perceptible way over in our yard. Sometimes the giggling and shrieking didn't stop until late at night. Other than this cluster of three houses, our street was remarkably empty, vacant lots, largely devoid of trees, stretching endlessly in all directions.

Father was too busy and sensible to go in for the pseudomystical line that California was other than another state of the Union, full of promise, all right, but without very strong metaphoric meaning. For him, it was not a place for exotic dream fulfillment but for profitable investment. For a short while he found himself in a group called Native Sons of the Golden West, but the lapel pin of this organization, complete with sturdy golden bear, he kept buried in his shirt-stud box. He died in 1973, providentially escaping the California that seemed to offer a natural theater for sillies like Zsa Zsa Gabor and crazies like Patricia Hearst. I doubt that he knew that Christopher Isherwood and Don Bachardy lived nearby and seemed to many to establish the appropriate California tone. For Father, California was a place more like, say, Oregon than Oz. It was a place for grown-ups well past the mental age when life could be conceived of as an animated cartoon, or the state imagined as a magnet for every pothead, drunk, egotist, and eccentric in the United States, an El Dorado of fools, Charles Mansons, and O. J. Simpsons.

Father was always formal, and except at the beach, he wore a dark blue or gray suit. His normal spoken idiom seemed to combine the genteel-euphemistic with the legal. He was fond of saying "save" instead of "except," and in identifying people in group snapshots by writing in white ink on the black pages of photo albums, he'd specify himself not as PF but as *Self*. He was not exactly a philistine, but he had virtually no interest in art or any music but light classics and operettas like *The Desert Song*. His views of painting and sculpture adhered to the strictly representational. He could stomach a bit of impressionism, but painting in cubist and surrealist modes struck him as simply "perverted." Some of his pronunciations marked him as careful and slightly archaic. "Chocolate" became *chack-let,* and in "doctorate" (a word he loved), he gave the final syllable the sound of *ate.* As he aged, "language" became *langridge.* As his abstention from profanity might imply — obscenity was simply unthinkable — he controlled anger, and he was amazingly good-natured, and to his relatives, including his children, astonishingly kind and generous. To his issue, stock certificates and trust funds became familiar, and there were large and unadvertised benefactions to charities and colleges.

But to me, his and my mother's greatest gift was a constant moral emphasis. This or that film was forbidden as "not suitable." Lying, stealing, cruelty, damaging property were sins not to be toyed with or easily expiated. The idea of *conscience* was to Mother as real as the idea of *the soul.* The two were innate and intimately related to each other. For me, there's no difficulty following Auden's advice to himself in "A Lullaby":

praise your parents who gave you
a Super-Ego of strength
that saved you so much bother.

That "English" house was our family headquarters until the end of the Second World War, and we children grew used to space and

18

comfort. Each of us had a bedroom, and in mine, the largest, there was room for, ultimately, a film and magic-show "theater," a darkroom, and a print shop, in addition to a double-deck bunk, where I entertained overnight guests. The house was only two blocks from an excellent grammar school, to which we walked with ease, the weather being usually benign, requiring no wraps, overshoes, or similar "East Coast" impedimenta. At Hamilton School it would seem that the main emphasis was on "creative" work, and my memories are less of the multiplication tables (which I never really mastered) than of poster paints, easels, and pots of clay covered with damp cloths. One unforgettable event was a kite-flying competition, with the kites made and decorated by ourselves.

I loved this school without reservation until the bugle-blowing humiliation. Somehow, I found myself furnished with a bugle and with it the obligation to play every morning "To the Colors" at the base of the school flagpole while Old Glory was slowly pulled to the top by two boys — who broke into uncontrollable giggles when they perceived that I couldn't play the bugle at all. I had grossly insufficient lung power, and nothing came out but a series of fartlike toots, in the proper rhythm but all on the same "note." Finally I was relieved of this daily humiliation by some music lover tossing a marble down the bell of the bugle. It stuck and entirely resisted removal, and that was the end of bugle blowing. After this shame-making proceeding (it must have lasted two weeks), I became less enthusiastic about infantine group life and its invitations to show off.

But there were other humiliations not my fault. One Halloween my loving mother decided that I should be costumed as Mickey Mouse. A whiz with the Singer, she ran up an outfit involving black tights, outsize shoes and gloves, and a little pair of red shorts with two large yellow buttons in front that made me cringe with shame.

It was at this school that several unattractive aspects of my character became apparent, at least to me. One was impatience and boredom, leading to anger at the slowness of others. In a class in "painting," I was once publicly shamed for applying paint without waiting for the undercoat to dry.

Miss Weatherhead: "Class, remember what I told you. Wet paint upon wet paint does what?"

Class (in delighted unison): "SMEARS!"

I also lied very often, and was often found out. It was that habit, together with my physical and intellectual vanity, that triggered one memorable occasion.

The desks we were assigned were arranged in permanent files, with about eight desks lined up behind one another. They all looked the same, and it was not easy to remember which desk was one's own. Behind me sat a very cute blonde girl I had a crush on, a feeling I imagined she reciprocated, and in spades, since I was really, I knew, better looking even than she was. She was extremely proud of one of her possessions her doting parents had given her, a green fountain pen that wrote with green ink.

One day I was thrilled, if not exactly surprised, to find that she had secretly made me a present of this precious thing, placing it without explanation (none, I conceived, was needed) in the drawer of my desk. When no one was looking I slipped it into my pocket, elevated by all the erotic and social self-satisfactions a ten-year-old could be expected to feel at such a loving gift. But the next day, all was revealed: the teacher announced that the girl's treasured pen was not in her desk drawer — she was crying bitterly — and had anyone seen it? Silence. And on my part, horror. Impossible to confess what had happened, that she had merely mistaken my desk for her own, for then my intense self-love would be revealed to all. The search for the pen went on for several days, during which I saw with terror some faint stains of green ink on my fingers. Finally, afraid that it would somehow be discovered at home rolled up among the clean handkerchiefs in my dresser drawer, I seized a moment when no one was around and buried it in a vacant lot behind our house.

My later hatred of compulsory "physical education" I can date from Hamilton School. Once we were commanded to remove our shoes and grasp a marble in the toes of each foot to carry across the floor. My marbles wouldn't stay picked up, and hostile questions were asked as to why I couldn't perform this simple exercise. But if I failed there, I managed to succeed elsewhere, especially in reading and spelling, and spelling was still taken very seriously as an intellectual achievement. My distinction in the language arts resulted in my skipping a grade, gratifying at the time but ironically a lifelong curse, making me always a year younger than everyone else wherever I found myself, especially the army.

But to Hamilton School I owe a great deal, not least because it inadvertently provided my first orgasm, suggesting thereby some of the delight and wonder available in the future. It was when I was about twelve, enjoying a bus excursion to the Los Angeles County Museum, a fascinating eclectic showcase of Indian artifacts, early Hollywood memorabilia (Chaplin's large black shoes, for one thing), and prehistoric animal skeletons dragged from the La Brea tar pits. The afternoon, which I'd enjoyed mightily, was over and it was time to return to the bus. I was late and fearful of a reprimand, and I ran breathlessly down a hill to the bus below. Suddenly, I was seized by the oddest, most magical, most powerful, most delicious spasm of pleasure in my loins. There was no ejaculation, but an unmistakable foretaste of something valuable, mysterious, and profoundly private. When my friends asked why I looked so odd, I knew I'd felt something I could never convey to them. Had God — in whom I didn't believe — visited me with a sign of His love and power? Or was I some sort of freak, destined to hover always on the outskirts of humanity?

There was no audible answer then or later, for Mother and Father were as shy as I was in bringing up such topics. Indeed, in those days, no one seemed willing to explain intimate details, and those of us who did learn (sort of) had our schoolmates for teachers. Public school teachers never dealt with such topics, and certainly Sunday school teachers did not.

Urged by Chickinanna, the family attended the Pasadena Presbyterian Church regularly, where we were regaled with fairly dignified music and high-class sermons by our venerable Scottish minister. To sustain group piety during the week, there were also dismal "Father-Son" suppers on Wednesdays, with group singing of "Marching Along Together" and similar Kiwanis favorites. These occasions might have been a good time for a bit of instruction in sexual hygiene, but no such thing took place. These meetings were conducted by a very nasty Christian Education young man with curly yellow hair and a goody-goody rhetoric passing belief. Cocoa was served, and its being made with water instead of milk established for me a model of Protestant meanness, confirmed later at numerous church sales as I noticed the absolutely minimal padding vouchsafed the expensive pot holders on sale, making them quite useless, tokens merely of fraud and pretentiousness. Could it be that churches cheated, like virtually everyone else? I'm afraid this early acquaintance with the Scottish Presbyterian spirit, as I understood it, quite turned me off not just church for life but Scotland as well. I found it easy to embrace the formulation Scotland is to England as Alabama is to Connecticut. Unfair, admittedly, but I can't help it, and perhaps the fault is less mine than Pasadena's.

After church, Chickinanna accompanied us home for quite a fair imitation of the British Victorian Sunday: no games, with card games especially to be watched out for; improving reading and very quiet outdoor activity barely permitted. At noon, a stultifying family dinner, consisting of overcooked vegetables, roast potatoes, and an overdone lamb roast. Chickinanna's contributions to the conversation were largely attempts to mend the pronunciation and language of her grandchildren, thus implicitly reproving her daughter-in-law's slackness in performing an essential duty. Don't say "Cream *uv* Wheat." Say "Cream *ov* Wheat." Never utter such indelicacies as "belly," or even "shirttail." The postprandial comment "Boy, I'm full" was especially warned against. As a result of this campaign, I became acquainted early with the whole lexicon of gentility and euphemism. Don't speak of cancer, speak of "a tumor." When you say "This room seems rather close," what you are understood to mean is "Someone's farted in here." As Chickinanna's instructions went on over the years, it was easy to understand why Father's brother had taken to Seattle, liberal journalism, cigars, and an occasional drink. By the time I grew up, the only thing Presbyterianism needed to blacken it forever in my view was the totalitarian-puritan mind and behavior of John Foster Dulles, the humorless Presbyterian secretary of state from Princeton. To this day I can't pass a Presbyterian church anywhere without a crushing feeling that boredom, rigidity, and fraud lurk inside.

My boyhood was excessively happy, but now and then this idyll was compromised by unpleasantness. Mother had read somewhere that a cause of juvenile misbehavior was the accumulation of unclean matter in the bowels, and that a timely enema was an aid to virtue. It was enema time whenever I'd engaged in particularly heinous conduct, like throwing kumquats at passing cars or stabbing to death the toads that flourished in our backyard pond with the bayonet-shaped tines of the gardening fork. After a while I didn't need to do anything wrong to earn a disciplinary enema. But I loved Mother regardless and could never have suspected that something was perhaps psychologically curious here. In those days boys assumed that what their parents did was right, and wouldn't have thought of suspecting in them ignorance, sadism, or simply error. If my anger at these enemas lasted more than an hour or so, it could be laid to rest when Mother came to my bedside to hear my "Now I lay me down to sleep."

If Mother tended to our clothing, feeding, and bowels, Dad supervised the operations of our minds. He made it clear that reading was not just a pastime like basketball or playing with tops but an obligation never to be neglected. Our household took in (for Mother) *Reader's Digest*, the *Ladies' Home Journal*, and the *Saturday Evening Post*, which Dad also read sometimes, especially when a comical story about the tractor salesman Alexander Botts appeared. For himself, he took the *Atlantic* in the days when a table of contents on the front cover was a sufficient come-on, an illustration being thought quite unnecessary and insulting to the intelligence of the *Atlantic* audience. But his weekly mainstay was *Time*, which he read religiously from its first number until his death. *Life* magazine he scorned, designating this pioneer of "photojournalism" "a magazine for people who can't read." Among the favorite reading of his children was one of his brightest investments, the multivolume *Book of Knowledge*. Originally published in England in 1912, this set was constantly revised and updated and given an increasingly American tone. The last revised edition, of 1966, contained almost four million words. Its articles were arranged not alphabetically but by topic, retailing notable facts about geology, biology, botany, anthropology, literature (heavy British emphasis), art history, travel, distinguished men and women, poetry (narrative, heroic, and sentimental), even an introduction to elementary French. One of my favorite selections, as I spent hours reading on my belly on the carpet, was "Things to Make and Do" (how to put on magic shows, make a cigar-box guitar, raise bees). Everything that would fascinate a preadolescent boy or girl was there, and the three of us read and reread these volumes constantly.

But just as Dad allowed himself a respite from *Time* and the law to frolic in P. G. Wodehouse, I turned often to lighter stuff, particularly *Penrod* and *Penrod and Sam*, which I knew almost by heart. Soon Ed and I became devotees of the Big Little Books, which conveyed the adventures of Superman and similar comic-strip characters, as well as books about more plausible people like Jerry Todd and Poppy Ott, boy detectives whose exploits ran to about forty bright red volumes. One of the best, I remember, involved the disappearance of a mummy from the museum of a small college and the acute processes of "deduction" Jerry and Poppy employed to get it back. And one evening each week or so Dad would designate Library Night, and the whole family would go off and spend a couple of hours at the nearby branch library. It was a breakthrough when I learned that you could actually buy books and own them forever instead of borrowing and then returning them. Matching Ed's and my passion for boys' adventure stories was Florence's devotion to a novel by Mariel Brady, *Genevieve Gertrude* (1928), which introduced us all to the important distinction between Funny Ha-Ha and Funny Peculiar.

Old men forget how intense taste and smell were before sex eclipsed them as delightful sensations. For boys, taste and smell were crucial ways of knowing the world before gentility forbade their use, at least in public. What boy can forget the taste of tennis-racket strings or violin-bow resin, or the tar used for road repairs? Wool tastes different from cotton, and both from paper, and paper from cardboard; licking wood is nothing like licking a tennis ball, and the rubber strings inside a golf ball taste entirely different from rubber bands. Until the practice fell under family prohibition, one smelled every dish of food, extensively, before tasting it. The conventions of popular folklore depict growing boys as tough and insensitive, but my friends and I spent hours registering our unaffected disgust at the loathsome language and imagery of adult health advertising. "Are you pained by stomach GAS?" "PILES: Don't be cut!" "RUPTURED? Thousands Thank God for the New Magic Truss." Our disgust often took physical form, moving us to actual nausea, in a way a few years of adult coarsening and cynicism would make a mere memory.

Secretly sensitive as they are, boys hate to be touched by strangers. This fact made my fortnightly haircuts an agony, especially when the barber folded my ears back crudely and painfully or carelessly nicked a mole whose tenderness he'd been specifically warned about. I've found that it wasn't until the haircutting classes spun off a subgroup designated Hairstylists that subtlety and art began to attend their procedures. Before that, all barbers seemed to me close to morons, and of the clumsiest sort. The sign of their union, glass and gilt and depending from a little chain, suggested their offensiveness:

it proclaimed. That's a significant bit of Americana: everything must pay. The pretentious-genteel and illiterate *well* instead of *good* is worth study too. The haircuts visited on boys in those days looked intentionally humiliating: too short on the back and sides, when we all wanted to resemble the full-haired boys in English or even "historical" movies. The American boys' haircut seemed to me a visible counterpart of the disciplinary enema.

Locked into the American late twentieth century like this, with no experience yet of Europe, how did I acquire the rudiments of a primitive historical sense? Partly by plowing through the vast collection of Victorian artifacts stored in Chickinanna's attic. There could be found wonders stranded by time: magic lanterns with kerosene lamps and glass slides, as well as stereoscopes with hundreds of double views of the pyramids and sphinx and forgotten world's fairs and exotic animals and people. In that attic I discovered long-disused children's toys in tin, not plastic, wood-burning sets, even a printer's cut constituting the top-of-the-front-page logo of a onetime boys' newspaper, *The Enterprise,* produced by Edwin Neal or perhaps Charles Fussell. Later, I appropriated it for a home-produced newspaper of my own.

Indulging my developing passion for the past, Father allowed me, after considerable teasing, to explore his "Army Trunk" stored in our attic. In the war (no question yet about which one), as a junior officer of ordnance, his duty, finally, was to preside over an ammunition dump near Bordeaux. This entailed riding a horse daily around the perimeter, and, as far as I could ascertain, little else. But there in a footlocker in the attic was all his stuff, complete except for a sidearm.

In that war officers had to buy their equipment, including helmet and gas mask, and it was all there, carefully laid up in mothballs: high shoes, puttees (both leather and wool), breeches, Sam Browne belt, jackets, and insignia, together with a notebook dating from father's passage through an Officer Candidate School, containing copious details about various kinds of artillery shells and explosives, all wonderfully hard to believe as subjects once significant to this notably peace-loving man.

As I examined and of course tried on these items, it was strikingly clear that they would be wonderful for play. Thus in one neighboring vacant lot my friends and I dug a system of three-foot-deep trenches, roofed with boards, old newspapers, and dirt, and lit by candles. Here we played trench warfare, bombarding one another's positions with dirt clods, blowing whistles to signal attacks, and coming as close as possible to miming the actualities of the Western Front as we'd seen them depicted in books. There, kitted out in Dad's uniform, with helmet and gas-mask carrier in place, I played boy officer, uncannily foreshadowing my destiny.

It was axiomatic among the Pasadena gentry that in the summer the heat made residence there physically — and socially — impossible. And the temperature did stay in the nineties for weeks at a time in a day when only movie theaters were beginning to install air conditioning. Cool summerhouses were indicated, and Father bought one, at Balboa, right on the ocean an hour and a half's drive away. There we spent every summer for fifteen years or so, years of absolute ecstasy for me as I sailed, rowed, attended wienie roasts, joined nighttime scavenger hunts, roamed the immense, largely deserted beach, and cultivated a special set of summer friendships centered on the Newport Harbor Yacht Club. Newport Beach had not yet become stylish, nor Orange County, where it was situated, a byword for political reaction, and the summer population was notably middle class, unsophisticated and unpretentious, with many families coming from the citrus and ranching areas of Riverside and San Bernardino.

The beach house, white clapboard with green trim, had many bedrooms and "sleeping porches" — it included the inevitable maid's room — and it was often filled with Pasadena friends. Dad bought it furnished, and among the furnishings was a large hand-cranked "His Master's Voice" Victrola with some records: "Lover, Come Back to Me," the "Anvil Chorus," and a "Negro" number, "Climbin' Up the Golden Stairs." Indoors, there was little to do but play cards (on weekdays only), and since poker chips were forbidden, we used kitchen matches. Of course America, like the rest of the civilized world, was still distinctly "sexist," and no explanation was needed when Dad supplied each of us boys with a twelve-foot sailboat, which we raced every weekend, while Florence had to be content with a ten-foot rowboat. Balboa was managed by a vigorous chamber of commerce, which was perpetually stimulating tourism by devising "events." The Flight of the Snowbirds was one. This was a sailboat race involving over a hundred children's boats at once — a farcical proceeding, really, but said by watchers on shore to be very pretty. The Tournament of Lights was another tourist enticer. Here, owners of yachts were invited to compete for trophies by dressing their vessels in lights and being towed slowly around the bay to the wonder of onlookers. Florence and I once won a prize by transforming her rowboat into a tropical scene with plywood palm trees and monkeys, lighting the whole thing with floodlights powered by car batteries and playing on a wind-up phonograph "Sweet Leilani."

Another event was Pirate Days, featuring a mock-up of a pirate

29

ship built on the ocean beach, populated without pay by a horde of shouting boys comprising a large part of the young male population of Balboa. I was allowed to tie a red bandanna around my head, remove my shirt, apply colored-pencil tattoos, and sport a rubber dagger in my belt. All these civic publicity events I enjoyed mightily, and I realize now how exciting a part of my prewar idyll they were.

Not least as a cause of delight at the beach was secretly learning to smoke cigarettes. Low brands like Wings cost only a dime, and no one supervised or even observed the relation between underage boys and cigarette machines. I took my smokes out on the wide ocean beach, and hiding the materials from the parents was a large part of the whole joyous exercise. The smell of cheap tobacco will bring back instantly idle Balboa afternoons when I smoked on the beach and returning home, imagined that Sen-Sen would cover my crime. The eucalyptus smell of the salve Noxema, which soothed my sunburn, evokes paradisal boyhood as well, like the scent of the thin army blankets we were allowed to build ad hoc tents out of on the beach. Cooking chicken thighs recently, I caught the exact aroma of a Balboa wienie roast, when the fire was ready and the first wienies were deployed above it on long forks with wooden handles. The wienies split and crackled, and were finally encased in buns and devoured, with Cokes and orange sodas, by a crowd of always barefoot but nicely dressed middle-class quasi guttersnipes.

For some reason, the standard adolescent crushes I began to develop — at first, only on boys — occurred at Balboa, never at Pasadena. For several summers I enjoyed a purely platonic passion for one younger boy. Whenever he appeared or indicated a desire to hang around with me, my heart leapt up. There was no sex involved, and we never touched each other. When the film *The Prince and the Pauper* was shown at a Balboa theater, I was thirteen, and I was simply ravished by the looks and charms of the Hollywood twins who played the two boys. I wrote them a mash note, disguised as a fan letter, and received a photograph in return. (Their "medieval," all-but-page-boy haircuts were exactly what I'd always fantasized for myself, but of course never got.) About these boyish obsessions I felt puzzled, until much later I grew familiar with Gerard Manley Hopkins and A. E. Housman, and preeminently the Virgil of the Second Eclogue, and came to realize how conventional and harmless they were. The passage of time has revealed how little they interfere, ultimately, with fully adult heterosexual life and happy marriages. As I developed, girls soon replaced boys as my passions, but I have never lost my sense of the attractiveness of such boyish characteristics as unexpected sensitivity and vulnerability, as well as courage and loyalty. Clearly, I could never have written the chapter "Soldier Boys" in *The Great War and Modern Memory* without this adolescent experience, nor identified myself in so many ways with Robert Graves, in his roles both as a student and a young infantry officer. When after my war I read in Graves's *Good-Bye to All That* of his falling in innocent love with a younger boy at Charterhouse School, and found his view that after five months of combat duty, a front-line officer is used up, neurasthenic beyond saving, I felt I was reading not his autobiography but mine. He also wrote about meeting by accident his schoolboy crush long after, in adulthood, and he emphasized how clumsy, ugly, and charmless an adult he'd grown into. I had the same experience with my young friend. I saw him with his wife many decades later and could think only of the words of Ogden Nash,

The trouble with a kitten is
That
Eventually it becomes a
CAT.

But I anticipate, and must get back to my prewar world of "youth's primordial bliss," as Kingsley Amis has put it, a world I barely understood until much later, when I began to encounter literary pastoral and to experience Eden, as mediated by Milton.

The beach house was also the theater of my early musical operations. I don't mean pounding away at the out-of-tune upright left by the previous owners, but something more genteel. Mother was "musical" in a highly amateur way. As a pianist she could read scores and play them at sight, and she was notably susceptible to sentimental performance. Once she took me to the Pasadena Playhouse to hear a recital by the Russian cellist Gregor Piatagorsky. He played soulfully, and his dark good looks were no impediment to Mother's admiration. One summer at Balboa, she decided that I must master the cello. A teacher, Mr. Edward Burns, was found in nearby Santa Ana. He was on his uppers, employed only in a WPA orchestra consisting of out-of-work musicians on the musical dole. He was delighted to help us buy a cello for me and come to Balboa once a week to initiate me into its mysteries. He was a good teacher, and after a bit of instruction and much practice, I could perform, Mother accompanying, a Mendelssohn cello concerto to plausible effect, if with excessive sentimental vibrato, a Burns specialty he passed on to all his students. "Make it sing," "Play it with soul," were his frequent injunctions. Playing the cello was fun, although daily practicing was not, and for the next several years I played in school orchestras and chamber groups, but not terribly well, for I never really learned to read music (it was the multiplication tables all over again) and was faking most of the time.

The first student orchestra I played in was at my next school, McKinley Junior High School. Like other "progressive" cities, in 1928 Pasadena had adopted for its public schools the six-four-four plan. This meant that a pupil spent six instead of eight years at grammar school, then four years at a junior high school, and finally attended a junior college for either two years (for the college bound) or four (for those earning associate degrees and going to work right away). At McKinley, the student orchestra specialized in the "Poet and Peasant Overture," over and over, but we also rendered the "Light Cavalry Overture," "My Little Gypsy Sweetheart," and my favorite, the Fest March from *Tannhäuser*, act 3, scene 4, with its nifty cello part. My four-year experience with this orchestra and with the tenor clef accustomed me to the support line in music, and today the melody line in any music interests me less than the bass and baritone background. Thus in college I chose to play the tuba and the sousaphone, which, unlike the bugle, had large mouthpieces requiring minimal lip muscle.

At McKinley the academic work was serious and not easy. Idle by nature and experience, I now had to confront not clay and poster paint but Latin, algebra, geometry, and history. I slid through English easily, largely through the kindness and skill of the teacher, Mr. Bishop, from whom I learned that if you know your stuff, you can get away with unidiomatic stunts like "At the end of the play Cleopatra suicides." In 1936 Great Britain was still a highly important, unbankrupt imperial power, and what happened there was still interesting to Americans. When Edward VIII abdicated in

December, Mr. Bishop regarded the moment as significant enough to justify installing a radio in his classroom to enable the assembled twelve- and thirteen-year-olds to hear the outgoing monarch say, "We all have a new King. . . . God bless you all. God save the King." But Mr. Bishop's easygoing approach and interest in the real world contrasted with the pedagogic rigor of Miss Riley, the Latin teacher, whose courses I barely passed and in whose classroom I suffered numerous defeats:

"Will you translate the next lines for us, Paul?"

"I'm sorry. I'm not prepared."

(Long pause, with tight pursing of lips and reaching for her gradebook.) "That's unfortunate."

But McKinley had a vocational as well as an academic emphasis, and there I was lucky to be inducted into the arts of pleasurable work with my hands. Boys were required to take a "shop" each year: wood, printing, sheet metal, and mechanical drawing. I joyously learned to measure, cut, sand, nail, and glue wood; to set type in a composing stick and to run off and correct proofs; to cut, bend, solder, and rivet sheet metal; and to write letters and figures according to the conventions of architectural and mechanical blueprints. And I learned something equally important, namely, to respect the shop teachers as much as the others. Both kinds had knowledge and a mastery of technique, and both impressed me as professionals: none was silly or superficial or cynical about the work. All made us want to do well, whether making artifacts like a wooden file box, a faultless printed copy of a four-line poem, a kitchen flour scoop (mother proudly used mine all her life), or a blueprint for a storefront ready for the builders.

My favorite place was the print shop, presided over by Mr. McNary. The main school font of type was twelve-point Caslon Old

Style, and we were exercised in setting up "The day is done," which Mr. McNary knew would produce instructive comical versions like "The pay is gone" and "The bay is pone." Much later, I wondered where these shop teachers came from. Was able, calm, tolerant Mr. McNary a printer who had gone into teaching, or a teacher who'd learned, surprisingly well, printing? The fonts of type we worked with became for me archetypes of beauty and deserved longevity, never forgotten. Later, when one publisher kindly asked me what body-type I'd prefer for one of my books, I chose Caslon Old Style. I've always been ravished by the dignity of the numeral 1 in this font. It's not an Arabic numeral but a "Roman" one, a small capital *I*, and for me it stands as a near-secret aesthetic rebuke to "efficiency," scientism, and the more utilitarian elements of modernism.

When another publisher asked what type I'd like for the large initials at the beginning of chapters in *The Great War and Modern Memory,* I specified Bodoni Open Face, a favorite of mine for decades. It was Mr. McNary's print shop that told me that whatever I did with my life, it would have to involve words and their public presentation. And in those days there was a special magic about the way writers and printers produced words for an audience. Cold type and desktop methods may be efficient, but if anyone can master them, the trade mystery that used to attend the old journalistic and hot-type world vanishes. And a lot else changes too. John Leonard has confronted the issues. Gone is

> an older idea of newspaper work as a craft or trade, not a profession with white-collar civil-service perks like summer homes . . . and private schools for our sensitive children. [Once,] our fingernails were dirty, and we knew the romance of ink, and we

lived in the high school print shop and could read the type upside down, and the belching machine seemed somehow to connect brain and word, muscle and idea, hot lead and cool thought, before we got into the information-commodity racket.

It wasn't long before I'd set up my own print shop in a well-lit large closet off my bedroom, complete with hand press (with a five-by-eight-inch chase), imposing stone, several fonts of type, composing stick, leads, borders, cuts — the whole works. It all came by freight from the Kelsey Press Co., Meriden, Connecticut, and for years I badgered people to let me print their business cards, labels, flyers, tickets — anything five by eight inches or smaller. Over the years my boyish job-printing business probably recovered less than 1 percent of my investment, but profit was the fiction, not the point. The point was to be a printer, to live amidst type cases, ink, paper, solvent, and lead, tin, and antimony. My behavior here was typical of the way I pursued all my "hobbies" — as my parents to my annoyance tended to refer to my enthusiasms. I was indeed incapable of moderation. I had to hurl myself totally into what I was excited about, impatient of any sort of restraint or good sense.

This long run of boyish happiness was not entirely free of darker moments, but even these did nothing to damage my inbuilt optimism. One bad period lasted for several months. I had been troubled by earaches that seemed to grow more frequent and worse and worse until an infected mastoid was diagnosed, and under ether — which of course made one throw up — I underwent a mastoidectomy at the same hospital where I was born. (Penicillin would have cured the ailment without the surgery, but there was no penicillin then.) As a result I convalesced at home for a semester, keeping in touch with schoolwork by means of a tutor, the amiable, not excessively bright or demanding Mr. Renner, who even brought along a drawing board, T square, and triangles so I could catch up with mechanical drawing. The only permanent damage wrought by this illness was a bit of bone loss behind my right ear. Psychologically, I remained unmarred, and if anything more cheerful and sanguine than ever.

Except for another threat to perfect felicity. I began to grow fat. Avid for soft drinks, hamburgers and hot dogs, candy, cake, ice cream, and Horlick's Malted Milk Tablets, and equally enthusiastic about abstaining from exercise, I became "a soft kid, thirty pounds overweight at the age of fourteen." I'm quoting from David Guy's novel *The Autobiography of My Body* (1991). His description will do perfectly, for his adolescent situation matches mine in an uncanny way. His father like mine wanted his son to become a lawyer, and like me, when the rest of the boys were joyously developing into athletes, he stayed soft and flabby. As he notes, fat boys try to defend themselves from ridicule and contempt by learning to be funny, and that's rather fun, but, as he adds, there's "a dark side of being fat . . . the big blubbery fifteen-year-old waddling through the locker room with his tiny little dick. Why does nobody ever bring that subject up, the single most obvious fact about fat boys?" My shame there was exactly like Guy's, and the communal shower after gym became a daily torment. All boys suffer from a degree of penis anxiety, and as Farley Mowat has observed, even in adulthood "a primordial fear haunts most men . . . that their organ is smaller than it ought to be." For years I've wondered why suddenly, and without explanation, I quit the Boy Scouts. Lately, I've come to realize that the cause was an announcement that on a forthcoming camping trip, swimming would be done without bathing suits. The degree to which adolescent boys are ashamed that their bodies — the only thing that, at that age, they might be proud of — aren't like some fancied norm has never been sufficiently emphasized. But at least I wasn't as fat as another boy, a genuine freak, cruelly denominated by his classmates Mount Flab.

One physical norm was supplied by the numerous Mexican boys, the Manuels and the Jesuses, at the school. They seemed fully mature to me, with their frequent injunctions to "Chinga tu madre" and their clear success with girls. "Chicano" culture, not to mention Chicana, hadn't yet been deemed worthy of learned attention. The Mexican youths had to struggle through geometry like the rest of us, although they didn't do as well, a fact we others imputed less to native dullness than to their more vivid social and sexual lives. One Mexican boy proudly brought to school an eloquent novelty, an eight-inch statuette of the Blessed Virgin. When reversed, the back side became an eight-inch penis, sculpted in startling detail. Such sophistication was quite beyond the reach of the more fortunate Pasadena boys.

And indeed, Southern California in those days was a place where it was possible for Anglo-Saxon youngsters, especially those from well-to-do families, to feel like aliens. There we were, playing at our pseudo-British culture, while all around us spread the enchilada-and-refritos, day-laboring world with place names like Costa Mesa, San Diego, Los Angeles, Palos Verdes, and the Santas Monica, Barbara, and Ana. No one in my family spoke Spanish at all and I "took" it for two years in junior college and only because I had to study a language and it seemed easier than French or German, and certainly preferable to going on with Latin. There were obviously no Mexican boys or girls attending Miss Travis's Friday afternoon dancing classes, regarded as socially indispensable for the rest of us.

Much as I liked, or at least tolerated, school, most of my pleasures were domestic: collecting stamps, playing with Erector sets and electric trains, making blue ink and other commodities from Gilbert Chemistry Sets, and collecting old newspapers in the area, tying them up, and selling them finally to the junkman, who paid handsomely for each hundred-pound bundle. Like all boys, I was constantly in need of money, and this early effort at profitable recycling was only one of my many attempts to augment the scanty, puritan allowance paid weekly by my father. Every year brought a new wild enthusiasm. Once I went overboard for spinning tops, and once I could think of little else than making from clothespins guns that would shoot wooden matches striking-end first, to hazardous but thrilling effect. Hot weather brought its own special delights: the nightly visit of the ice-cream man's white truck with its tinkling bell, or roller-skating and drinking ice-cold draft root beer at a nearby rink with our nicest maid ever, blonde and buxom Emma Anderson — soon to marry and join the Rosies riveting planes for the Second World War.

One treasure dear to every boy was a Johnson Smith catalog, from a mail-order company in Detroit. This was our source for saucy "novelties" not available in Pasadena: whoopee cushions, dribble glasses, artificial dog turds, and "plate lifters," small flat rubber bladders that could be surreptitiously inflated beneath a tablecloth to rock dinner plates and puzzle diners. "Sending away" for such things involved the excitement of filling out the order form, enclosing the money order, dropping the envelope into the mail slot, and then waiting with mingled anxiety and hope for the plain-wrapped package and the final ecstasy of baffling Chickinanna as her dinner plate wobbled inexplicably and ominously during the canonical Sunday dinner.

This diddling of Chickinanna manifested, I'm sorry to say, the boyish will to power propelling most of my enthusiasms. Even so apparently neutral an activity as printing assumed the act of dominating an audience with words. When later I began to throw myself into putting on magic shows, the object was, as a literary critic might put it, rhetorical — the management of others' perceptions and (if possible) the aggrandizement of my own power over them. My later enthusiasm for something like "press" photography involved the privilege of going where others could not go, resulting in a product that imposed my vision on others. And finally, what was university teaching but a high-class version of something similar? Much later, studying Jacobean drama at Harvard under Harry Levin, I learned to think of this urge as the *libido dominandi*. If the United States should get into the war, clearly I would have to be in a position to impress and manage others while, in my fantasy, enjoying their admiration. That is, I'd have to become a young officer. But that identity lay ahead. I was only fifteen and the new European war was very far away. Pasadena and Balboa were still entirely secure precincts of Paradise.

⧉ II ⧉

BROTHERLY LOVE, as in the word *Philadelphia,* is what motivated my brother Ed to take care that I arrived well briefed on the customs of the schools where I followed him, from Hamilton to McKinley, to Pasadena Junior College, to Pomona College, and even to Harvard's Graduate School of Arts and Sciences. All the hints he supplied I was grateful for, but for none so much as those preparing me for Pasadena Junior College, for it proved startlingly different from junior high school. At McKinley, administrators and teachers had been the only ones in charge. But at Pasadena Jaycee, it was as if the students were running things, and running them very well. It was like a large university with impressive new white buildings set down in the middle of the city, and it offered "university" features unknown at my earlier schools, like a student-produced yearbook and deans of this and that subject and division, as well as extramural heavy sports like football, together with basketball, baseball, track, swimming, tennis, skiing, and boxing, all sustained by cheerleaders in neat red-and-white sweaters and trousers and skirts. The athletes wore letterman's sweaters, and their public exertions were accompanied by the university-quality music and precision marching of the Bulldog Band. (On January 1 it doubled, in different uniforms, as the Tournament of Roses Band.) Everything the college undertook had a professional, nonchildish air: the orchestra, with eight cellos, where I occupied the last chair in the section, was comparable in size if not quality with the New York Philharmonic. The ROTC unit enrolled three hundred fifty cadets wielding Springfield rifles commanded by twenty-seven much-envied cadet officers with sabers and Sam Browne belts. There was a student legal system for the adjudication of misdemeanors, and virtually every student interest was represented by a student-run club, from art and journalism to electrical technology and aviation (some students actually flew). In the absence of fraternities and sororities, there were "restrictive clubs" for men and women (no longer "boys" and "girls"). Because I was overweight and an ROTC nerd, I was never pledged, but Ed belonged to "M.O.S." (Mystic Order of the Sphinx), and his future wife, Jean Tupman, was a member of "The Club." (Pin: a playing-card club surrounded with pearls.) There were of course plays elaborately mounted by students and performed on a technologically sophisticated stage. The women students were remarkably good-looking, or was it just my rapid maturation that made them seem so? Whatever, the college produced the most erotic-looking nurses I could ever imagine. It was the college's privilege to elect, on the basis of beauty (as defined by contemporary Hollywood), the annual "Queen" of the Rose Parade. Riding on her flower-decorated float, she looked like the kind of white-robed Statue of Liberty that could occasion erections all the way down Colorado Street. In short, Pasadena Jaycee offered what could be considered a thorough preparation for adult communal life.

Intellectually, it was perhaps less impressive but still not easily dismissed. In a history class I learned as much about the Hohenzollerns as I could decently pack in, and the offerings in science, although I merely skated through the bare requirements there, were respectable, with impressively equipped laboratories. If I had something like a "major," it was journalism, taught by an unforgettable ex-newspaperman named Wayne Hodges — the spitting image, I later found, of trombonist Jack Teagarden. He was appropriately *Front Page* in his cynicism and skill.

This whole costly package was proudly supported by the taxpayers of Pasadena, happy to have something called a "college," if only junior grade, in their town. To be sure, the California Institute of Technology was there too, but it enrolled few Pasadena students and seemed quite out of reach. Local pride centered on PJC, and to go there was to feel you were accomplishing something valuable and admirable. I never heard the place condescended to.

By this time, although I kept up my print shop at home, I had added "news photography" to my enthusiasms — great for exercising the *libido dominandi*. With this act I actually made some money, selling a picture now and then to the Pasadena *Star-News* or to a trade journal. One of the eight-by-ten glossies from my home darkroom, depicting a new shoe-repair business, was bought and published by a shoe-repair monthly. And the first substantial amount I made — I think it was fifty dollars — came from a large-circulation magazine. A Boy Scout Jamboree was taking place in nearby Arcadia, and I decided to exploit it in full professional fashion. I equipped Mother's Chevrolet coupé with an immense windshield sign reading PRESS and set off with notebook and serious-looking camera with flashgun. Returning with pictures, I wrote up the event in journalese, with which I'd become proficient writing practice news stories for Mr.

Hodges, and sent story and prints to the Scout journal *Boys' Life*, where it appeared a month or so later. Joy! I was launched on a career, if I wanted it. And photography opened other avenues, perhaps less decent, to income. I used to get the car all ready, camera and equipment in place, parked facing outward in the driveway, ready for a rapid getaway. Then I would listen to the police calls on the short-wave radio, which the family Zenith brought in, waiting for news of a major auto accident nearby. I would rush to the site and photograph all the damage, both human and automotive, in the expectation that the litigants-to-be would buy my photos. They did.

Because Jaycee had no student residences and because it was located smack in the middle of the Southern California auto culture, most students drove to school and used the extensive parking lots provided. Not to arrive in your own car was to suffer moderate social demotion. The favored auto was a Model A Ford roadster in perfect, shiny condition, with windshield raked back. Dark blue was the best color. Next in desirability was some form of Model T, with the original matte black paint unrecognizable under many coats of red, green, or yellow, perhaps with satiric stripes or polka dots. Ed and I, and Florence later, were (wisely) not allowed our own cars. I had to make do with Mother's. When I took her car to school, I dressed it up by affixing a removable foxtail to the radiator ornament with a rubber band.

I entered Jaycee just as the Wehrmacht entered Poland, but my joining the ROTC had less to do with any sense of forthcoming military activity than with the welcome news that after their twice-weekly drills on the parade ground, the ROTC cadets, sweaty as they might be, were not forced to strip and shower. We performed in full dress uniforms, which we were proud to wear all day. They resembled the actual army's except for the bright blue lapels on the jackets and the brass insignia bearing not "US" and crossed rifles but torches of learning. Keeping those insignia bright and our belt buckles burnished was our sole ROTC homework. Actually, we learned nothing but the nomenclature and handling — not, of course, firing — of the Springfields, and the rudiments of close-order drill. I think it safe to say that as long as danger and fear are not imminent, soldiers generally like, or at least don't mind, close-order drill, if performed with some style and snap to which all can contribute. It is, after all, a form of showing off. Style and snap were our constant aim, and we did get quite proficient at drill, marching in columns of three alongside an overdressed boy officer counting cadence and swinging his saber on his arm. At such moments, it was possible to believe we were doing something worthwhile, or at least sensible. Because we were in a "junior" college, the ROTC unit was officially a junior unit. Senior units were at senior colleges, which awarded bachelor's degrees and, for the ROTC faithful, officers' commissions. But if junior, this junior ROTC was an infantry unit, although none of us exercised enough imagination to conceive of what infantry might mean in the future.

We were, as if carefully, shielded from the truth. Tactics was a topic never addressed, neither of attack nor defense, nor were foxholes mentioned. About tree bursts and Graves Registration, malaria and trench foot, our instructors were silent. Occasionally we were allowed to gather that bullets might come toward us, but we had no idea that we would also have to cower from mortar and artillery shells, which would drive some of us to tears, some to madness. Later, we were absolutely astonished to discover how much blood could come from a human body, and to hear at night cries of "Mutti!" from the German boys we'd shot, dying in front of our position. We did not learn in the ROTC that the official first-aid packet might do to cover a bullet hole but would do nothing for a foot blown off by a Schu-mine. The ROTC was, in short, a wonderland, just another subdivision of the Pasadena Paradise.

By the time I got to PJC, it seemed axiomatic that girls were for taking out on Saturday night, boys for horseplay the rest of the time. Girls I took to dances, parties, and sometimes for hamburgers and Cokes at a drive-in across the street from PJC. The girls I liked best were those who seemed to view the whole conventional relation between the sexes as rather funny, and my favorite girl regarded it as sidesplitting. We laughed more than we kissed. In those days, "dating" had a meaning quite different from the current one. It implied flirting, not fucking. The fear of pregnancy lurked in all relations between the unmarried young. Contraception was difficult: there was no pill, condoms were not to be had without great embarrassment or sometimes exposure by a pharmacist who knew your parents, and a diaphragm had to be fitted by a doctor. Thus both intense desire and intense frustration characterized the junior sexual scene. Girls who got pregnant were socially ruined, but those who didn't allow boys freedoms verging on the immensely risky were "unpopular," destined to spend many Saturday nights in shameful loneliness.

Safer, and less structured, if quite devoid of the erotic kick, were male friendships, of the kind and intensity that can be enjoyed only once in life, in adolescence and in one's late teens. Total honesty, we found, was possible only there. Parents would be shocked at what you really wanted to say, girls repelled. "The best of adolescence," Phillip Roth agrees, "was the intense male friendships — not only because of the cozy feelings of camaraderie they afforded boys coming unstuck from their close-knit families, but because of the opportunity

46

they provided for uncensored talk." Laugh as you might with your date, for cascades of laughter continuing through gasps, holding of sides, and falling down, you had to be with your friends. And you saw them often enough to carry on with them a protracted continuity of allusion, to persevere in the same jokes for weeks and to augment them into deep fantasies of the preposterous and the outrageous. All boys are satirists by instinct, but the satiric impulse survives boyhood in only a few who decline ever to abandon their initial conviction that the world is, though delightful, in essence absurd.

Although not exclusively pivoting on magic or photography, most of my male friendships came about because of a common interest in such enthusiasms. But I never found anyone interested in printing. It kept its hold on me all through PJC — so much that in the summers I conveyed my whole print shop to Balboa and installed it in my room. There I issued a weekly two-page newspaper, *The Enterprise*. The news I printed consisted wholly of sailboat-racing results, and printing and distributing them fast was what I did to simulate the excitement of a real newspaper deadline.

One close friend I lost suddenly over the European war. He had British ties somewhere in his family, and once, when I was uttering my vigorous isolationist sentiments, he suddenly seemed to realize that in idea at least I was condemning his relatives to death or slavery. By that time the British cause was so automatically honored in the United States that he struck out with, "You're not a very good American, are you?" We never saw each other again.

In 1940 Ed went off to Pomona College, where I joined him a year later. But first I underwent the ritual concluding my first two years at PJC, elsewhere called "high school graduation." There were so many of us graduating that only the Rose Bowl could hold us, and there one evening, in dark suits and white dresses, we listened to the speeches and sang "Land of Hope and Glory," whose British colonialist sentiments no one apparently found inappropriate or anomalous. We pretended to find the whole proceeding ridiculous, but no one snickered, and we behaved ourselves as we'd seldom done before as we formed two long lines on the grass and filed by to be handed our diplomas. It would only be a year and a half before such gatherings would be prohibited, lest, it was held, Japanese bombers seek out such large crowds.

This seventeen-year-old boy's initial suitability for the higher learning may be gauged from his answer to the question "Why are you going to college?" when he applied to Pomona in June 1941:

> *I am going to college for two reasons. The first is to complete my education in such a manner that I will be well suited to face the world in years to come. The second is to gain valuable friendships and experiences that will prove exceedingly valuable in later life.*

He was wrong on both counts, as we shall see. And the reader should resist the temptation to interpret his canting words as satiric or ironic, clever send-ups of the sincere style. Actually, he was being perfectly genuine and guileless.

Pomona College, which had no relation to the nearby small city of Pomona, was about twenty-five miles east of Pasadena. It was located in the high-minded town of Claremont, a place committed to churchgoing and local option — local prohibition of alcohol persisting long after the repeal of the Eighteenth Amendment in 1933. The college was founded in 1887 by a group of Congregationalists seeking to establish in the moral wilderness of Southern California "a Christian College of the New England type," and the seal of the college denominated it as "Our Tribute to Christian Civilization." The catalog for 1890 specified that the college "requires for admission a course of study substantially identical with the old academies of New England. . . . It is a Christian college. Its teachers are appointed with reference to their large personal influence in the foundation of character." That was still true when I was there, although *character* was now conceived as wholly secular, intellectual, and moral. Classes were small. The faculty, at least those who influenced me, were young, learned, serious, and friendly, and many held class in their living rooms. If by "the old academies of New England" places like Amherst and Williams were meant, Pomona constituted, despite its palm trees and Spanish tile roofs and neighboring orange groves, a plausible imitation.

Except that it was coeducational, and had been since its founding. It was distinctly antivocational, and until 1926, daily chapel attendance was compulsory. When a year later the custom of opening faculty meetings with prayer was dropped, the college was in a position to realize its full potential as a liberal arts institution, its very nature a celebration of the absolute freedom of the mind. As E. Wilson Lyon, the president of the college who arrived at the same time I did, once emphasized, "The independent liberal arts college . . . has the transcending merit of independence from any outside body — whether church, local, state, or national government" — and, I'd add, corporation or profit-making business.

The formal entrance to the college (on "College Avenue," of course) was a solemn gateway displaying on one side the words "Let only the eager, thoughtful, and reverent enter here," and on the other,

"They only are loyal to this college who departing bear their added riches in trust for mankind." Both messages were composed by James A. Blaisdell, president of the college from 1910 to 1928, and ultimately he had second thoughts about the *Let only* injunction, which came to seem to him "a trifle too prohibitive," demanding "too much of the entering student." He allowed the words to remain, however, and they have provided — espécially the *eager* and the *reverent* — an occasion for student levity ever since. The other set of words, insisting on lifetime intellectual obligation, I have taken more seriously, although I would have felt embarrassed saying so until now. As I have over and over weighed those added riches, I've realized powerfully and gratefully that they were provided by others, not learned by myself, and provided not in expectation of payment or self-promotion.

Physically, the college, which enrolled about eight hundred, could be mistaken for a sort of mini-Stanford, with its white buildings and red tile roofs. Its immense eucalyptus trees conveyed an impression of age and permanence. Proximity to Hollywood would suggest some leanings toward show business, and among Pomona graduates are Robert Taylor (original name, unbelievably: Spangler Arlington Brugh), Joel McCrea, Richard Chamberlain, Kristoffer Kristofferson (his original spelling), and Twyla Tharp. Symphony and choral director Robert Shaw is an alumnus, and so are writers Ved Mehta and Wright Morris.

From September 3 to 5, 1941, at Auschwitz I, Zyklon B (prussic acid) was first tested as an exterminating agent for undesirable human beings. The cellars of Building 11 were chosen for the experiment on six hundred Soviet prisoners and two hundred fifty sick Polish inmates. Although it took three days to do the job, it was clear that gassing would be an effective way of getting rid, forever, of things like Jews and Slavs. On September 5, young Paul Fussell Jr. arrived at Pomona in his brand-new clothes, found his room and met his roommate, had his first college dinner in the large dining hall, and prepared for a week of settling in. If he'd known anything about killing people with Zyklon B, or killing people at all, he'd not have understood.

For him, all was joy. He was close enough to home to have his laundry done, but far enough to avoid parental censure for his mild experiments with drink. The men's dormitories featured maid service, and I never had to make a bed or clean a room. The college food was excellent, with ice cream twice a day. Service was normally cafeteria style, but there were frequent formal dinners, with obligatory jacket and tie, served by students beautifully trained and disciplined as a corps of waiters. On these occasions, we had steak or roast beef. The suite I shared with my roommate featured a fireplace and a curious upright piano acquired by my brother. It was stuck all over with dried glue and bits of flowers. He'd bought it off a Tournament of Roses float, where it had been covered with fresh blossoms. On that piano I learned to play boogie-woogie by ear. Ed played more sophisticated popular numbers, while I specialized in imitating Meade Lux Lewis, Pete Johnson, and Albert Ammons. My "Yancey Special" was the pride of my (repetitive) repertory.

If Proust's memories could be triggered by the taste of a madeleine dipped in tea, mine are awakened as automatically by certain sounds and smells. The sound that brings back my first college semester with uncanny accuracy is the melody and words of "Blues in the Night." The smell: that of Mennen Brushless Shaving Cream, which I used once a week whether I needed it or not.

My roommate was a hyperenergetic young man whose father in

Pittsburgh had sent him to Pomona apparently in lieu of a reform school or military academy. He was comical, noisy, and subversive, and clearly not thoughtful or reverent, or even very eager. He flunked out spectacularly at the end of the first semester, although his academic achievement wasn't dramatically worse than mine. Specializing in history and government, I racked up a series of C's except in English, spending more time on the piano bench and bar stool than the study chair. Several of my required books remained unopened during the semester (a selection of Plato's dialogues was one), but I found that quickness of mind and skill in fraud could earn passing grades, at least in the humanities.

At Pomona one got along happily as long as one adapted to the group and played the game. For men, the local sumptuary laws required fairly strict costuming, at least in the trouser department. This depended on seniority. Freshmen were advised to wear "moleskins." Sophomores could slum in blue jeans, but they were inevitably long enough to make rolled-up cuffs necessary. Juniors and seniors were permitted corduroys. Freshman had special, would-be humiliating headwear, little green flannel "beanies" or "dinks" with the class-year "45" in yellow on the front. To omit the dink was to risk punishment, e.g., push-ups, from all upperclassmen.

For most of us, women as well as men, Pomona was our first heady experience of release from close parental supervision. It was a joyous theater of freedom and privilege. Were most of our parents Republicans? (They'd have to be, to pay the fees.) Then we imagined ourselves their class enemies, and we sang union songs like "Joe Hill" and "You Can't Scare Me, I'm Stickin' to the Union." Were most of our parents conscious of their superiority as members of the Caucasian classes? Then we threw ourselves into "Negro" jazz and

Trinidadian calypso, and affected "solidarity" with the clusters of poor Mexicans living near the campus.

If the men cast themselves as opponents of political reaction and respectability, the women had their own work of opposition to perform. The brighter ones ridiculed official attempts to instill in them the standards of Gracious Living. They were supposed to embrace without objection or satire the lore of flatware patterns and flower arrangement, tea pouring, and appearing always in exactly the right clothes. All in aid of early successful marriages and subsequent hostess-ship. It's a wonder any woman emerged from Pomona unscathed.

As a gesture of freedom, I was fond of cutting classes. But I didn't cut English. In those days English tended to mean "English"—not American. American literature hardly got a look-in and was taught by the dumbest man in the department. Its sudden ascendancy after the war and the appearance of "American Studies" and "American Civilization" as legitimate ideas would have astonished people in 1941. British literature was the thing, and no one thought an injustice done. The term "elitist" was never heard, and if it had been, most of us would have rushed at a chance to earn that title. My English professor the first semester was Ernest Strathman, an expert on Sir Walter Ralegh. In second semester I was taught by Frederick L. Mulhauser, a devotee of Victorian literature, later the wonderfully learned, conscientious editor of the works of the British poet Arthur Hugh Clough. These responsible professors required of us a theme every week, which they returned promptly, thoroughly marked and evaluated. No teaching assistants read our papers, for there was no graduate program to justify them. Every professor, regardless of rank or seniority, taught at least one twenty-student section of Freshman English, and taught it as if he enjoyed it.

Intellectually supine and incurious as I was, preferring "laughs" to thought, now and then something encountered in a class, especially an English class, would ignite a tiny flame of something like enthusiasm. In Strathman's class our textbook was J. D. McCallum, ed., *The Revised College Omnibus,* a one-volume anthology of all sorts of stuff, including a biography (Lytton Strachey's *Queen Victoria*) and a novel (Hardy's *The Return of the Native*). The essay section contained one piece that powerfully arrested my vagrant attention. It was James Truslow Adams's "The Mucker Pose," which aimed to stiffen the will to courageous individuality and contempt for the herd wherever pressure to the contrary might be found by the entering college student. Why, asked Adams, do even educated men "try to appear uncultured?" He urged his readers to beware the American quest for "popularity" at the expense of one's real character. Posing as a mucker, i.e., a lowbrow, is not, he pointed out, "a question of a mere decline in manners but of consciously striven-for pose." Why, in short, do American men act as if afraid to appear educated, and why do they "assume as a protective coloration the manners and level of thought of those who are beneath them"? Slovenly language is one symptom of the mucker pose: vogue words and clichés "corrode the mind," and the Babbittry of business is a main cause of this appalling habit among those who know better. The sad fact is that in business "one has to conform or one is lost."

It was Adams's essay almost alone that persuaded me that I might come clean about my total lack of interest in athletics and be satisfied to be myself. No more would I affect concern about things that others were concerned about. But my transformation was not immediate. It took some time to learn to forgo popularity of one sort and to solicit popularity of a different kind, and from a much smaller audience. But Adams had planted a seed, definitely. His implicit snobbery (if that's what it was) found an echo too, and seemed a relief from the notion of human uniformity and consequent dullness being insisted on widely, at Pomona as elsewhere.

If Adams's essay became an important part of my personal baggage, so did another item in that freshman anthology, Sir Arthur Quiller-Couch's "On Jargon." For me that comical assault on clichés constituted a footnote, or more than that, to "The Mucker Pose" and got me ready to love, finally, Orwell's "Politics and the English Language." I suspect that a reading of Stuart Chase's essay "The Luxury of Integrity," in the same volume, also left something behind. But the prose in the *Omnibus* offered more than moral stiffening and hints toward dictional consciousness and discrimination. Hanson Baldwin's account of the sinking of the *Titanic* is so consummately well done that a recent reading brought tears to my eyes — as it doubtless did not when I first came upon it.

Feeble as my intellectual interests were at this point, these early classes were my introduction to notions of intellectual curiosity and intellectual ambition. I've wondered why hints and personal examples of such things seemed not to have been conspicuous at PJC. Perhaps one reason is that at Pomona for the first time I encountered teachers who had been liberally educated. Never having been subjected to training in "education," like so many of their lower-school counterparts, their intellects had not been dulled nor their curiosity dampened. If at Jaycee the idea was to embrace what could be obviously useful "in later life" (see my canting letter, above), at Pomona the idea seemed to be to regard one thing as fascinatingly related to all other things and to seek the meaning of the relationship regardless of consequences. At Jaycee I was never invited to probe for the embarrassing truth and to distinguish it from the popular lie. I was ushered into a world of certainties, not ambiguities. Dim as my mind was, I perceived now that I was in quite a new scene, even if I didn't know what to do about it. And I don't want to suggest that the PJC teachers were "bad" or lazy or incompetent. Just the opposite. They were excellent teachers of what they knew. They just didn't know enough, or they didn't know enough about ideas and values and their shifting history. Or if they did know, they didn't regard that as the most compelling focus for those learning to be grown-ups. To sum up the situation, they'd not been persuaded that their most important responsibility was criticism — artistic, literary, intellectual, political, and social.

In the second semester of Freshman English, Mulhauser conducted us through *The Return of the Native*, *Henry IV, Part 1*, and poems. I'd paid no attention to poetry since, in junior high, I'd been required to memorize and recite a poem by an English teacher at wits' end and ignorant of what else to do with the class. My choice was Leigh Hunt's "Abou Ben Adhem," which persuaded me that poems contained moral instruction and were to be valued for that reason. As I moved on, PJC left me quite innocent of poetry, as it did of all art except music, and my real introduction to it came from Pomona, not just from Mulhauser's tough-minded explications and queries, but, later, from moments like Joseph Angell's unequivocal assertion, "The most masculine thing in the world is poetry." In *The Revised College Omnibus* we read Browning's "Caliban Upon Setebos," Hardy's "The Darkling Thrush," Housman's "Loveliest of Trees," Frost's "Mending Wall" and "Stopping by Woods on a

Snowy Evening," and my first Eliot, "The Love Song of J. Alfred Prufrock," an early experience of a poem loaded with what was to become indispensable to me, irony. Even without a teacher, the *Omnibus* itself served as an elementary school of taste because in addition to these poets, it included as unwitting contrast poems by Edna St. Vincent Millay, whose banality, emptiness, and sentimentality were especially on view in her once very popular poem "Renascence." An encounter with it prompted me to suspect all poems, or even propositions, that seemed "beautiful" (in the pejorative sense) or excessively solemn. "Renascence" also bolstered my view that except as material for metaphors, physical nature contained little of interest.

In revenge against Millay, I liked to play on the piano and sing "Renascence" as allegro as possible to the tune of "Little Brown Jug":

All I could see from where I stood
Was three long mountains and a wood;
I turned and looked another way
And saw three islands in a bay.
So with my eyes I traced the line
Of the horizon, thin and fine,
Straight around till I was come
Back to where I'd started from;
And all I saw from where I stood
Was three long mountains and a wood.
Over these things I could not see;
These were the things that bounded me;
[Ha ha ha! Tee hee hee!
Little brown jug, how I love thee!]

This raucous act of subversion, one of my standard turns for amusing friends and callers at my room, I regarded less as the philistinism it was mistaken for than as an act of criticism and an exposure of phoniness and artistic incompetence. It could have been interpreted as a necessary prolegomenon to my ultimate taste for Eliot, Pound, and W. C. Williams, poets specializing in historical awareness, ironic analysis, and satire.

At Pomona, required physical education offered further opportunities for idleness and subversion. For their first semester, freshmen had to choose a "self-defense" activity, either boxing or wrestling. Not wishing to risk a broken nose and terrified of facing the slightest pain, I chose wrestling. I soon located a fellow malingerer able to simulate strenuous exertion without expending any effort at all. During the semester we learned to rest, almost to sleep, holding each other inertly in our gray sweatsuits, feigning taxing grips, which we varied now and then convincingly. It didn't take long to discover that physical education was very largely a fraud, "attendance," not activity or achievement, being the thing that mattered. My subsequent experience with the easiest possible compulsory group game, volleyball, confirmed this conviction.

"Extracurricular activities" proving at this point much more attractive than classes, I hurled myself into student theater, appearing in Maxwell Anderson's *High Tor* — I played one of the gangsters — and in a farce by Norman Philbrick, Pomona '35, then a teacher of theater at Stanford. In his *The Sky's the Limit*, I impersonated a crazy furniture mover, and to make myself look fatter and even funnier than normal, used grease pencil to overemphasize my double chin and jowls. It was simply an extension of my standard role of laugh-producer among my friends, and because the audience was larger, this act was eminently satisfying.

Although my heavy and not yet completely developed body was not, I knew, the thing to attract girls without a generous admixture of "wit" and "humor," I did pursue several young women, but without a lot of sexual success. What with constant supervision, signing out, early return to their dormitories, and lack of private places, it was difficult for girls to gratify even attractive men, that is, football players and the like. I found that girls were best when you got them to the beaches at Balboa, Laguna, or Corona del Mar, some forty miles away. Distance from chaperonage and minimal beachwear encouraged lots of necking in the sand, followed by exciting underage beer drinking at dinner before the perilous drive back to Claremont. For something close to genuine sex, a car seemed necessary, and the favorite spot for night parking was an unkempt, rock-strewn sandy area east of the campus, providentially equipped with olive trees to serve as screens. Here I sometimes took a date in Ed's 1939 Plymouth sedan and tried my luck. Girls were also fun in a different way at college dances and at the twice-yearly concert nights. Then, the boys dressed in their tuxedos — their particular contribution to Gracious Living — and the girls in long dresses. Many wore corsages to lighten the duty of attending to Rachmaninoff and Tchaikovsky as played by the Los Angeles Symphony, or other Russian favorites sung by the Don Cossack Choir. The concert was preceded by a formal dinner where you and your woman for the evening could converse about your class work. I'm sorry to say that the accessories for my tuxedo included a snap-on purple ("burgundy") bow tie, then all the rage, matched by a purple boutonniere made of feathers. (The two came in a boxed set.)

Another device for putting study in its place was drinking. I began not with the college boys' favorite, beer, but with Scotch, and many uncomic moments resulted. Since we had to drink very much off campus, sometimes driving many miles to a place known not to demand documentation of birth dates, driving home at least a bit drunk was an exciting part of the exercise and enjoyed by all. Mothers Against Drunk Driving hadn't even been thought of yet, and we drove drunk without fear or shame. And we were remarkably lucky. I know of no auto accident occasioned by drink while I was at Pomona, and that contributed to the feeling that we were indeed inhabiting Paradise. We could do anything and get away with it.

Not that there weren't plenty of close calls. Once I skidded on a graveled mountain highway, returning from an evening of boozing, and the car just avoided going over the edge. And once, driving back from the town of Pomona late at night, with the car full of drunken friends, we encountered a dense fog on the outskirts of Claremont. I slowed to about five miles an hour but even then could barely see the road directly ahead. Suddenly the right front wheel struck something palpably alive and before I could stop ran over it. Its bones crunched. Cold chills in the car. Was it a person asleep on the road? Trembling, I got out to look. The thing was silent and inert. It was the body of a large mongrel dog. I drove back to college silent and quite sober.

Centers of alcoholic culture were the six local fraternities tolerated by the college. (There were no sororities.) The fraternities were not just tolerated: they occupied for their meetings and high jinks large basement rooms officially granted them in the men's dormitories. There they performed their rituals and conducted their meetings, Ping-Pong games, and all-night poker sessions. One didn't drink there, but that was where we often assembled to plan drinking parties off the campus. In the spring of my freshman year Ed succeeded in persuading his fraternity to pledge me as a "tribute," and I cheerfully endured a week of humiliation, exhaustion, and paddling, thrilled, despite my secret disdain for the mucker pose, to be included in a set of athletes and future businessmen. Paddling was not as bad as it looked and sounded, and indeed had some usefulness: it taught me to bear pain almost with enjoyment, a lesson that was to come in handy in the spring of 1945.

Pomona offered no opportunities to continue my obsessions with magic or printing, or even photography. The student photographer who served the newspaper and yearbook was much more professional and able than I. But writing for the student publications was a further way of having fun quite outside the classroom. Providing prose for newspaper and yearbook soon enabled me to master all journalistic clichés, and I found I could spin out three hundred words on any topic almost instantly, and enjoy it. Writing not classifiable as reporting I put into the college humor magazine, *The Sagehen*, which Ed and I edited jointly. Once a semester we distributed it in the dining hall and then watched surreptitiously to see if anyone laughed. Few did. The would-be funny pieces with which I filled this magazine bring today a profound feeling of shame. How could I have thought them funny? Since Ed was partial, there was no one to tell me that this piece might do, but never, never that one. We desperately needed an editor-in-chief, but all we had was a moral censor, to whom all copy had to be submitted. He was alert only to obscenity, and we tormented him by submitting each time endless galleys of filthy and obviously unprintable jokes, just to see what he would do. (As a Christer and teacher of "speech," he clearly deserved punishment.) Like all conductors of college humor magazines, we thought we were imitating *The New Yorker*. Instead of "The Talk of the Town," we opened with "And So It Goes," where we imitated our New York betters by deploying freely the hallmark *we*. Our pages were thick with bad imitations of Thurber and Perelman, mock-pedagogic diction, and funny names (e.g., Mortimer Flywheel). The best things about the magazine were the covers and cartoons of Gordon Ingram, a shy and brilliant artist we found among the students. He specialized in splendid, rather cruel caricatures of campus personalities, including members of the faculty, and I gratified my hatred of gym by assigning him the task of ridiculing one of the coaches who had become my special bane.

At Pomona, opting for ROTC did not get one out of gym, but since I'd started with it at Jaycee, I went on into the "Advanced Course." It was wholly preposterous, taught by a senile, never very bright colonel and his nice, kind assistant, a Pomona graduate who was a regular army captain and the most benevolent officer I ever met. He also had the distinction of sporting the very last Sam Browne belt I saw worn (sabers went first, then Sam Brownes). The ROTC class work was farcical, focusing on the generalities of military sanitation (we never used a straddle trench or saw a Lister Bag) and wholly abstract map reading (we never used maps of our actual location so that we could compare visible features with their symbolic representation). Antipersonnel mines were not mentioned, nor were booby traps. The program assumed that we were all going to become infantry officers. This was clearly, for most of us, a ridiculous idea, although we were already equipped with a uniform allowance that we spent on real officers' outfits. One afternoon a week we had close-order drill on the football field, providing fun for satiric wits in the bleachers. Drilling with our World War I Springfields, we might have seemed, for the moment, almost plausible, but in 1942 the ROTC

Springfields from all over the United States were collected and donated to Britain. They were replaced by clumsy one-piece wooden simulacra. Marching with these on our shoulders, not to mention presenting "arms," drew especially raucous laughter from the stands. I was not the only one, I'm sure, who was convinced that prepared this way, we could never actually fight in any war. For me, I knew, the Pasadena-Pomona Paradise would go on forever, becoming richer, funnier, and more satisfying all the time.

Just before the outbreak of the Great War, British artist, novelist, and critic Wyndham Lewis had felt that way too. Indeed, in August 1914, like me in early December 1941, he had felt so precisely like me that what he says in his memoir *Blasting and Bombardiering* (1937) will do for both of us:

> *Life was good and easy, and I called Life 'friend.' I'd never hidden anything from him, and he'd never hidden anything from me. Or so I thought. I knew everything. He was an awfully intelligent companion; we had the same tastes (apparently) and he was awfully fond of me. And all the time he was plotting up a mass–murder.*

⊰ III ⊱

$\mathcal{T}$HUS, INTO THIS silly Paradise, a serpent crept — or rather, dropped. Levity over our ludicrous weekly drill couldn't survive the implications of the message received at Naval HQ in Washington on December 7, 1941:

AIR RAID ON PEARL HARBOR THIS IS NOT A DRILL.

Nor could it mitigate the president's words, especially his "very many," addressed to Congress on Monday, December 8: "I regret to tell you that very many American lives have been lost." All eight hundred of us Pomona students heard those words outdoors, assembled at 9:30 in front of the Carnegie Library, where normally we gathered for football rallies. It was a cold morning for Southern California, and I was wearing my snappy reversible windbreaker jacket, beige on one side, light blue on the other. We all agreed with the president when he said, "No matter how long it may take us to overcome this pre-meditated invasion, the American people in their righteous might will win through to absolute victory." He went on to express "confidence in our armed forces," which, some of us couldn't help noticing, included, in a way, the ROTC, and revealed thus a degree of severely misplaced confidence. Given the impudence of this "dastardly and unprovoked attack," it was clear that Japan must be not just defeated but severely punished. The common feeling among the assembled students was simply intense hatred and an urge to destroy. Few thought anything wrong in the subsequent rapid roundup of Japanese Americans and their enforced removal from the West Coast.

Why had Dr. Lyon assembled the college that morning? To listen to the call for a declaration of war, of course, but also to hear his own plea to the male students not to rush off to the recruiting stations but to wait, for months if necessary, to be called up — as officer material, of course. The general campus tone was one of deep gloom, as registered in an editorial in the student newspaper on December 9. "The time has come for hard work, for sacrifice, for unhappiness." Indeed, "we are going to get our pants burnt." But I was privately rather exhilarated by this new turn of events, for I knew that I could come to no harm. I was too rich, too well looked after, too well groomed, too fortunate in every way to be damaged. My unvoiced conviction was close to W. H. Auden's when he went to the Spanish Civil War. When friends wondered if he wasn't afraid of being killed or wounded, he said, "No. Nanny wouldn't allow it."

Except for a few hotheads, athletes and the like, many of whom dashed off to join the Marine Corps, most of us were content to wait, and within a few months, every male in the college, the physically unfit excepted, was enrolled in some national program exempting him from the draft and allowing him to continue in college until finally called up for officer training. Popular were the Navy V-1 and V-12 programs, which seemed to promise a fairly clean and civilized future. Popular also was the Army Air Corps, whose officers' chic, droopy visor caps, silver wings, and melodramatic song, "Off We Go into the Wild Blue Yonder," young men with a flair for engineering and romantic personal display found hard to resist. All these fantasized wartime careers as dashing pilots, or at least navigators and bombardiers, but a great many disgraced themselves by washing out of flight schools and becoming enlisted gunners, or even — the ultimate disgrace — ground crew. There was hardly a more flagrant social demotion than flunking out of officer training, regardless of branch of the service, and victims littered the premises during the forties and fifties. Some have never recovered. One Pomonan, extremely intelligent and believed to possess striking literary talent of a Hemingway kind, foundered in Air Corps officer training within a month or so. Thoroughly demoralized, he wrote one bad novel, generated a few unproduced screenplays, and disappeared into Mexico, never to be heard of again. Those of us in the Infantry ROTC signed up for the Enlisted Reserve Corps, which guaranteed a few more months of college before call-up, which we assumed meant immediate automatic entry into Officer Candidate School at Fort Benning and rapid transformation into second lieutenants. Boy, were we wrong.

Soon the college was operating year-round. The former summer school, long a shameful recourse for delinquents, now assumed the status of a regular, honorable term, and most of the men and some of the women opted for "accelerated programs," at least hoping to graduate before more unforeseen and terrible things happened. From the end of 1941 to spring 1943, I was in school constantly, although I remember little of what I learned. I was taught Shakespeare by an extremely lazy and "charming" former Rhodes Scholar who set us objective tests (easier to grade) instead of essays. At his hands, we confronted literary challenges like the following, which persuaded most students that the study of English was indeed fatuous and quite useless:

Shakespeare was born at Stratford-upon-Avon, which is in the county of (a) Sussex (b) Warwickshire (c) Somerset (d) Stratfordshire.

During these empty months, the war was always there in the background, prompting a flux of earnestness threatening to my devotion to "gags." We had constant scrap drives and blood drives, bond drives and don't-waste-food drives. Ed's and my pleasure with *The Sagehen* was spoiled by the news that all editors of college humor magazines were expected to welcome an official eight-page "Victory Section," prepared and printed elsewhere and shipped to us in bales for local insertion. While seeking, clumsily, a light touch consistent with the tone of the magazines, these unwanted pages were relentlessly unfunny and merely morale boosting in the crudest way. I was so opposed to accepting them — comic-magazine editors were assured that the scheme was entirely voluntary — that I objected vehemently to the administrators supervising the business end of college publications. I was listened to, then told by a red-faced jingo that my want of patriotism was a disgrace. I can't remember exactly what he said, but the substance, if not the language, of an exhortation to Get on the Team! was a large part of his message. Defeated, I slunk away, perceiving early the damage the war was bound to do to intellectual independence and self-respect. Of course we had to accept the Victory Section, and *The Sagehen,* while still pretending to be critical, independent, and subversive, became something quite opposite, a government mouthpiece where even our almost-dirty jokes were tainted by neighboring high purpose.

In January 1942, Reinhard Heydrich was convening the Wannsee Conference to plan the extermination of the Jews of Europe. Faint echoes of this sort of thing reached us from time to time, and we wondered what Grover Magnin, '42, one of the few visible Jews at Pomona, made of it all. No one knew him or even talked to him. He was identifiable only as a relative of the famous I. Magnin. We pursued our quiet way, frightening ourselves now and then by wondering how we might protect ourselves if the Japs should drop bombs or poison gas on the West Coast. The Fussell family deplored having to black out the front windows of the beach house. The beach in front, where we used to cavort in innocence and toast our wienies, was now a sinister place, patrolled by soldiers in the new pot helmets and bearing M-1 rifles with fixed bayonets. They were accompanied by savage dogs, clearly avid to tear apart any Jap venturing ashore from a submarine or a disguised fishing boat.

Waiting to be called up was a universal experience of college males in 1942 and 1943. Threatened by something more serious, college was really over, and yet the more serious thing hadn't arrived. We were locked into a great national holding pattern, and I can never forget the boredom of the long afternoons when to have something to do I walked to the student union for a lemon Coke and to see which girls were around. We listened to the jukebox playing "Praise the Lord and Pass the Ammunition," "American Patrol," or "Buckle Down, Winsocki!" That song I mistakenly took to be a spirited attempt to raise the morale of a serviceman, perhaps Private George Winsocki, addicted to sleeping past reveille and thus retarding the victorious ending of the war ("We can win, Winsocki, if you'll only buckle down"). Or the song might have alluded to the idle Able-bodied Seaman Leonard Winsocki, always late leaving his hammock and nowhere to be found when the deck needed scrubbing. Much later, indeed, only in 1994, did I find out that *Winsocki* is not the name of a fictional person at all but of a fictional secondary school, Winsocki being Winsocki Prep of Winsocki, Pennsylvania, as depicted in the Broadway musical *Best Foot Forward* (1941). Regardless, the song, whatever its original implication, is unforgettable, and I can hear it now, as I can feel those long, warm, vacant afternoons when we were all waiting to go to war. My luck so far suggested strongly that it would be safely over before I had to go.

While waiting, we rolled our own cigarettes, the manufactured kind having grown as scarce as gasoline. This we procured from a black-market operator who had a filling station on the road to the city of Pomona. There was clearly some collusion between him and enforcers of the rationing law, for cars backed up dramatically from his station for a quarter of a mile while nearby honest, patriotic gas outlets went visibly unpatronized.

One recourse against the tedium of waiting was practical joking, of which we became, in our own view, distinguished practitioners. My self-destructive roommate had been replaced by another, smart and gifted in the arts of quiet outrage and general sabotage. He and I invented an imaginary student named Philip Phallus, whom, with utmost solemnity, we enrolled in various classes and activities, hoping to hear sometime a comic roll call. Philip was a nerd — a chemistry major — who played the violin. Often we volunteered his musical services in his own pitiable telephone voice to local academic and community gatherings, offering to play the violin free in return for tea and cakes. Other cruel jests involved a thick, slimy, gelatinlike substance we manufactured from jellied soap. Sticky, streaky, and gray, this looked like a satire on semen, and we deposited generous helpings in many beds during 1943. What with the claustration of women a quarter-mile away, there was so much masturbating and wet-dreaming that we knew we could count on numerous shocked recoils as men encountered our product in their beds and leaped out, thinking, "God, did I do *that?*" Our behavior, illustrative both literally and figuratively of the team *sophomoric,* sent us into paroxysms so violent and prolonged that we collapsed onto the floor, our whoops echoing through the dormitory.

Waiting entailed other forms of idleness, like the hours I spent with Ed refining definitions — trying especially to specify precisely the difference between an *asshole* and a *shit,* with examples drawn from male students of our acquaintance or our imaginations. Philip Phallus was clearly an asshole, dumb, sincere, dull, and harmless. On the other hand, ——— was undeniably a shit, pompous, pretentious, selfish, and mean. And with nothing but schoolwork to do, there was a temptation to idle somewhere else. The father of one of my funnier friends was an engineer at the Basic Magnesium plant at Las Vegas. The demand for magnesium, used in flares and incendiary bombs, was such that this immense plant operated twenty-four hours a day. For us, it was fun after a night of drinking to hitchhike to Las Vegas, some 275 miles away. The uncertainty of rides was what made it amusing. More than once we found ourselves, on a distinctly chilly morning, stranded in Barstow, less than halfway to Vegas. Once we walked to a base of the Civil Air Patrol and, outside its gates, lied to a passing driver that we were pilots in training. He began to see through us before we reached Las Vegas, and we narrowly escaped a beating-up. Upon our arrival at Vegas, my friend's parents, clucking tolerantly at our folly, let us eat and rest. We returned to college on a bus. Did we miss some classes? No matter: military discipline would have us in its grip very soon.

For me, waiting was partly alleviated by my discovery of the delights of H. L. Mencken. How did I find him? Did a teacher drop his name and suggest that I'd like him? Did a friend? Whatever, I took all his books out of the library and for many weeks regaled myself with his battle against the morons. Prepared for Mencken by "The Mucker Pose," I was exactly ready to gather self-identity and strength from Mencken's wit and uncompromising contempt. He firmed me up remarkably: "Perhaps the most valuable asset that any man can have in this world is a naturally superior air, a talent for sniffishness and reserve." (I was already working on that.) "The generality of men are always impressed by it, and accept it freely as a proof of genuine merit. One need but disdain them to gain their respect."

The wartime idolizing of the common man was beginning to grate on me, and I welcomed Mencken's comment on George Washington: "He had no belief in the infallible wisdom of the common people, but regarded them as inflammatory dolts, and tried to save the Republic from them." Having observed the proceedings at Aimee Semple McPherson's Angelus Temple, I agreed enthusiastically with Mencken's explanation of the reason Aimee decided to promulgate her mystery in Los Angeles. She perceived that "there were more morons collected in Los Angeles than in any other place on earth." Indeed, once she blew her clarion, "the half-wits were flocking in from twenty states." With Mencken's observation on America's "capital defect" I agreed then, and my agreement has grown stronger the more I have seen the ideal of liberal learning displaced by vulgar utilitarian exercises: "The capital defect in the culture of These States is the lack of a civilized aristocracy, secure in its position, animated by an intelligent curiosity, skeptical of all facile generalizations, superior to the sentimentality of the mob, and delighting in the battle of ideas for its own sake."

The rigid uniformity the army was about to impose made highly pertinent this Menckenism of 1922:

All government, in its essence, is a conspiracy against the superior man: its one permanent object is to oppress him and cripple him. . . . One of its primary functions is to regiment men by force, to make them as much alike as possible . . . , to search out and combat originality among them.

I vibrated sympathetically to Mencken's contempt for athletics, his rejection of "the common delusion that athletics, in themselves, are uplifting and hence laudable." Likewise, I constructed my "religious" understanding after Mencken's: "The most satisfying and ecstatic faith," he declared, "is almost purely agnostic. It trusts absolutely without professing to know at all." Mencken alerted me to the appalling ugliness of the America that men had built, the positive "Libido for the Ugly" presiding here, the love of the unbeautiful apparently for its own sake. For twenty-five miles out of Pittsburgh, Mencken notes, the traveler by train is confronted only by sights that "insult and lacerate the eye." Conclusion: "Out of the melting pot emerges a race which hates beauty as it hates truth." I confess that the exaggeration there became a stigma of my own style, like, alas, Mencken's prolixity, occasioned perhaps by his delight in showing off his command of languages and idiom, and in engineering surprising collocations of high and low styles. From him also I borrowed the trick of tossing in the archaic subjunctive, especially in not entirely appropriate contexts, like: "The mind, where there be any, finds thinking impossibly hard work."

All this Mencken was hardly the best preparation for my becoming a docile common soldier in the largest, most uniform army ever fielded by the United States. This happened on May 6, 1943, a date for me as unforgettable as December 7, 1941, itself. On May 6, the fifty-five of us enrolled in the Enlisted Reserve Corps were "called to active duty." This began quite merrily with an informal early morning march, band playing, down College Avenue to a Pacific Electric streetcar drawn up at the tiny Claremont rail station. After many waves and facetious shouts, we were conveyed to Fort MacArthur at San Pedro, the nearest army reception center. There, illusions were shattered from the very start when we were treated not at all as officer material but as ordinary drafted scum. We were lined up, insulted, shouted at, numbered, and hustled into a barracks building by contemptuous sergeants. Next day, conditions did not improve: we were put through a physical examination featuring scrutiny of one's anus ("Spread those cheeks!") with, sometimes, public critical commentary. After that, we were rudely supplied with basic uniform, in the traditional wrong sizes.

I can still smell the synthetic-rubber odor of the stiff olive drab raincoat, and I remember my surprise on learning that the helmet liner, which I'd seen looking like a bellicose helmet in countless photographs, was made not of metal but merely of something resembling plastic and was designed to be worn inside the real steel helmet. Since as ROTC students we had always worn dress uniforms complete with neckties for all our outdoor exercises, the components of this new uniform were a shock. They were so clearly designed not for show but for hard, unheroic labor. We'd never worn dark green cotton working-class fatigues before, nor heavy high shoes, nor canvas leggings. Clearly the soldiers we'd seen in public and depicted in propaganda pictures were notably different from ones like us now, manhandling garbage cans, cleaning out kitchen grease traps, and picking up cigarette butts from wide, wide parade grounds. Unbelievable that we were ever considered, in our satisfactory former lives, incipient officer candidates. Here, we were serfs, or even lower than that: we felt the dog tags issued to us accurately named. Even our overseas caps lacked class. They were plain, devoid even of light blue infantry piping. That would come only after we'd completed basic training and had earned the right to be designated soldiers, rather than shitheads, assholes, and dumb fucks.

We knew now that we'd been cruelly duped, and our ever emerging from our current social status seemed quite impossible. Our inquiries about when we would head for OCS triggered the most obscene sarcasm and abuse. I have no evidence, but I feel certain that one or two tears were shed once we were safely put away in our cots at night. But worse was to come. Far worse.

Like the others', my first army duties were distinctly unofficer-like: carrying heavy bales of clothing around in a warehouse and, as if I were a sad-sack character in an army musical, peeling endless potatoes. I wrote home:

This KP is really a drudge. An illiterate mess sergeant . . . was quite profane. . . . When I reached the kitchen, I was immediately assigned to the vegetable (potato) room. I peeled potatoes all morning, after which I washed, mopped, and scrubbed the floors and porches. . . . This morning I passed out sausages (two for privates, three for corporals and sergeants). That's the way everything works around here. In the mess hall, the non-coms sit and eat steaks all afternoon while we work.

But there were only six days of this, and what came next made it seem like heaven.

Camp Roberts, an infantry basic training center, was 225 miles north of Los Angeles, near the town, now transformed into an army town, of Paso Robles. We were conveyed there by bus.

May 13, 1943

Dear Mother and Dad,

    There is plenty to complain about at this stage of the game. First, we're not told what to do but required to guess. This is essentially a combat training course, and the whole object of the training is to become toughened in body and calloused in mind. We are forbidden to drink water from breakfast (6:00) until supper (5:30). Anyone caught sneaking a drink of water is punished.

    Almost all the instructors are 2nd Lieutenants, and most of them are plenty tough. . . . I miss you all a great deal.

Love,

Paul

Our seventeen-week "course" was not to begin for a day or two, providing time for a number of painful injections, hours of equally painful calisthenics, a viewing of a "Why We Fight" film, a well-intentioned but wholly unbelievable "welcome" speech by the commanding general, and issue of serious martial equipment: steel helmets, gas masks, cartridge belts with first-aid packets and canteens, packs, and rifles, whose serial numbers we were enjoined to memorize instantly and recite on command. One of us who mistakenly grabbed his sergeant's rifle instead of his own was required to expiate by wearing his own rifle for a week, slung diagonally across his body, whether at meals, on the toilet, or in the sack. The rifles were rigorously locked up whenever not in strictly supervised use. I don't remember when bayonets were issued, but they probably did not appear until the loonies among us had revealed themselves and been quietly removed.

These few days before our training began allowed us to contemplate the various Camp Roberts usages different from those appropriate to young gentlemen from Pomona College. Communal toilets, for one thing, a long row of commodes devoid of stalls or partitions. Communal showers, for another, where we bathed before shaving — always at night, there being, in the frantic hustle with whistles blowing all over the place, not enough time in the morning. Another novelty was going to sleep surrounded by thirty other people, twisting, turning, muttering, snoring, masturbating, and farting. Many of us had brought pajamas. We quickly learned to sleep in our underwear. Years later, I realized what a lot I had in common with Robert Graves, who wrote in *Good-Bye to All That,* "What I most disliked in the army was never being alone, forced to live and sleep with men whose company, in many cases, I would have run miles to avoid."

In the odd moments allowed us for "recreation," we were permitted (after 6:00 P.M.) to visit a local PX, where a bottle of watery 3.2 beer could be enjoyed to the accompaniment of hillbilly jukebox music, like "Lay That Pistol Down." But the only time of day or night that did not invite to either satire, desertion, or suicide was the thirty seconds before sleep after the barracks lights were turned off. Then you heard, for the first time seriously, taps played not on a record as you might expect but on a nearby bugle, and played beautifully, with the right emotional retards in the right places. That nightly moment might persuade you that you were really a member of an organization proposing to extirpate totalitarianism and brutality, no matter how brutally one or more of the Four Freedoms that organization had violated during the day.

August 12, 1943

Dear Mother and Dad,

We had an all-night hike and bivouac problem last night. . . . I got one blister and am the envy of the platoon. Some men's feet look like beefsteaks.

I was more tired today than ever before in my whole life. We worked on the obstacle course most of the afternoon, and I kept going to sleep. Very funny!

To the torments of the obstacle course and the weekly ten-mile night march with rifle and full pack were added regular all-night guard duty and twenty-four-hour KP. One Pomona friend almost had his head knocked off for failing to understand immediately the harsh command of an immense Filipino mess sergeant, who shouted at him, "Bring brass!"

"What?"

(Augmented volume.) "BRING BRASS!"

It turned out that *brush* was the thing meant.

And how shocked we were by our first shortarm inspection, to be repeated monthly. The purpose was to detect symptoms of gonorrhea. It began with the ominous order, "Put on raincoats and shoes!"

"Is that all?"

"Shut up. Do as you're told, and don't ask questions."

In a nearby recreation "hall" we lined up and passed before medical officers, who commanded each man to open his raincoat and then, unbelievably, to "skin it down." No yellow matter appearing, we were allowed to return to barracks and to change into our normal proletarian work clothes. In the ROTC no one had told us about the institution of the shortarm inspection. Did officers, we wondered, have to do this too? Did we really want to be in the army, even as lieutenants wearing, on dress-up occasions, snug-fitting dark green tunics and pink trousers? How could I ever tell Mother about the shortarm business, or such upper-middle-class Pasadena dates as Louisa and Nancy, who wrote me loving and innocent letters? How could I tell sister Florence, now attending the University of California at Berkeley, a mere eighty miles away but in quite a different universe? It was little comfort to know that brother Ed was experiencing similar shames, but in the navy. He was being tormented at midshipman's school near Chicago, and later would undergo antisubmarine training in Miami and other places. He ended as a lieutenant junior grade on a destroyer escort in the Pacific, and miraculously survived the kamikazes, the subs, the mines, and the typhoons.

But all this time I was undergoing a remarkable metamorphosis, turning rapidly from a fat boy into a thing that would be called, in later wars, a lean, mean killing machine. In seven weeks my waist went from thirty-six to thirty-two inches, and for the first time actual muscles began to appear, causing one Pomona friend to sing loudly in the latrine, to the tune of "John Brown's Body," "Fussell's getting muscles in his back." I lost my double chin, and now, blond as I was, began to look like an SS man of the better sort, with a jaw-line suggestive of a character in *Terry and the Pirates*. And I became a killing machine by no means abstract. I learned to kill with a noose of piano wire and with a sudden knife-thrust up under the rib cage. And I learned more. I learned to relish the prospect of killing this way and to rejoice in the conviction of power and superiority it gave me.

The extravagant physical demands produced further changes. "I have noticed one thing," I wrote home. "I am becoming absolutely fearless. I will now *run* very fast down a steep hill covered with sharp rocks that I wouldn't have *crawled* down a few months ago," and I could now throw myself around on an obstacle course that would have terrified me at Pomona. Unafraid, I entered the tear-gas cham-ber without a mask, which one put on only by command, playfully and painfully delayed. The daily heat was almost unbelievable, 110 degrees most days, and we sweated until our clothes were completely wet. My face and hands grew tan, and I felt wonderful. On the rifle range, I attained the grade of Expert Rifleman and won thereby a carton of Chesterfields. Scared of loud noises as a child, I grew to love them. I enjoyed the bang of the rifle in my ear, as well as the kick against my shoulder. On realistic maneuvers, I found I was most comfortable when the artillery shells were landing very close. The crack of the shells soothed me, reminding me that the infantry had plenty of support that would never let us down. Camp Roberts was only twenty-five miles from the ocean, and it was impossible to for-get that we were in a killing war, for when marching, each platoon carried a red wooden box of rifle ammunition, to be expended when called for on Jap invaders or aviators. Because of a Japanese invasion scare, our passes for July Fourth were canceled, and I don't think we cared a lot, so pleased were we to imagine ourselves indispensable to the national defense.

Those of us fantasizing becoming officers someday had before us plenty of examples of bad and good. Most of the officers training us were apparently from the National Guard and the Reserve, and some were so bad we couldn't refrain from rude audible laughter. Our platoon leaders came and went, each staying only a few weeks. One was Second Lieutenant Williams, a scandal at that rank because fully fifty years old. He was intolerably stupid and witless, and we enjoyed picking on him, calling him Bolo Willie within his hearing. "How many of you wants to go to religious services?" he would ask, and one of our college wits would raise his hand and say, "Sir, I wants to." Another, fond of acting British and educated, asserted at a political orientation session that Winston Churchill is without doubt "the greatest man of our area." To be unique, he pronounced "discipline" with the stress on the middle syllable. Another, explaining that when saluting, one keeps the fingers of the right hand extended and joined, always said extended and "jointed." Where did such people come from, we wondered?

But there were good officers too, distinguished by modesty, respect for the men, and smooth mastery of their duties. One we loved was Lieutenant Jacobs, Jewish, flat-assed, and kindhearted, for whom we would have done anything. Thirty-five years after the war I caught sight of him near New Brunswick, New Jersey, where he managed an interurban bus company. I wish I'd told him then how much we'd admired him and appreciated his kindness to us, but somehow I didn't have the nerve. What was this nice, sensitive person doing as an infantry officer? Instead of rebuking us, he would smile appreciatively as we sang on the march the impudent songs we'd made up. Some nights a loud siren signaled an imaginary Jap air raid on the camp, requiring all the troops to disperse rapidly into a nearby sand flat smelling seriously of raw sewage. This exercise was known as Dispersal Rehearsal, and we sang

The Dispersal-Rehearsal Song
(Tune: "Mad'moiselle from Armentières")

Dispersal rehearsal tonight at eight, parlay voo,
Dispersal rehearsal tonight at eight, parlay voo,
  Dispersal rehearsal tonight at eight,
  We'll sit in the sand and masturbate,
Hinky dinky parlay voo.

Twelve weeks of the Camp Roberts treatment — largely, hiking with fifty pounds of pack, plus rifle — were so humbling that they almost erased from the mind the idea that we might some day achieve officerhood. Thus we boys from the Pomona ROTC were surprised to be informed that we were to appear before an Officer Candidate Board to be passed or failed, after a brief oral examination, as fit for Benning. The board consisted of six lieutenants, captains, and majors and met in an empty barracks. There were four windows along each side, and the board asked each of us to imagine that these windows were the four platoons of a rifle company commanded by us, lined up at attention, rifles at order arms, waiting for our close-order-drill commands. The trick was not just to pitch one's voice at proper command volume but to keep in mind that the imaginary soldiers had to be right-faced and right-shoulder-armed before they could be marched away for further evolutions. I went through this, I think, without major gaffes, returning the nonexistent troops finally to their starting positions and instructing them to stand "at ease."

This was only the first part of the examination. The final part was "intellectual," requiring, presumably, quickness and accuracy in answering quite unexpected questions. I was asked, "How many sides on a pair of dice?" (Six was the answer that had sunk countless candidates.) I was also asked to describe the size of a seventy-two-hour-old human embryo. I guessed that you'd need a very powerful microscope to see it at all. That was apparently correct enough, and after a few minutes' consultation, the board kindly ignored my looking like a fifteen-year-old kid and called me back to tell me I'd passed. Much 3.2 beer was consumed that night.

The final ordeal for infantry trainees was a two-week bivouac away from cots, floors, toilets, water faucets, hot food, and similar comforts.

Sunday, Sept. 12, 1943

Dear Mother and Dad,

I got back from the bivouac yesterday morning. It turned out to be the toughest thing we've had to do. We walked two hundred miles in two weeks. We slept on the ground, went without water, and endured treatment calculated to wear us down and tire us out. We hiked 34 miles to the first bivouac area.

The 34 miler was supposed to be 20 miles, but the battalion got lost in the mountains for two hours. We'd drunk our canteens at 20 miles, and at about 30 miles nearly a quarter of the battalion had dropped out, or passed out cold from the heat or just plain exhaustion. I went the whole distance. When we finally reached our area, we were allowed no water but had to dig slit trenches immediately.

Although the first week was not so bad, the second was hellish. Very little sleep, and when I did sleep I just lay on the ground fully clothed and put my raincoat over my head. We went through artillery attacks, gas attacks, and every other kind of attack to rob us of sleep. We lived on C and K rations. The officers and non-coms were as tired as we were. One sergeant with eight years in the army broke both his arches on the 34-mile march and will never walk normally again.

We felt proud of our battalion coming in, because only one man fell out on the 20-mile march, and he broke his leg on one of the mountain trails. A band met us when we returned and escorted us back to our barracks. Everybody cheered and applauded us, and we felt pretty good. The officers congratulated us and said that our march back was something of a triumph. It certainly was for me, because my feet were so sore when we started that I thought I'd never make it. You should have seen us when we got in! Haggard faces, torn clothes, feet dragging, but everyone in step with the music and marching straight and proud.

Recalling that moment reminds me of many more when pleasure and pride in the army outweighed my customary repulsion and shame. The boy from Pomona College was learning that happiness consists not entirely in doing as one wants. It can be consistent also with deprivation and pain, exhaustion and tears — so long as self-respect is intact, and even, as here, augmented.

Training concluded a few days later, and we had a "graduation" ceremony where we were all presented with Certificates of Accomplishment. They represented, I wrote home, "more sweat and wrenched muscles than anyone will ever know." Immediately our training battalion broke up. Most of the trainees were shipped off as replacements to infantry divisions, where I'm afraid very many were killed and wounded (as they were trained to be) in the battles in France and Italy in 1944. The fifteen or so Pomona ROTC boys who had survived the OCS board enjoyed for a while a very different, almost unbelievable, fate: the Infantry School at Benning was overcrowded at the moment, and we were sent into a comfortable waiting period back at Pomona College, where we resided for two months pursuing an irrelevant army engineering program to keep us busy. It was now that my utter incapacity in the higher, or even moderately high, mathematics exposed itself. I never understood what a trigonometric "function" was, for no one troubled to explain, and although I wielded an expensive slide rule and a book of sines, cosines, and tangents, I never got it. I received a gift grade of D in that subject, but since it didn't matter at all — these grades, being "army," were not considered significant for our real Pomona records — I was not bothered. Besides, we'd all been promoted to private first class, and the minute our orders came through to proceed by train to Columbus, Georgia, we became corporals. That, for former infantry privates and trainees, accustomed to being shouted at and demeaned, was now the only sort of thing that mattered.

If at Camp Roberts our implicit social class had been deep plebeian, at Fort Benning it was, if not precisely patrician, certainly middle class, or even upper middle. Although we had to make our beds, and tautly, we no longer were obliged to clean the barracks weekly with brooms and wet mops and window rags: Black troops did these things, and picked up outside too, facts that never let us forget that if we were in the army, we were also in Georgia, where movie theaters and drinking fountains were segregated and no one thought anything wrong. As officer candidates, we were excused KP and guard duty, and our bunks were farther apart than before. We were presumed to be in good physical shape now, and thus we were not marched out, burdened with heavy weights, to field problems. Instead, carrying clipboards rather than rifles, we were trucked out to the field and back. And another novelty: all the officers treated us decently. Here, it would have been unthinkable for a company commander, marching his troops, to shout — like our captain at Camp Roberts — "What're you looking down at the ground for? There are no holes there, but if there were, I'd march you into them, I assure you!" At Benning, there was ample civility behind the toughness, and it was assumed that backward and clumsy as we were, we resembled, in a way, gentlemen. We were organized in three platoons instead of four, each under the constant scrutiny of a lieutenant called a tactical officer, who was often to be seen making entries about us in his pocket notebook. Simulated command positions rotated. One day a candidate might pretend to be the platoon leader, another the platoon sergeant or a squad leader. Every command these gave, every reprimand each administered, every scintilla of praise each doled out, was noted by the TO. He observed also hesitations at the more hazardous and demoralizing features of the obstacle course, or delay or "I think" or "It seems to me" in answering hard questions at lectures. We were addressed not as "Corporal" or "Soldier" or by last name but always as "Candidate," and we were never allowed to forget that we were not

Father

Mother

Mother with Edwin, Florence, and PF.

The Pasadena "English" house. On the steps,
Florence, PF, Edwin, Mother.

In 1931 boys like PF wore white
shirts and neckties very often
(G. Edwin Williams).

Sailing at Balboa in the 1930s. The boat originally belonged to the French sailing team at the 1932 Los Angeles Olympics. Hence the *O* and the *F.*

PF and Florence in the Balboa Tournament of Lights, summer 1937.

With Edwin, putting
together *The Sagehen*
by appropriating ideas
from the University
of California *Pelican*
(Photo: Pomona College).

The Pomona ROTC with
the embarrassing wooden
rifles, 1942. PF is in the
middle of the front row
(Pomona College).

Trainees at the Infantry Replacement Center, Camp Roberts, California, summer 1943. PF is second from left, top row.

At Camp Roberts, summer 1943. The archaic long bayonet is the sixteen-inch 1942 model, later reduced to ten inches when it was found that the shorter version scared the enemy just as badly with less risk of damage to friendly eyes, hands, and clothing. If the bayonet had ever been plunged into a German, Italian, or Japanese torso, two inches would have occasioned sufficient internal bleeding to do the job.

PF, at right, straightening out fellow ROTC students waiting at Pomona to go to Fort Benning, fall 1943. The service flag shows the number of Pomona students in the armed forces. The man seated on PF's right survived Benning to be killed on the line in France *(Pomona College)*.

May 1944, just commissioned *(Noel Studio)*.

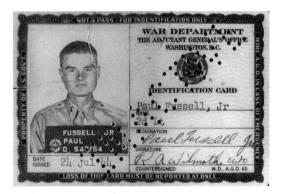

The spelling error at the top of the official officer's identification card might suggest to skeptics that the army would make many more mistakes *(US Army Signal Corps)*.

PF's hammertoes, whose excessively delayed recognition might turn any boy toward irony, satire, and general contempt for authority.

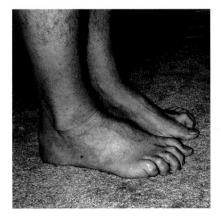

Troops of the 2nd Battalion, 410th Infantry, on December 15, 1944, after searching a fort of the Maginot Line near Climbach, Alsace, for Germans in hiding. None was found. Far right, standing on elevated ground, Sergeant Hudson. Fourth from right, in light-colored trench coat with hood, PF (US Army Signal Corps).

On leave in Paris, July 1945.

student officers or officers-to-be but merely candidates for possible, but not very likely, commissioning.

It was emphasized that only a third of us would survive the course, failures being dispatched immediately to fill the enlisted ranks of infantry divisions. Benning was a school of ethics as well as "leadership" and tactics. Cheats and liars were sent away instantly. Three boys from a university in New York poked fake bullet holes in their machine-gun target with a pencil. They were expelled on the spot. At the Infantry School, the focus seemed less on winning the war by leading troops effectively than on simply surviving the course, and in this emphasis on survival, Benning resembled the combat culture of the larger war. Here our battle was between ourselves and the school standards, and so much trauma had been occasioned by anxiety and the desperate cutthroat atmosphere that the school issued to all candidates a booklet explaining why most aspirants failed and how to avoid that fate. It was titled *The Selection System of the Officer Candidate Course . . . and an Analysis of Officer Candidate Failures.* There was an attempt here to portray the tactical officers as kindly advisers and encouragers and to underplay their function as spies and hostile critics:

> *From the moment candidates report they are constantly and continuously under observation. . . . Officers of the company to which the candidates are assigned are in continual close association with them and observe all phases of their conduct and work. . . . The candidates' attention to lectures and their response to the training received . . . is carefully noted. . . . They interview the candidates frequently, correct observed mistakes, and advise and otherwise assist in every way possible.*

But others were watching too:

The candidates are also under the direct observation of the members of their own class, and, most particularly, the members of their own platoon and squad.

Three times during the seventeen-week training cycle each candidate executed a confidential form rating the others on his floor of the barracks, attesting to his view of their potential as combat officers. "Fuck Your Buddy" sheets, these forms were called, but we undertook this task seriously, knowing that it was a test of our own judgment and objectivity as well as of our acuteness of perception. There were also frequent written tests designed to reveal the incompetent in simple mathematics, map reading, aerial photo interpretation, and the writing of field orders.

But "more candidates fail because of lack of force and aggressiveness than for any other reason," the pamphlet informed us, and vocal skills were crucial here. Every night you heard from the nearby pine trees the strained voices of candidates working on the volume and timbre of their shouted commands. "Double time, MARCH!" had to sound as if it came from someone who meant it. That held true even more for "Follow me!" with which, it was proposed, one was going to lead men into rifle and machine-gun fire or get them to cross a field being, at the moment, cratered by artillery.

Physical incapacity was the second most important cause of failure, and it was for that reason that I almost went out. The terrible obstacle course had to be negotiated within a certain time, and I didn't seem able to make it fast enough. Our tactical officer, not much older than I, devoted a lot of effort to getting me over that hurdle, working with me in the evenings after supper, watching me go through the obstacles over and over and timing me with a stopwatch. He finally declared that I'd passed, although I suspect that his timing was not cruelly rigorous and that the prize was awarded for my persistence rather than my agility. Regardless, I was ecstatic to know that the main impediment to my graduation and commissioning was now overcome. I was learning something important: it was becoming clear that felicity dwelt only in things you'd earned yourself, and especially in obstacles and difficulties overcome — not an easy lesson to learn for a boy who'd always had life his own way.

For those who busted out, the Infantry School offered a not terribly convincing consolation:

> *The standard is high and many candidates with a number of excellent qualities and characteristics have failed to meet it successfully. Such failure is not necessarily a reflection upon the character or the ability of the individual. Many men who do not possess the qualities of leadership which are indispensable in an officer are capable of outstanding performance in many other types of valuable service.*

As the weeks passed, our quarters took on an aspect increasingly melancholy, for the cots of the failed remained in position, their mattresses grotesquely turned back on themselves, as if their hopes had been ruined too. Some men were removed only a week before graduation, too late for their names to be deleted from the souvenir program. In this anxious atmosphere, our being allowed to go into Columbus to buy our uniforms and insignia was almost an assurance that we were safe, but men were known to be plucked out at the last moment because of venial acts of dishonesty or cowardice, and we didn't feel entirely secure until we'd taken the oath and pinned on our gold bars. This we did in the sight of greedy enlisted men skilled in locating and saluting fledgling officers and receiving from each one dollar, the conventional reward for the first salute.

At OCS I made no permanent friends, and indeed I made none in the army. Taught by James Truslow Adams and Mencken, I was too censorious to be good company, as well as, at Benning, too scared of flunking out to waste time in frivolity. I was deadly serious. Of my co-candidates I remember very few. One, a wry little man handicapped by a plaintive look and a weak voice, was tossed out four days before graduation. His bunk was next to mine, and many times I'd listened to his quiet fears of not making it and letting his family down. Another last-minute casualty was the barracks wit, who had entertained us for months with ribald jokes and hilarious mimicry. He proved finally to be merely an entertainer, and the TO fired him too. But if I forgot most of my classmates, I would never forget the unique smell of Benning that winter, the smell, unfamiliar to me, of coal smoke on icy mornings as we fell in on the company street to begin another day's schooling. Nor can I easily forget the unique music of Benning that winter, "Mairzy doats and doazy doates and little lamsy divey," faintly audible from somewhere on Sunday afternoons as we wrote our optimistic letters home or labored over our Fuck Your Buddy forms.

If we had been more imaginative or less proud of ourselves, what might have darkened our outlook was confronting some elementary and obvious facts. Here it was April 1944. The army had already reached its full wartime strength, and therefore infantry second lieutenants were needed now only as replacements for those being constantly killed and wounded. If this many were needed — a new class of almost one hundred graduated every week, and our class was the 321st — the rate of destruction was much greater than we'd ever allowed ourselves to contemplate, and the fact was that few of us could look forward to a long life undamaged. We were meant to be expended, and that's why there were so many of us. (I learned much later that our TO who'd helped me succeed on the obstacle course went from Benning, newly married, directly to an infantry division. Shipped to France, he was killed in due course.)

Up to this point we'd had little actual experience of death and destruction. There was the memorable image of the sergeant at Camp Roberts who was emplacing a block of TNT in a simulated shell crater in an exercise featuring live ammunition. As he bent over his work, someone back at the electric control panel accidently threw the crucial switch, and his body flew into the air. When he landed, it was clear that he was not alive. And at Benning, in the combined artillery-paratroop-infantry exercise designed as the climax of our course, one of the light artillery-spotting planes flying at two thousand feet was struck by a shell from the plane's own guns. The only human thing that fell to earth was a shoe containing some bones and bloody meat. But we were too proudly young and successful, so far, to regard these events as in any way portents of our own future. At this stage, we were like the eighteenth-century British prep-school boys in Thomas Gray's "Ode on a Distant Prospect of Eton College." There, we are warned not to spoil the boys' happiness by informing them of what lies ahead, for

why should they know their fate,
Since sorrow never comes too late,
And happiness too swiftly flies?
Thought would destroy their paradise.
  . . . where ignorance is bliss,
'Tis folly to be wise.

"You'll work like the devil here," said the captain welcoming us to Benning, "but in the end, you'll be a good bunch of fighting lieutenants." The word *fighting* reminded us of something some of us wanted to forget — that the junior officer in the infantry, in addition to the impressive uniform and the "Sirs" and salutes, is in essence a soldier, whose ability to kill with rifle and grenade, piano wire and trench knife, must be as efficient and as untroubled by scruples as the lowest GI's. He is really little more than a grunt with gold bars, and the minute he forgets this, he is useless.

As we fanned out to lead rifle platoons in the infantry divisions, our main stock-in-trade was the elementary fire-and-flank maneuver hammered into us over and over at Benning. It was very simple. With half your platoon, you establish a firing line to keep your enemy's heads down while you lead the other half around to the enemy's flank for a sudden surprise assault, preferably with bayonets and shouting. This tactical operation is said to have been the one tirelessly emphasized by General George C. Marshall when he served as assistant superintendent at Benning. Faced with the task of transforming hordes of military sows' ears into silk purses, he decided, as he said, that "we must develop a technique and methods so simple and so brief that the citizen officer of good common sense can readily grasp the idea." We all did grasp the idea, but in combat we found that it had one signal defect, which quite effectively prevented its being applied. Namely, the difficulty, usually the impossibility, of knowing where your enemy's flank *is*. If you get up and go looking for it, you'll be killed. If you don't find it or just assume that you know where it is, you'll lead your flanking troops directly into his fire. Like so many of the "School Solutions" we were taught, the standard small-unit attack was a nice abstraction, but perhaps its function was rather to raise our morale and confidence than to work as defined. It did have the effect of persuading us that such an attack could be led successfully and that we were the people who could do it. That was good for our self-respect and our courage, and perhaps that was the point.

⊰ IV ⊱

No WONDER PEOPLE at the Dallas bus station giggled when this boy lieutenant asked for the bus to Camp "Howzy." How was he to know that Howze was pronounced *Hows?* Seriously overdressed in his natty tropical worsted jacket with its excessively shiny gold bars, he was on his way to his first assignment with troops. He was headed for the 410th Infantry Regiment, one of the three composing the rifle power of the 103rd Infantry Division. Its emblem ("patch") was a green cactus against a yellow background, and thus it was referred to, sometimes, as the Cactus Division. Camp Howze, near the Texas town of Gainesville, was aesthetically much worse than Camp Roberts. There, the barracks were two stories tall and faced with white clapboard. Here, they were one story and faced with tar paper, ostentatiously momentary. (Recently, in Denton, Texas, I asked if Camp Howze still existed. I was told it had entirely disappeared decades ago, leaving not a wrack behind.) Reporting at midnight to regimental headquarters, I was assigned to Company F, whose CO in turn designated me the leader of the second platoon. It consisted almost entirely of hillbillies and yokels (or so they seemed) who had been in the army longer than I and some of whom were close to twice my age. When I presented myself to thirty-six-year-old Technical Sergeant Edward Keith Hudson, my immediate subordinate, I could read in his expression a combination of weary disbelief and outrage that a creature so babyish was now in charge. My light blond crew cut made me resemble a week-old chick. But after a few days, both he and the almost forty members of the platoon seemed reconciled to the inevitable, and we got along fairly well, although there was occasional stifled laughter from the ranks, immediately repressed by the loyal Hudson, when I shouted a command and my voice suddenly went treble.

Preposterously young as I was, I was not the most conspicuous for boyishness in the battalion. There was child lieutenant Matt Rose, from Atlanta, in charge of the antitank mine–laying platoon, who had never shaved at all, his cheek and chin displaying only the lightest blond fuzz. (I at least shaved every week.) How we boy lieutenants got away with our act I don't know. I'd chalk it up to the decency and generosity of the men we commanded. As we used to repeat when the troops complained of having to salute some officer detested for incompetence or cruelty, you don't salute the man, you salute the uniform. You don't obey the boy, you obey the lieutenant. And Sergeant Hudson, bless him, required that I be taken seriously. "Say 'Sir' when you speak to the lieutenant," he would admonish some thirty-year-old long-service regular-army buck sergeant writhing with hatred and contempt.

The quarters for junior officers were also tar-paper shacks. When it rained, water came through my ceiling onto my bunk, and I had to shift cans around to catch the drips. Indoors, mice devoured my candy bars. Outdoors, mosquitoes swarmed, and chiggers liked to ascend our calves under our leggings. As we sent men overseas as emergency replacements, casualties proving worse than anyone had estimated, we received hundreds of very angry young men from closed-out units of the Army Specialized Training Program, who had been luxuriating in colleges. They had now to be quickly trained as infantry replacements, a fate that (justly) horrified them, for they were bright and had imaginations and could interpret the casualty figures. Also cast down were hundreds of former Air Corps youths suddenly shifted to infantry units, their hopes of romantic and clean battle action quite evaporated. I was put to teaching these pissed-off newcomers the art of bayonet fighting, and I made one man so angry that he came at me with a naked bayonet, which I luckily knew enough to parry with my hand. Reassignment to the infantry was so appalling that one man on a train carrying soldiers from Howze to another camp in Texas decided to end it all with a gross overdose of aspirin. In charge, I stopped the train and ran into a small town to find a doctor, with whom I left the weeping wretch and reported him AWOL.

The only exercise we underwent at Howze that was any fun or even interesting was flying in troop-carrying gliders at a nearby airport. But the six months' training the 103rd Division went through now was for the men and certainly for the officers a tedious repetition of things already boring: weapons disassembly, lectures on military sanitation, small-unit tactics (practicing over and over General Marshall's fire-and-flank maneuver), and long marches under the hot sun with full packs, weapons, and equipment. The Second World War has so rapidly joined the deep past that it's not easy now to convey a vivid sense of the futility and waste of training and retraining and finding some work to do for the expendables awaiting their moment to be expended. It would be hard today to comprehend the rationale of the daily training schedule and the exhaustion, inflexibility, and uselessness of the training day.

For me and other platoon leaders, a typical day would go like this: up at 5:00; shower if lucky; dress in fatigues with web belt, canteen, first-aid pouch, and helmet liner with fatuous gold bar on the front; then hurry to battalion officers mess with contemptuous glances from field-grade officers resentful at having to share space with underlings. Then, a rapid visit to the communal toilets, followed by a dash to one's company for a day of elaborately organized wasted time. Lunch (i.e., "dinner") in the company mess hall at the table labeled Officers, where one did not go through the normal chow line but was ineptly served as if a gentleman by a snotty mess sergeant. Then, the torrid afternoon spent lecturing the troops on hygiene, map reading, or the techniques of small-unit action. Sometimes one of us junior officers would be commanded to read aloud the Articles of War to the whole company, the assumption apparently being that few could read for themselves. Some of these articles were heart stopping in their calm rigor, like the one promising that anyone convicted of "lurking" about military premises could be punished by "death, or such other punishment as a court-martial may direct." Finally, in late afternoon, "home" on the run, dripping with sweat, to shower again and change to khakis and necktie for retreat ceremony back at the company. Dominating all this is the ever-present, ludicrous, murderous heat. The training day is so inherently ridiculous that the only half-significant part is retreat, where after standing silent and stiff for twenty minutes, we all present arms and salute while a bugle plays "To the Colors." That makes you feel almost good because you are at least wearing clean clothes, and you can feel some pride in associating yourself with the flag. After that, dismiss, and the fast supper and the wasted evening at the bad movie. Did we ever discuss the ideological purpose of the war? Never. We took it for granted that we were engaged, somehow, in opposing totalitarianism, both German and Japanese, and we were willing to do that, but what it was all about interested us hardly at all. What concerned us was when it would end and who would get promoted first, and what an ass the battalion commander was.

In the midst of such silliness and boredom, I deeply envied the men of the Counterintelligence unit, which had the interesting, cretive task of generating plausible Top-Secret rumors to be fed to the enemy. These were cleverly planted among the troops with the certainty that strict warnings about absolute confidentiality would guarantee their wide circulation among the home folks. One bit of bogus planted intelligence, which we all believed, was that the division would go overseas in the middle of August. Another, even more credible, had me exhorting my mother and father to observe the strictest secrecy. I wrote them on July 23:

> To tell anyone might cost the lives of a good many men, including myself, so keep [this news] strictly between the three of us. . . . We expect to leave in the middle of September to a port in Calif., thence to the South Pacific theater. . . . Please destroy this letter when you have both read it. Do not mention this in your next letter or ask questions about it.

The Counterintelligence Corps knew that within minutes the news would spread widely in Pasadena and environs and quickly work its way east as well, presumably to be conveyed by shortwave to Tokyo and Berlin.

D-Day of course excited us, but the thrill was less in the Allied success than in the excitement we felt at the likelihood that the war would be over before we could be sent to it. At moments when we felt especially victorious, we persuaded ourselves that we'd probably do no fighting at all. I wrote home on August 13, "It looks like the Germans are on their last legs. Bets are being made here that the European war will be over in six weeks." A lot of hope was invested in that remark, like the comfort derived from telling the folks, "This is a very messed-up division. It will never go overseas as a unit, and is now serving mainly as a replacement training center, disguised as a combat division."

But "messed up" (euphemism) as we were, we did go overseas as a unit, just as if we were a serious threat to the Axis. We were doubtless no more messed up than all the other ad hoc infantry divisions would have appeared to a twenty-year-old Pasadena perfectionist. In September we packed up and went east by train, company kitchens cooking away in baggage and freight cars, men sleeping two to a berth. Our destination was Camp Shanks, near New York City, where we were issued all new equipment, which no one needed or wanted and which made us feel strange and uncomfortable. To everyone's annoyance, the new rifles, infinitely less familiar and respected than the old ones, had to be zeroed in on the camp range. At this stage of the war, it was still thought that rifle fire had to be accurate rather than simply copious. As the war ground on, sheer volume of fire, frequently shot from the hip, was what we depended on instead of precision of aim. Thus, all the repetitive weeks of aiming instruction, firing in different body positions at targets at different distances, learning to estimate distances and to give the correct firing commands, together with the mock-academic pedantry of "qualifying" as a rifleman of certified adequacy — all proved to be largely a waste of time.

You can take the boy out of Pasadena and Pomona but not the reverse. As the 103rd Division sailed away on the troop transport *General Brooks*, I simply radiated college-boy optimism. Later, I would tell encouraging lies to Mother and Dad in my letters, but now I was honest when I wrote home, "I feel very confident and safe." I had undergone nineteen months of verbal abuse and humiliation, exhaustion, anxiety, muscle pain, and boredom. In barracks I had listened to hours of the nastiest raised-voice slander of "kikes" and "niggers." And yet, if you'd asked me, I still would have proclaimed the world a benign place, inhabited by creatures sincerely concerned about the dignity and welfare of their fellows. If I'd known Tennyson's *In Memoriam*, I would have enthusiastically agreed "that somehow good will be the final goal of ill."

It takes a heavy load of optimism to find happiness on a troop transport, but I was so accustomed to accentuating the positive that I found a great deal. Even though six of us lieutenants were jammed into a cabin designed for two, it was at least a cabin, and our situation, as always, was better than that of the troops, sardined six bunks deep in the vomit-smelling hold. In a lounge on the upper decks someone in charge of "recreation" had provided instruments for an officers' jazz band. When no one confessed to an ability to play the bass viol, I volunteered, assuming that pizzicato there was similar to pizzicato on the cello, and assuming also that my skill in musical faking would carry me through without disgrace. Besides, I reasoned correctly, the function of the bass was not melodic but percussive, and as long as the rhythm was right no one would notice that the notes were wrong. This proved correct, and I managed to fake my way even through the obligatory bass solos. But I didn't notice that the resin on the strings was at work quite abrading the fingertips of my avidly plucking right hand, and when our little band finished to wild applause, my fingers were painfully raw and bleeding. The Band-Aids I wore for days were a fit advertisement of my pretension and vanity.

The *General Brooks* made the crossing in fifteen days, blacked out at night and surrounded with escort vessels. During those endless days I was presented with a duty the Infantry School had never even hinted might be mine: censoring my platoon's letters home. This seemed then, and still does, an appalling invasion of privacy, and further, a grave insult: normally officers' letters were not censored, an officer's signature on the envelope testifying on his honor that the letter contained nothing to compromise security. But the men, it was implied, had no honor, and they felt the insult deeply, if silently. I wonder if anyone ever thought of a simple method for avoiding the embarrassment of one's officer knowing about one's private life. Namely, censoring the letters of a unit different from one's own.

The night before we landed at Marseilles there was some nervousness and the blackout was enforced more strictly than ever. We were now within range of a German air base at Genoa. But nothing happened, and next day down the cargo nets we climbed into landing craft, just like the marines. Marseilles was peaceful, having been subdued days before, and we marched from the monstrously damaged port to a muddy bivouac fifteen miles away, our only enemy so far the weight of the packs, duffel bags, and weapons we had to hump. Much of the division's transport, like its rifles, was new and unused and even unassembled, and before long we were spending days and nights at a covered dock in Marseilles putting together with bolts, nuts, and wrenches crated trucks and jeeps. This work took place on an immense floor that had once served as a storage place for live poultry, and some observed that the odor of chicken shit was all too appropriate.

But there were occasional trips into the city, its bars and whorehouses distinctly French in style. To an American youth, there are two classic initiatory experiences, sex aside. One is his first acquaintance with France. The other, his introduction to war, involving the constant risk of his own early death. For me, these were roughly simultaneous. France was my first experience of Abroad, and my lifelong affair with that country dates from the moment I encountered such welcome un-American phenomena as formal manners and a respect for the language; a dislike of all forms of violence except verbal; a well-founded skepticism about proclaimed human motives and rationalizations; real red wine and real bread; the convenient *pissoirs,* correctly named and right out on the sidewalk, unashamed; and the smell of Turkish tobacco when I'd been brought up to conceive that all burning tobacco smelled like Virginia and Burley. Not to mention the French obsession with the cuisine.

The initial stages of my introduction to war were equally pleasant: the truck ride up the Rhône Valley, the flowers thrown to us by lovely girls, the bottles of wine proferred by smiling and nodding old men, the cheers and applause, which we accepted as if we'd earned them. We arrived finally at a bivouac area near Épinal, at the foothills of the Vosges Mountains. (At first, we pronounced it *Voz-jees.*) We could now hear artillery, our own, we hoped, quite close, but I remained cheerful and secure, persuaded that my background, good looks, and mental and physical agility would keep me safe. And besides, I was sure the war would be over very soon, perhaps in a week or so. Also, I had been trained at Fort Benning and knew that I could perform properly and help win the war.

On the night of November 10, we were introduced into the line in a forest overlooking the city of St. Dié, relieving a filthy, battle-beat-up company of the Third Division. The Germans we were facing had been in the war for five years. We were all new to it, and our inexperience, despite our affectations of adequacy, was the most conspicuous thing about us. I was so dumb that I was wearing my costly officer's short overcoat, with gold bars winking on and off on the shoulders. Experienced troops know that a night relief is among the most difficult of infantry procedures. Especially in a forest, where contact between leaders and led is a frustrating problem even in daylight. As beginners, we expected the night relief to go according to plan, but when we stumbled forward in the pitch black trying to find our assigned places, we were astonished to be cleverly and severely shelled: it was as if the Germans a few hundred yards away could see us in the dark and through the thick pine growth. When the shelling finally stopped, at about midnight, we realized that although near the place we were supposed to be, until daylight we would remain hopelessly lost. The order came down to stop where we were, lie down among the trees, and get some sleep: we would finish the relief at first light. Scattered over several hundred yards, the two hundred of us in F Company lay down in a darkness so thick you could see nothing at all but black. Despite the shock of our first shelling (and several people had been hit), we slept as soundly as babes.

At dawn, I awoke, and what I now saw all around me were numerous objects I'd miraculously not tripped over in the dark. These were dozens of dead German boys in greenish gray uniforms, killed a day or two before by the company we were replacing. If darkness had mercifully hidden them from us, dawn disclosed them with staring open eyes and greenish white faces and hands like marble, still clutching their rifles and machine pistols in their seventeen-year-old hands. One body was only a foot or so away from me, and I found myself fascinated by the stubble of his beard, which would have earned him a rebuke on a parade ground but not here, not anymore. Michelangelo could have made something beautiful out of these forms, in the tradition of the *Dying Gaul,* and I was astonished to find that in a way I couldn't understand, at first they struck me as awful but beautiful. But after a moment, no feeling but horror. My boyish illusions, largely intact to that moment of awakening, fell away all at once, and suddenly I knew that I was not and would never be in a world that was reasonable or just. To transform silly conscripts into cold marble after passing them through unbearable humiliation and fear seemed to do them an interesting injustice. I decided to ponder these things. In 1917, shocked by the ghastliness of the Battle of the Somme and recovering from a nervous breakdown, Wilfred Owen was seeking relief by reading a life of Tennyson. He wrote his mother: "Tennyson, it seems, was always a great child. So should I have been but for Beaumont Hamel." So should I have been but for the forest overlooking St. Dié.

Until that moment in the woods, the only dead people I'd seen had been Mother's parents, placid, dignified, cosmeticized, and decently on display in their expensive caskets at Turner and Stevens Mortuary in Pasadena. Unlike these ill-treated youths, they had been gathered full of years, cooperative participants in the inexorable process by which the universe deals with its superannuated organisms. These boys were different. They had been not fulfilled but cheated. But worse was to come almost immediately. The captain called for me, and as I ran toward him down a forest path, I met a sight even more devastating. The dead I'd seen were boys. Now I saw dead children, rigged out as soldiers. On the path lay two youngsters not older than fourteen. Each had taken a bullet in the head. The brains of one extruded from a one-inch hole in his forehead, pushing aside his woolen visor cap so like a schoolboy's. The brains of the other were coming out of his nostrils.

At this sight, I couldn't do what I wanted, go off by myself and cry. I had to pretend to be, if not actually gratified, at least undisturbed by this spectacle of our side victorious. Such murders, after all, were precisely what my platoon and I were there for. Here for the first time I practiced a defense against visible signs of emotion. I utilized it often during the coming months. I compressed my lips very tightly and kept them that way for some time. This ritual tightening-up constituted my sole defense against all my natural impulses to weep, scream, or run away.

At Sevastopol, almost exactly a hundred years earlier, Leo Tolstoy was a young officer like me, and I can thus adapt his version of first combat to make it uncannily like mine:

A lad fresh from [the Infantry School] finds himself [on the line in Alsace]. A few months ago he was as merry and happy as girls are the day after marriage. It seems but yesterday that he first donned the officer's uniform an expert tailor had skilfully padded with wadding, arranging the thick cloth and the shoulder-straps to mask the boyish and still undeveloped chest and give it a brave appear-

ance. . . . It is no longer he who has to be on the watch lest he fail to notice and salute some passing officer; it is now his approach that is looked out for by the privates, and he carelessly raises his hand to his cap and commands 'at ease.' . . . Was it not yesterday . . . his mother was so touched that she wept for joy, kissing and caressing him . . . ? It was only yesterday that he met a lovely girl . . . and he knew that she (and not only she, but hundreds of other girls a thousand times better) might, and must, love him. It all seems to have happened but yesterday. It may have been trivial and absurd and conceited, but it was all innocent and therefore pleasing.

And now he is in [the line], and suddenly sees that something is not right, something is happening that is not at all as it should be. His commander calmly tells him that he — whose mother so loves him, and from whom not she alone but everyone expected so much that is good — that he, with all his special and incomparable physical and mental excellences, is to go where men are being killed and crippled. . . . His heart contracts with a double fear: the fear of death and the fear of shame. . . . He goes to the place where men are killed, and hopes it is only said that men are killed there, but that that is not really the case and things will turn out otherwise. But half an hour [in the line] is ample to show that the reality is more terrible and more unbearable than he expected.

Tolstoy's boy officer now realizes that he is precisely as vulnerable as the boys he's seen killed, and he thinks,

'Why should [the enemy] try to do it to me — to me who was so good, so nice, so dear, . . . not only to my mother . . . but to so many people — to almost everybody?'

It wasn't long before I could articulate for myself the message the war was sending the infantry soldier: "*You* are expendable. Don't imagine that your family's good opinion of you will cut any ice here. You are just another body to be used. Since *all* can't be damaged or destroyed as they are fed into the machinery, some may survive, but that's not my fault. Most must be chewed up, and you'll probably be one of them. This is regrettable, but nothing can be done about it."

Exhorting me, "Be careful! For God's sake, be careful!" the captain ordered me to sneak out between our woods and the Germans, occupying another woods a few hundred yards away, and to position myself in a two-story farmhouse out there, where through binoculars I was to observe enemy behavior and by sound-powered phone give the warning if an attack seemed imminent. I took with me a sergeant and three or four men, and by keeping the house between us and the Germans we got there without being seen. But of course they knew that the house, the only one in the valley, must serve as an important observation post in our outpost line. From a window on the top floor, staying well back as I'd been taught, I examined the forest across the little no-man's-land between us and the enemy. (We always called the Germans "Krauts," doubtless to bolster our sense that we were killing creatures very odd and sinister and thus appropriate targets of contempt. The more experienced troops of the Wehrmacht, not needing such bluster, referred to the Americans less offensively as "Amis," *Ah-mees*.) Although I could see only trees, I knew that somewhere over there was an 88-millimeter gun, because earlier it had fired at Sergeant Hudson and me when, frantically trying to get our platoon organized and positioned, we'd carelessly shown ourselves for a few seconds at the edge of our woods. This immediately drew a shell whose concussion knocked Hudson out for a few seconds, while a fragment cut a gash in the thick cloth of my stylish overcoat. By the time the Germans could reload, we'd scuttled back into the woods. The fact that one .88 shell was expended on a mere two men was a bad sign, suggesting no enemy ammunition shortage and plenty of acute observation.

The woods opposite were to be attacked next morning by another regiment of the 103rd Division, which would pass through us, and as it grew dark, I focused more and more intently on the German woods, searching for signs of German preparations.

And then, an absolute gift, the result of a terrible mistake unworthy of experienced soldiers. One elementary infantry principle is never at all costs silhouette oneself on a hilltop. While I was watching, the Germans began to burn the city of St. Dié behind them, presumably to deny us its shelter during the coming winter. The flames leapt up, and I saw the silhouettes of about a dozen Germans digging emplacements at the top of their hill. They didn't know that they were silhouetted from my position, and with a proud conviction that we amateurs had caught the pros in this elementary gaffe, I grabbed the phone.

"Fox Six, this is Fox Two."

"Yes, do you see something?"

"Boy, do I! Can you get me connected with the eighty-one-millimeter mortars? Fast."

"I'll try."

(Pause and clicks.)

"How company."

"Can you get me the mortar section?"

"Mortars, Lieutenant Crow."

"Hey, Crow, this is Fussell, observing from a house between the lines. I've got a great target, about a dozen Krauts digging in on top of a hill four hundred yards away. I'll give you an azimuth from where I am. Fire a round and I'll adjust."

(A minute's pause. It seemed too long. I was afraid the Germans would wake up and scent their danger, but as the flames flickered in the distance behind them, they worked stolidly on. Then, a muted *pop* from behind me. Ahead, a sudden crack and a smoke cloud to the left of the Germans. To my wonder, they seemed to notice nothing and kept digging.)

"Range is OK. Move it two hundred yards to the right and fire for effect." (Would the Germans hear the unmistakable sounds of the mortars firing and vacate the scene fast? But they still didn't catch on. They continued working like obedient soldiers. Suddenly, with no warning at all, the heavy-mortar shells arrived on them virtually all at once, and bodies and limbs flew up into the air.)

"Wonderful! You've hit them exactly! Great shooting, Crow!"

As we became more experienced, we learned not to do such showy things anymore. They inevitably brought retribution, and both we and the Germans found that in the absence of orders to the contrary, the best policy was to leave well enough alone. This attitude used to infuriate General Patton, who insisted on constant aggression everywhere. "We must be eager to kill," he emphasized, "to inflict on the enemy, the hated enemy, all possible wounds, death, and destruction." He went on: "Do not say, 'I have done enough.' See what else you can do to raise hell with the enemy." He also tried to forbid signs of prudence that seemed to border on cowardice, like officers concealing their insignia to avoid the special attention of snipers, and tankers augmenting their front armor with rows of sandbags. Proud of my success so far, I ignored the possibility of enemy revenge. In this first encounter, my cleverness had outwitted them so badly that I was sure I could beat them forever.

I was now hungry, and I went downstairs to the kitchen where the French farm family and my men were busy preparing food. Suddenly, a deafening *crack!* from above. An .88 shell had hit my window exactly. It was as if they'd known all along that I was observing there but had decided not to waste a shell on a single pismire — until it seemed absolutely necessary. If I'd stayed two minutes longer, I'd now be a mess of bloody bits. This, merely the first of my many close calls, left me white and shaken. One shell fragment had come through the kitchen ceiling and lodged in the thigh of one of the French girls. We tied up her wound as well as we could, and her father, trembling with fury, ordered us out of the house. We compromised by moving for the rest of the night into a part of the cellar the family was not occupying. The father kept a sharp and hostile eye on us all night, clearly expecting rape next from this gang of careless, brutal foreigners.

That night I was ordered to send the sergeant and a couple of men on a patrol to find out the depth of a stream the troops attacking in the morning would have to cross. In due course the patrol returned with an encouraging report: the stream was so shallow that it could be crossed with ease. Because I always obeyed orders, I assumed that others did so too. It was only after the war, drinking beer with a member of that patrol, that I learned the truth. "You didn't actually think we went all the way out to that stream in the pitch dark, did you?" I answered that yes, I actually did. Terrified, they'd gone about twenty yards from the house and after a plausible interval, returned with their agreed-upon lie. But luckily they'd guessed right, and it turned out that the stream was shallow.

In the morning the attack went forward all around us, and watching from the farmyard, we had our first experience of the most awful thing you can see in combat — your fellow GIs savaged by machine-gun and mortar fire, screaming, bleeding, thrashing about on the ground in agony, crying, calling on Mother. We stared horrified, helpless to do anything. Later, returning through the forward edge of our woods, one of my men saw something he'll never forget, if he still lives. He saw on the ground a bloody liver or kidney or similar organ, blown out of one of our attacking soldiers.

From what I'd seen so far, and I'd been on the line only two days, I realized that Mencken would be very little help here. For all his wit and penetration, he was limited by a very American malady: skilled as he was with comic irony, he was deficient in the tragic sense. He didn't respond to the classical understanding that all human life is destined to failure, and that only tragic irony is capable of offering a grown-up vision.

And as I became more familiar with war up front I perceived that in addition to being a theater of terror and mortality, war is an exemplary theater of the absurd. Witness what I found as, looking for hidden Germans, I explored the downstairs of that farmhouse between the lines. Entering a small private chapel, properly furnished with altar and lace altar-cloth, what did I see but a live, fused artillery shell five inches in diameter, resting ridiculously on the carpet. There was no visible way it could have entered through wall or window. Someone had carried it in, and it was simply stupidly, mysteriously there. Was the object to sell it some day for scrap? A total mystery.

Similarly absurd was an occasion on the march some days later. For a couple of weeks we engaged in no large attacks but took part in a number of small-scale actions in the Vosges Mountains —

patrols, raids, reconnaissance. The official history of the 103rd Division provides the context:

> *The scourge of the infantryman — the 'G.I.'s — hit the 103rd about its second week of combat. Theories concerning the cause of this strength-draining, stomach-sickening diarrhea were varied — dirty canteen cups, unwashed apples given by the French, overly sweet 'D' ration chocolate bars, mouldy 'K' crackers.*
>
> *During this epidemic, which reached its peak in late November and early December, it was not uncommon to see platoons of men fall out of a marching column and run for the brush.*

One night I was marching with my platoon toward a town where we were to be billeted. Suddenly, with no warning at all, my stomach churned and terrible cramps forced out a cascade of liquid shit before I could scuttle to the side of the road and drop my trousers. While the company marched stolidly on, I spent fifteen minutes in a rutabaga patch trying to clean myself up. I first used my trench knife to cut off my soaking, stinking long underwear. I then tried to wipe off my legs, not with toilet paper, which I'd not yet learned never to be without, but with the only paper I had, some fancy stationery I'd bought in a town we'd passed through. That exhausted, I had recourse, finally, to the pages of my official Field Message Book, a useless Benning item some of us were still naive enough to carry. This cleanup was only barely successful: socks and shoes were still wet, brown, and offensive, and when I finally got myself more or less together again (three pairs of trousers, two shirts, two sweaters, raincoat, then over the whole, belt with canteen, first-aid packet, and extra clip for carbine), I went on to follow the company, long disappeared. I prowled the blacked-out town until I finally found the company billet. The first thing one of my men said was not "Where've you been, Sir?" but "Lieutenant, you stink!" "You're so right" was the only thing I could say. I have not often been so miserable, so humiliated, so profoundly unable to put on an impressive front. In the next few days, I somehow found washing water and a few clean articles of uniform. But there was a bright side: this episode, illustrating my comical vulnerability, quite cemented my relations with the platoon. Many of the men had suffered similarly, and my mishap reinforced the impression that we were all, really, equals, closer to each other than we'd ever thought before. Needless to say, Benning had in no way prepared me for an event like this, nor offered any sort of School Solution.

The narrative structure of "war stories," even mild and comic ones like that, has caused skeptics to suspect that raw events have been managed, and even invented, to point a moral or to heighten irony or melodrama. Tim O'Brien, who fought in Vietnam as an infantry sergeant, has gone so far as to declare, "A true war story is never moral. It does not instruct, nor encourage virtue, nor suggest models of proper human behavior." He concludes: "If a story seems moral, do not believe it." But I can offer a couple of factual reports for which, in different ways, the term *redemption* seems the only way to suggest their literary themes and their permanent attractiveness.

Back at Camp Howze one man in Company F was convicted of stealing money from a barracks mate and was properly punished by court-martial, after which he became the company pariah. Men turned away as he walked down the company street, and his bunk was distant from others'. Later, in France, a call came down for three enlisted men to volunteer with an officer for a hazardous twenty-four-hour patrol behind the German lines. One of our officers, our former first sergeant who had won a field commission, volunteered: none of the rest of us did. The author of a moral short story would have to invent at this point the motive of the pariah in volunteering for this dangerous mission — to "clear his name." But that would be the truth. He did volunteer, he did go on the patrol, and he was effective and brave during it. He returned to become one of our few company heroes, his disgrace entirely forgotten. To talk with him now and to walk beside him was recognized as a privilege. It is impossible not to notice how often actual military situations approximate fictional melodrama or can be understood and made useful by sensing the melodramatic content in them.

The case of Second Lieutenant Abe Goldman is also instructive. He had joined F Company at Howze in April and was assigned to lead the third platoon. His arrival brought joy to every anti-Semite in the battalion, for Lieutenant Goldman seemed an absolute slob. He was short and fat, and he wheezed when marching. His khakis were not just ill fitting and unpressed. They were dirty. His stumpy legs were encased in puttees too large, and his trouser legs were never bloused. On his collar his gold bar and crossed rifles were cheap and unpolished, as well as carelessly pinned on. His teeth were awful, and he smiled all the time and chewed with his mouth open. He had come from the National Guard, and the officers from colleges regarded him with mingled astonishment and disdain. Why was he in the infantry instead of where he belonged, the Quartermaster Corps, the Finance Department, or the Medical Administrative Corps? Although we were often amused by him, regarding him as a cheerful company mascot, we were really deeply ashamed to be associated with him, and many times the company commander tried to get him transferred. But the news had spread, and it seemed that getting rid of Lieutenant Goldman was impossible. He shipped out with us, he came on the line with us, and he was with us still.

Fighting in Alsace in the fall kept us too busy to take much unfavorable notice of him, but he did seem more plausible as an infantry officer once he'd exchanged his filthy garrison uniform for the slovenly grease-stained dark green fatigues with helmet nets we wore now all the time. When we all looked crappy, he seemed almost to fit in. On November 30 we were to attack in the afternoon a German-occupied town called Nothalten, located just where the Vosges give way to the Rhine plain. Following the Benning received wisdom, which called for reconnaissance before an attack, the captain gathered a group of about ten officers and NCOs, with a few riflemen and an automatic rifle man as bodyguards, to go forward and look over the scene.

Led by the captain, we sauntered out, gaping about us, trying to locate "terrain features" on the map and the aerial photographs, just as we'd been taught. We assumed that the Germans were some distance in front of us and we talked and joked in normal voices. Suddenly, just as we approached a low mound with a small tree and some scraggly bushes growing on top of it, rifle shots cracked directly in front of us, and terribly close. No one was hit, by some miracle, or more likely because the Germans, terrified at seeing this heavily armed gang coming so near, couldn't shoot straight. We all threw ourselves down behind the mound, which provided a bit of cover. As I hit the ground I had a quick glimpse of a short trench about fifty yards ahead with two German-helmeted heads peering up out of it.

We were now all on the ground, paralyzed by surprise and fear into total inaction. It was the perfect moment for a "leader" to appear, but none of us elected to play that role. "Anybody got a grenade?" asked the captain fuzzily, his face pressed to the dirt. No one did. He finally ordered the automatic rifle to lay down fire, but the soldier in charge of it luckily found it "jammed," and he soon had it stripped down, ostentatiously looking for the cause of the stoppage, while the captain cursed and swore at him. Did one of the lieutenants resolve the situation with a crisp and brave Benning decision? No, no one did anything but lie there and hope.

Except Abe Goldman. He suddenly said, "Let's get those sons of bitches," and crawled forward with his carbine to the top of the mound. Just as he settled himself to fire, an immense crack split the air and Abe gave a little sigh and settled back behind the mound again. The back of his field jacket was ripped open from neck to waist, and out of that long rip steam was rising and blood was welling. As the person next to him, I inspected the damage while keeping my head well down. The bullet had somehow missed his head, but it had entered his fleshy back just below his neck and torn a straight two-foot-long bloody channel down his back from his shoulders to his ass. It must have hurt terribly, but except for an occasional quiet "Ohhhhh," Abe said nothing.

Aware that at any moment I might be called upon to return fire and invite Abe's fate, I set to work instantly at the self-appointed diversionary task of helping Abe Goldman, my equivalent of the mythical repair work conducted by the automatic rifle man. With impressive verisimilitude, he was now searching in the grass for dropped parts and blowing into the weapon's interstices to dislodge fictive dirt particles. Meanwhile, I was conveying the impression that without my total attention to his wound, Abe might bleed to death.

Reaching under him, I managed to find his first-aid packet, to extract the rectangular metal box, and to open it. I took out the envelope of white sulfanilamide powder, tore off a corner, and sprinkled it like a condiment into the long bloody wound down Abe's back. When I opened out the white bandage pad, I found that it covered only about a quarter of Abe's wound, which was now bleeding freely all down its long course.

"Fussell, take Abe back and get help," said the captain. Turning Abe around toward the rear — that took five minutes, he was so heavy — I very slowly, moving one knee and one elbow at a time, crawled back, guiding and pulling Abe along with one arm across his back and being careful not to be seen from the other side of the mound. During this antlike progress, I whispered to Abe, encouraging him to crawl as well as he could and assuring him that he was going to be all right. I believed this, for my view of the wound disclosed no bones or internal organs, only bloody meat. During this clumsy, agonizing passage back, he uttered no word or sound of complaint.

We must have crawled together for fifty yards before I felt far enough from danger to kneel and pull him up onto his knees and guide him into a little clump of trees. There I left him while I ran back to the company several hundred yards to the rear. I found that our little recon group had not been missed at all and that no emergency was expected. After dispatching litter bearers for Abe, I sent a squad with a bazooka and grenades around to the right flank of the German trench. Almost immediately they blasted it, killed the two Germans, and released the pinned-down group. Relieved that the problem had been solved so satisfactorily, I sat down and ate a small can of K-ration cheese. My hands were still red with Abe's blood, but of course there was no place to wash them, and I eagerly consumed a mixture of cheese and blood. One of my sergeants told me later that it was the most brutal and insensitive thing he'd ever seen me do. Later, in deep winter, I had to go to the rear on some errand for the company. The only transportation available was a truck in the service of the Graves Registration outfit, and the only place I could sit during the hour-long drive was atop a pile of stiff German corpses, frozen hard as stones. The truck unloaded them at the Graves Registration depot, where I passed the time with the soldiers in charge. They were hopelessly drunk, and they had been for many weeks. It was the only way, they explained, they could do their work. Among their collected cadavers, it emerged, was one of a member of our Pomona College ROTC unit. I regarded it entirely unmoved, by this time conscious only of a feeling of relief that the cold body was not I. As time went on, there were fewer and fewer moments when I had to clamp my lips tightly together. I was becoming a fighting lieutenant in every respect.

Abe's instructive courage was not wasted. The anti-Semitic innuendos stopped dramatically. We all knew that Abe's behavior, both before and after being shot, did encourage virtue and constitute a model of proper human behavior. Six weeks after the war in Europe ended, I took a jeep into Innsbruck on some errand and caught a quick glimpse of his squat little figure on the sidewalk. Abe was just disabled enough not to return to a line company but was now doing some work with a motor pool or something like that, perhaps in the Quartermaster or Medical Administrative Corps. His uniform was still a mess and his gold bar was still dull and scratched. I stopped to chat. He said how much he missed the company and his soldiers and his fellow platoon leaders, and when he said how much he wanted to be back on the line again, I had no trouble believing him.

Abe was not the only one of us damaged in that attack on Nothalten. We fought on its vineyard-covered hills from midafternoon until pitch dark, and when we'd finished, of our six officers only two remained. I was one and the company executive officer and second-in-command was the other. Because the captain had had his knee shot off, the exec replaced him as company commander. My platoon, once forty strong, was reduced to twenty-seven men. Anxious to do well, I had led them so far into enemy territory that I had to be stopped and ordered not to bring them back until darkness could cover our return. There was a great deal of machine-gunning that day. Running gung ho to the attack at a vineyard corner, I passed one of the company's sergeants, a tough olive-skinned Italian American, writhing in agony. He'd been machine-gunned through the leg and had had enough. The little battle concluded with our pot-shotting a few middle-aged Germans trying to flee in their long, clumsy overcoats up a steep hill. Sharpshooting, we brought down a couple with pride and delight.

I perceived that despite my unwillingness to act the hero behind the mound in the morning, I had plenty of courage when violently attacking, worked up to anger and high physical excitement. This is why I felt fully adequate, even enthusiastic, when around this time I was ordered to lead my platoon in a night seizure of a town reputed to have been recently vacated by the Germans. I hadn't yet learned that when undertaken by my battalion, night operations inevitably failed. I might have understood that from our experience the first night on the line, near St. Dié. Regardless, brimming with confidence and a high sense of adventure, we set off late at night on this mission. And within an hour we were hopelessly lost. Sergeant Hudson and I huddled with the map under a raincoat and lit match after match without discovering where we were. The town at issue was there on the map all right, a few miles away, but where were we? We spent most of the night in a ditch, scratching our heads. When it finally began to get light, a nearby hill covered with woods offered at least the hope of elevated observation in daylight, and we got up there as fast as we could move. On the hill we split into two parties to search in different directions. Hudson took a large group, leaving me near a tree with a smaller group, which I sent off to explore for a few minutes. I was now alone. After fifteen minutes, I saw some soldiers returning and to make sure they recognized me, I greeted them with a wave. Three of them, who had their rifles slung, looked at each other wonderingly, and as they turned their heads I saw that their helmets were square cut on the sides, not rounded. Fortunately, some of my men had gone off without their rifles — moving around un-armed was the worst military sin, but we, being new, didn't know that yet — and they had leaned their guns against the tree where I stood. Now the question was: could I kneel down, grab a stranger's rifle, and fire before the Germans could get theirs off their shoulders and aim at me? Miraculously, I won this little speed and agility con-test. The rifle I grabbed had, luckily, a round in the chamber. I knelt, snapped off the safety, and fired the whole clip of eight at the three Germans. One fell, one limped away at speed, and one ran — and ran straight into my men, who returned at a rush with their prisoner, alerted by my frenzied rapid firing to something ominous going on.

It was another close call for me, and afterward I trembled for hours, prompting one of my squad leaders to counsel me quietly and gently, over and over, "Take it easy, Lieutenant. Take it easy." Convinced that these three Germans were a mere patrol and that there were no others nearby, we went forward to look at the one I'd killed two hundred yards away, exactly as if we were hunters going up to inspect the game we'd shot. The dead one was a large NCO, hit about five times, three times in the head, which was bleeding copiously. "Stuck pig" would suggest the appropriate image. He stared at me with dead, as if reproachful eyes, as I removed his papers from his pocket. I'd won because I was faster than he. If I were rewriting the motto of the United States Military Academy, I'd add to *Duty, Honor,* and *Country* a fourth charge, *Celerity.* It was just as well, by the way, that we got lost that night. It turned out that the town we were to capture in the dark was swarming with the enemy, of whom the patrol that ran into me was a tiny representation.

Before we'd finished in Europe we'd seen hundreds of dead bodies, GIs as well as Germans, civilians as well as soldiers, officers as well as enlisted men, together with ample children. We learned that no infantryman can survive psychologically very long unless he's mastered the principle that the dead don't *know* what they look like. The soldier smiling is *not* smiling, the man whose mouth drips blood doesn't know what he's doing, the man with half his skull blown away and his brain oozing onto the ground thinks he still looks OK. And the man whose cold eyes stare at you as if expressing a grievance is not doing that. He is elsewhere. The bodies are props on a set, and one must understand that their meaning now is that they are props, nothing more.

But there was one exception. One such prop did convey invaluable meaning. In Pasadena before the war, "Negroes" had seemed creatures quite alien, comical and harmless, not to be teased or tormented but also not to be taken on as intimates and hardly to be imagined as social equals. That is, they were not like us. Once, back in December 1944, I found myself alone, a bit behind the line, walking up a hillside path looking for a good position for a machine gun. Beside the path I suddenly came upon a six-foot-deep slit trench, dug earlier by the Germans. It seemed empty as I approached, but as I came closer and looked into it more carefully, I saw lying on the bottom the facedown body of a black American soldier. I knew he was dead because his skin was no longer dark brown but blue-black, or rather, dark brown with a dark blue, almost fluorescent, tinge. As I contemplated this sight, it came to me that Negroes were not at all what I'd thought them before. In important things, they were like us. In fact, they were us. The lucky among us, black or white, survived; the unlucky, black and white together, died in the open or under trees or at the bottom of slit trenches. Where it mattered at all, we were quite the same.

"The most extreme experience a human being can go through," says historian Stephen Ambrose, "is being a combat infantryman." Part of that experience involves, of course, intense fear, long continued. But another part requires a severe closing-off of normal human sympathy so that you can look dry-eyed and undisturbed at the most appalling things. For the naturally compassionate, this is profoundly painful, and it changes your life. In the First World War, platoon leader Wilfred Owen confesses at one point, "My senses are charred. I don't take the cigarette out of my mouth when I write Deceased over their letters." I don't wash Abe Goldman's blood off my hands before I eat the cheese.

And it was both illuminating and humbling to realize that I was not unique in what I was doing and in the way it was changing me. In Europe then there were 1,200 American rifle companies with 4,800 second lieutenants leading platoons like mine. Impossible for me, once so Pasadena-special, not to feel as murderous and cool as the other young officers. Earlier, there had occurred in F Company the event known as the Great Turkey Shoot. In a deep crater in a forest, someone had come upon a squad or two of Germans, perhaps fifteen or twenty in all. Their visible wish to surrender — most were in tears of terror and despair — was ignored by our men lining the rim. Perhaps some of our prisoners had recently been shot by the Germans. Perhaps some Germans hadn't surrendered fast enough and with suitable signs of contrition. (We were very hard on snotty Nazi adolescents.) Whatever the reason, the Great Turkey Shoot resulted. Laughing and howling, hoo-ha-ing and cowboy and good-old-boy yelling, our men exultantly shot into the crater until every single man down there was dead. A few tried to scale the sides, but there was no escape. If a body twitched or moved at all, it was shot again. The result was deep satisfaction, and the event was transformed into amusing narrative, told and retold over campfires all that winter. If it made you sick, you were not supposed to indicate. I was beginning to understand what a marine sergeant told Philip Caputo during the Vietnam War: "Before you leave here, Sir, you're going to learn that one of the most brutal things in the world is your average nineteen-year-old American boy."

Although many in my platoon were killed and wounded, not one was ever captured or ever ran away, and that was true of F Company as a whole. What did we think we were doing, and why would we never flee or give up? Some few may have been following the higher morality and offering their lives and limbs for the Allied cause and the Four Freedoms, but 90 percent of us were engaged in something much less romantic and heroic. We were maintaining our self-respect, protecting our manly image from the contempt of our fellows. By persisting without complaint, we were saving our families from disgrace. We were maintaining our honor by fulfilling an implied contract. We were not letting the others down. All of us desperately wanted to be removed from danger, but we now sensed that the war would not end in a few days and that only death or wounds would be likely to grant us our respite. We kept on, there being nothing else we could do. We knew the Germans had lost the war, and they knew it too. Our inexorable, if snail-like advance, told the story, as did the daily streams of dotlike silver bombers flying toward Germany with none coming in the other direction. It was the terrible necessity of the Germans' pedantically, literally *enacting* their defeat that we found so disheartening. Since it was clear that we were going to win, why did we have to enact the victory physically and kill them and ourselves in the process?

As we went on, we became always more aware that the idea of war is synonymous with the idea of mortal blunders. Experience taught us that being shot by one's own people was as great a hazard as being shot by the enemy, and at night we moved around carefully, clearly announcing our identity very often. Sometimes others were the victims of our blunders. F Company was once ordered to advance into a town at the bottom of a beautiful valley in the Vosges. The town was said by battalion intelligence to be occupied by Germans. To frighten them into leaving before we arrived, we dropped in a couple of 60-millimeter mortar shells. When we finally entered, we met a distraught woman wailing and wringing her hands. We had just killed her middle-aged husband, an architect working in his studio in the top floor of their house. There were no Germans in the town.

Of course we were all astonished and shocked to hear of the immense German attack in the Ardennes, and immediately the 103rd and other Seventh Army divisions traveled north to fill the space left by the Third Army as it rushed up to Bastogne. While the fighting there was going on, from mid-December to mid-January, we held a thin line near Sarrequemines, so thin that occasional patrols connecting a few strong points were our sole defense. My platoon spent most of the time trying to keep warm in a half-underground concrete bunker left over from the First World War. In the trees in front I set out elaborate booby traps and flares connected to trip wires. Typical of our lazy, careless, irresponsible procedures, I made no written plan of them, leaving it a possibility that in due course French men, women, or children would stumble into their deaths in the woods.

We had so few means of defending this line that we relied heavily on mines, especially antitank mines. This meant that Lieutenant Matt Rose, the child antitank officer from Camp Howze, had a lot to do, laying out his mines and from time to time checking on them. On one quiet morning, with nothing whatever going on and the Germans across the way more quiescent than usual, we heard an extraordinarily loud explosion several hundred yards off to our right. Soon there were hysterical shouts, getting closer and closer.

"Where's an officer? Lieutenant Rose has been killed!"

Taking along a couple of my men and heavily armed myself, I invited the shouter, quietly weeping by this time, to lead us back to the trouble. There at the edge of the woods, his body all loose and twisted like a blood-covered rag doll, lay Matt Rose. His head, neck, and the top of his shoulders hung behind him like a very red riding hood. Something had literally blown his head off. What had happened? We speculated at first that a single German shell had violated the local peace and scored a lucky direct hit. But the large black stain on the snow told the truth. Matt Rose had accidentally blown himself up with his own antitank mine, as his assistant, ordered prudently to kneel many yards away, confirmed. It was typical of the boy Matt Rose, and admirable, that he chose to do the hazardous work himself. As the winter went on, we gradually learned that the fuse in the American antitank mine, or its explosive, grew extremely unstable in subfreezing weather. Later, when I was in a hospital, a fellow patient was a young officer whose face was being rebuilt after it had been torn up by shattered glass. He had been looking out a picture window when a passing truck loaded with antitank mines hit a bump and the whole package blew up in front of him. The volatility of these mines remains generally unknown, and their devisers, manufacturers, and inspectors remain unnamed.

If the savaging of baby Matt Rose was awful — men from F Company had to remove his body, and they were sick at the sight — there were moments of coarse comedy equally crude that winter. Our gas masks were normally stored back with the company kitchens, well behind the lines, together with such other useless impedimenta as the officers' heavy bedrolls. But at the beginning of January some authority came up with the rumor that the Germans might use poison gas as a last-ditch weapon, and the gas masks were sent up to us on the line, where for a week we carried them. During that week one of my sergeants told me that a man in his squad had thrown his mask away and was using the carrying case as a repository for candy bars. We agreed to punish that man and create some amusement as well, and we let the rest of the men in on our plot.

Installed for twenty-four hours of duty in the front-line bunker, I affected to be talking to company headquarters on the phone and receiving frightening news of an imminent German gas attack. The sergeant and I ordered gas masks on and watched with delight as one soldier sat on the straw glumly, his gas-mask carrier unopened. We asked him mock-innocently what the trouble was and made him announce that at the moment he had lots of candy but no gas mask. He was beginning to get scared too. To calm him, I declared that it had been found that a handkerchief soaked in urine and tied tightly across the nostrils would serve as an effective emergency mask, and he hastened to apply this expedient. By this time the whole group, faces covered by gas masks, was snorting and puffing with laughter, which finally gave away the joke. But we'd at least had a quarter hour of comedy, involving a brief welcome satire of the war itself, its dangers and its solemnity. The miscreant finally forgave us our collegiate practical joke, but he was careful of his equipment afterward.

His Ardennes counterattack having failed, Hitler tried one more time to break out of the Western Front. He didn't expect to win the war, but he did hope to put himself in a better posture to negotiate with the West and perhaps persuade the Americans and the British to turn on the Russians. This time he projected Operation "Nordwind," a large attack on the American Seventh Army, including the 103rd Division, holding the southern part of the line. It was still deep winter, the coldest in Europe for decades, and this would be a battle in snow and ice, the German troops clad in white camouflage suits and wearing white-painted helmets, supported by white tanks. The importance of this desperate attack became clear when the officers unhappily destined to command it were called back in late December to be harangued by Hitler himself at Bad Nauheim, in the presence of Heinrich Himmler and Martin Bormann, together with such important military figures as Field Marshal Keitel and Colonel-General Jodl. In his fifty-minute speech, Hitler proclaimed, "I haven't the slightest intention of losing the war." He went on to emphasize that the Allied front in the south was now so weak as a result of stretching north to assist in the Ardennes defense that it was more vulnerable than usual. East of the Vosges, only four or five American divisions remained. He proposed to wipe them out with eight divisions, including some first-rate SS units. He concluded: "It must be our absolute goal to settle the matter here in the west offensively; that must be our fanatical goal." The commanders on the ground were not at all enthusiastic, but loyally determined to do their best. One said in confidence to a colleague, "Two things are being overlooked: we have no air superiority and nothing equivalent to set against the massive U. S. artillery. Our men are spent and the replacements have no experience." (Many were sixteen years old.)

Although our replacements were older than that, they were equally inexperienced, and they were shocked beyond measure when the Germans attacked all along our Alsace line on New Year's Day, 1945. The Americans retreated everywhere. Whole battalions were wiped out. Many men were captured. Quite a few deserted. The roads were icy and it was snowing much of the time. When the snow let up, the temperature dropped to twenty below zero. Pushed back and back, by January 20 F Company was in the town of Niederbronn-les-Bains, which we abandoned at night for a nine-mile march in a raging snowstorm back to the River Moder. There we set up what we hoped would be a final defense line between the towns of Mulhausen and Bischoltz. The retreat in the snow and ice was a nightmare: tanks and trucks skidded off the road and had to be abandoned — to the Germans. We had a day or so to slow them down as they pursued us, and at one point someone laid out on the road a number of inverted dinner plates, hoping that when covered with a bit of snow they'd resemble antitank mines and cause a brief German delay. While we were struggling back, our positions along the Moder were being prepared by engineers. The ground being frozen too solid for digging, they used blocks of TNT to blast out three- and four-man holes roofed with railroad ties. Three feet of snow quickly covered these emergency emplacements, leaving nothing visible from the front but a dark slit two inches high and ten inches long. Through such a slit for the next five days I watched the Germans on the other side of the river getting ready to attack us. I reported back regularly by phone to company headquarters, located in a hole an enviable four hundred yards behind us. Crowded into the hole with me (we dignified it by the designation Platoon Headquarters) were Sergeant Hudson, platoon medic Juan Medillin, and the platoon messenger, Larry Bishop. The only entrance was through a slippery slide at the rear, which became increasingly nasty because there we had to throw out our excrement, deposited first on a spread-out K-ration carton. To appear outside the hole in daylight was to be shot instantly.

What an attack would mean for us was too frightening to dwell on. We could fire only forward, out of the slit, and only one man could fire at a time. If the German attack were to come during snow or fog, we couldn't fire effectively at all. All the Germans would have to do would be to approach invisibly from a flank and toss in a grenade, either through the slit or the rear entrance. At night one of us was always on guard at the slit. It was terribly cold. The only warmth we had came from burning the K-ration cartons and lighting the little heat tablets we warmed coffee over. We tried various expedients to survive the cold: there was disagreement over whether sleeping with the hands in the crotch or the armpits was the best way to avoid frostbite.

On January 25 the attack came. It followed a really terrifying artillery preparation. We cowered at the bottom of the hole, dreading a direct hit, and dreading equally a German attack during the barrage, which would catch us utterly unprepared to repel it. In his pep talk to his generals, Hitler had emphasized that the main purpose of this attack in Alsace was not the recovery of lost ground but the reduction of American "manpower." The object was "the destruction of enemy forces." That meant us, trembling in our ice-cold hole. Juan the Medic happened to be a serious Christian and a gifted amateur minister. He consoled us with prayers, in which, believers or not, we others occasionally joined. Juan's favorite morale-raising passages were from the Ninety-first Psalm:

I will say of the Lord, He is my refuge and my fortress: my God, in Him will I trust. . . .

A thousand shall fall at thy side, and ten thousand at thy right hand; but it shall not come nigh thee.

He was also fond of quoting Romans 8:31: "If God be for us, who can be against us?"

The troops of the Sixth SS Mountain Division soon indicated that they were the ones against us. Stimulated by schnapps, shouting slogans and abuse, they swarmed toward us — to be torn to pieces by our machine guns. But thank God, who perhaps had heard Juan's prayers, the axis of the attack was five hundred yards to our right, and our hole remained unassaulted. Indeed, we watched proceedings from our filthy rear entrance. On the right the SS burst through our line, capturing a town behind, from which they were finally ejected after a brutal struggle. These SS men were the best troops we ever fought. They behaved as if they actually believed that their wounds and deaths might make a difference in the outcome of the war.

The SS attacks having failed, with corpses left all over our snow-covered hills, in our hole we resumed our quiet life of watchful terror until we were relieved by another battalion on January 27. Throughout, our problem had been less how to help win the war than how to survive the cold. The war was being won, actually, by the Russians, who at this moment were moving inexorably toward us, even if they were a thousand miles to the east. Since January 12, they had been exerting powerful pressure on their front, making dramatic daily advances of many miles. If they seemed not yet likely to appear at any moment coming over the mountains we were facing, wearing fur caps with red stars on the front and brandishing submachine guns, we could raise our morale by thinking of them as very near, and we gathered renewed strength from realizing the German dilemma, hopelessly trapped between two converging fronts. Why didn't they surrender? Why did we and they have to proceed with this nonsensical ordeal, repetitively killing ourselves, since the issue of victory in the war was already decided? When we were finally back in a town behind the lines, washing and shaving for the first time in many weeks, I came down with pneumonia, and with a temperature of 104 degrees was evacuated to a hospital where I spent the next two weeks imbibing antibiotics. It was warm and quiet and safe, and I hoped I'd never have to return to the line. But I did, and the winter war went on.

Probably because I was growing increasingly snotty and sarcastic toward the battalion staff, I always seemed to be the officer assigned to lead their patrols and raids, often at night. When I rejoined the company, the battalion staff chose me to go back to our just-vacated battlefield to lead a night patrol of twenty-five men in an assault on the town of Mulhausen. Why, no one seemed to know. I was issued a Verey-light pistol containing a colored flare with which to call down artillery fire on the town if needed. With my experience of botched night operations, I could have foretold what was going to happen. We tried to enter the town by the most obvious route, insisted upon by the battalion staff. Machine guns at the edge of town stopped us immediately, and I decided to fire the planned signal flare. But the Verey-light pistol didn't work, no matter how often and how violently I pounded on its firing pin. We retreated in disorder, carrying one man with a bullet wound in his thigh.

It was while retreating this night up the silent, snowy slopes that I saw a wonderfully absurd, bizarre, and unforgettable sight quite surpassing the keepsake artillery shell in the farmhouse near St. Dié. There was some moonlight that night, perhaps one of the reasons our raid so conspicuously failed. Climbing slowly up the hill, draped with a long belt of machine-gun ammunition like a German soldier in a cheap patriotic illustration, I came upon a perfectly preserved dead waxwork German squad. By this time the whole front was silent. There was no rifle or machine-gun firing, no artillery, no mortars, not even clanking tank treads or truck motors to be heard in the distance. The spectacle that caused my mouth to open in wonder, and almost in admiration, consisted of five German soldiers spread out prone in a semicircular skirmish line. They were still staring forward, alert for signs of the Amis. Behind them, in the center of the semicircle, was an equally rigid German medic with his Red Cross armband who had been crawling forward to do his work. In his left hand, a roll of two-inch bandage; in his right, a pair of surgical scissors. I could infer a plausible narrative. One or more men in the group had been wounded, and as the medic crawled forward to do his duty, his intention was rudely frustrated by an unspeakably loud sharp crack overhead, and instantly the lights went out for all of them. The episode was doubtless a tribute to our proximity artillery fuse, an invaluable invention which arrived on the line that winter, enabling a shell to explode not when it struck something but when it came near to striking something. Here, it must have gone off five or ten yards above its victims. Or perhaps the damage had been done by the kind of artillery stunt called time-on-target — a showy mathematical technique of firing many guns from various places so that regardless of their varying distances from the target, the shells arrive all at the same time. The surprise is devastating, and the destruction immediate and unimaginable. Whichever, the little waxwork squad, its soldiers unbloody and unmarked, had all left life at the same instant.

For a minute I stood and contemplated this weird tableau. It was a sight that somehow brought art and life into strange relation. If an artist had arranged these figures this way, with the compelling narrative element, an audience could hardly have refrained from praise. It was so cold that the bodies didn't smell, and they'd not begun visibly to decompose, but their open eyes were clouded, and snow had lodged in their ears and the openings in their clothes and the slits in their caps. Their flesh was whitish green. Although they were prone, their knees and elbows were bent, as if they were athletes terribly surprised while sprinting. They looked like plaster simulacra excavated from some chill white Herculaneum. No one but me, apparently, saw this sight in the moonlight. Had I hallucinated the whole thing? Or was it some kind of show put on for my benefit? Was I intended somehow to interpret it as an image of the whole war and its meaning, less a struggle between good and evil than a worldwide disaster implicating everyone alike, scarcely distinguishing its victims in the general shambles and ruin? Whatever it meant, this experience remained with me as a prime illustration of modernism, not that it occurred but that it seemed so normal, and that no one seemed to care. Pasadena seemed very far away indeed.

By the time I'd been in the serious war for a couple of months, I'd learned quite a bit. I'd learned for one thing that the proper function of a rifle platoon leader was much less exalted than I'd wanted to believe at Benning. I knew now that a platoon leader made practically no tactical decisions except on a patrol or raid, nor did much of anything that elevated him above the status of a passer-on of orders and information from the company commander to the squad leaders. His job was essentially to be there, physically, and to censor letters, serve as an authoritative backer-up of the platoon sergeant, intervene occasionally in disputes among the men that the sergeant couldn't handle, and "lead" the platoon in company attacks, which meant being visible and conspicuous and shouting a lot. The platoon leader's main function seemed to be that of an emblem, a visible testimony that officers shared the hardships of the men, an example of manly phlegm and "official" sanction. I'd also learned that there's one emotion a junior officer can never indulge, and that's self-pity. Combat makes you realize how unspeakably lucky you are to have lost, as yet, no limbs, to eat and sleep daily, and to be on the winning side. F. Scott Fitzgerald and Hemingway agreed that if you're any good, you understand that *everything* that happens to you is your own damn fault and you embrace that knowledge and go on from there.

More practically, I learned never to trust novel, exotic equipment but to keep things simple. It took no more than a week to discover that the classy little Handie-Talkie radios we'd been equipped with wouldn't work: in ideal conditions they might, but not in forests, mountains, or any of the places we were. We threw them away and regarded their use by others as evidence of dangerous incompetence and naïveté. Instead, we relied on sound-powered telephones, or even more simply, runners and messengers. Similarly, we got rid of all but essentials in our personal kits. I ended up carrying nothing but a rifle and a light sleeping bag, suspended from my shoulder by a piece of tent rope, like a tramp. The only item you needed for eating was a spoon, carried in the breast pocket. Mess kits, backpacks, and musette bags were simply an impediment and a bore. Anything you couldn't carry in a pocket you shouldn't be carrying. That's where we carried extra socks and gloves and cigarettes and matches and K rations and toilet paper and letters from home and V-mail forms for writing back and a pen to write with. That's where I carried the company's mail-censoring rubber stamp and stamp pad when it was my turn, and I plied them busily whenever we halted and settled down for a moment in holes or houses. Carrying a toothbrush was regarded as effeminate. My greasy field-jacket pockets were large enough to hold the food treats my parents sent from Pasadena. I asked them to send more or less exotic things to counterbalance the rigors of the line, and they sent stuffed olives in bottles, malted milk tablets, Mexican tamales in jars, and candy. Now and then a box of homemade cookies would survive the passage, but more often arrived shrapnel-nicked and snow-soaked. Most of us also carried amulets and charms as secret protection against wounds and death, but few ever talked about them or showed them to others. Although entirely a skeptic, I carried as if "faithfully" a small brown leatherette-bound New Testament in the left-hand breast pocket of my shirt. I conceived that even if it didn't provide magical, supernatural safety, it at least — it was a half-inch thick — might slow down shell and grenade fragments and deflect a bayonet thrust to my chest. I did look into it from time to time, noting the unequivocal Commandment, "Thou shalt not kill," and enjoying the poetic skill of Henry F. Lyte's "Abide with Me."

In addition to learning to live out of our pockets, we learned many simple survival techniques. One was never to assume that a friendly soldier knew who you were at night and in his nervousness would refrain from shooting you. We learned that "passwords" were seldom efficacious: you had to raise your voice to speak them, risking arousing the enemy a hundred yards away, and it was very likely that the password had been forgotten by one or both of you anyway. Officially, the password was changed daily, but if you were out of contact with your company for a few days, you knew no passwords and had to hope for recognition and goodwill, which were not always vouchsafed. As we grew more experienced, which meant less "GI," we became more aware of not just the danger but the probability of intimate "friendly fire," and moving about in a woods at night, for example, we spoke softly our own names repeatedly, loudly enough to be heard but not by the enemy. "Fussell approaching," one would say, and without any comic intent. We had long ago disused the honorifics "Lieutenant" and "Captain," persuaded that they would draw immediate fire just like the shining gold and silver bars on our collars, which we covered with wool scarves. The only time we spoke with normal volume was when we were well behind the lines. Up front, we spoke very quietly or whispered. The Germans, appallingly clever at concealment, and patient at waiting for you to blunder, were always very close, at least in our imaginations. They were our boogeymen and, like children, we believed in them.

A couple of months of war taught us a lot about courage too.

We came to understand what more have known than spoken of, that normally each man begins with a certain full reservoir, or bank account, of bravery, but that each time it's called upon, some is expended, never to be regained. After several months it has all been expended, and it's time for your breakdown. My reservoir was full, indeed overflowing, at St. Dié, and so certain did I feel that no harm could come to me — me — that I blithely pressed forward, quite enjoying the challenges and the pleasures of learning a new mode of life. At Nothalten, a lot of courage remained in my reservoir, and even the portent of Abe Goldman's blood didn't scare me badly. But at the Moder River line in the snow hole, some courage leaked away, and it was distinctly hard for me to leave the hole at night to go out and check on my men.

And some serious leakage occurred after I'd been back in the hospital with pneumonia. That seemed to break the rhythm and set me to thinking seriously about the physical risks I had been taking. I was really scared the night the flare-pistol didn't work: I was afraid the SS, knowing now how many and where we were, would counterattack and chase us back over the hills, intent on massacring the lot of us. But worse was ahead. I had not yet come to grips with the full force of President Roosevelt's words in his D-Day Prayer, where he referred to the assault troops as "Our sons, pride of our nation," and warned: "They will be sore tried, by night and by day, without rest. . . . The darkness will be rent by noise and flame. Men's souls will be shaken with the violences of war." He prayed, "Let our hearts be stout, to wait out the long travail, to bear sorrows that may come, to impart our courage unto our sons wheresoever they may be." That was the courage I was soon going to need.

As the days grew warmer and the snow began to melt, it became clear except to wild optimists that soon the Seventh Army would have to attack, this time en masse and seriously. No more of those little piece-meal attacks we'd been mounting. Nor could there be any escape or evasion: the war had to be won, and it had to be won by the infantry and the armor, at whatever cost. The whole Seventh Army, all twelve divisions of it, had to advance and keep going until the war was won.

But before attacking we had to capture prisoners to learn the strength of the immediate German defenses. A man I came to despise, a fat first lieutenant who was the battalion intelligence officer, charged me and my platoon with the task of locating a machine gun said to be operating at night just in front of the German line. And if possible, to bring back a prisoner or two. This lieutenant had never himself gone on a combat mission, preferring to remain in the rear marking his maps.

In deep darkness, the whole thirty of us set off down a convenient draw leading a couple of hundred yards to the ditch where we were to dispose ourselves in line and wait for the machine gun to manifest itself. I was carrying a phone and a reel of telephone wire, which squeaked loudly as the wire unwound, and we couldn't believe that the Germans weren't vividly aware of our clownish approach. Installed in the ditch, we looked for the German position but saw nothing. Suddenly, as in melodramatic fiction, a shot rang out. It came from one of my own men, whose rifle, he said, had gone off accidentally. Our position now obvious, there was nothing for it but to hightail it home and report the failed patrol to battalion.

This was the fourth time I'd been involved in a night operation that went awry, and most had ended in near disaster. I was learning from these mortal-farcical events about the eternal presence in human affairs of accident and contingency, as well as the fatuity of optimism at any time or place. All planning was not just likely to recoil ironically: it was almost certain to do so. Human beings were clearly not like machines. They were mysterious congeries of twisted will and error, misapprehension and misrepresentation, and the expected could not be expected of them.

Others in the war were learning this new, un-American view of the instability of human hopes and the unpredictability of human actions. A D-Day observer of the surprising sinking of the clever dual-drive tanks off the Normandy beaches, which went down like stones with the helpless, puzzled crews inside, said later that for him this catastrophe "diminished forever the credibility of the concepts of strategic planning and of tactical order; it provided me instead with a sense of chaos, random disaster, and vulnerability." Curiously, there seems something in the American character that makes it easy to believe that night operations can succeed. In the Normandy invasion, dropping the paratroops from the 82nd and the 101st Airborne Divisions at night practically guaranteed a fiasco, to the general astonishment of the planners.

Reporting our failed patrol at battalion headquarters, I was ordered, as if in punishment, to repeat the procedure the next night, and to use the same path leading to the same ditch. This in violation of an elementary infantry principle: never invite ambush by repeating the same patrol along the same route. I protested this plan but got nowhere. We were being forced to violate one of Patton's wise axioms, the fruit of knowing about, among other things, the fuckup called the Battle of the Somme. "Plans," he declared, "should be made by the people who are going to execute them." The battalion intelligence officer saw us off the next night, fantasizing that we were going to return with a string of prisoners, while we saw ourselves walking directly into a vicious ambush. But neither happened. The Germans must have been as scared as we, and if they knew we had moved that close to them, they decided to leave us alone. After two hours of waiting, we returned, with of course no prisoner.

The prisoners we did collar from time to time we usually took without effort. Most were pitiful youths who came across willingly, persuaded that the war was lost, and tired and wet and hungry and scared as well. I found that the productive way to deal with them was to treat them kindly. It was not just fun to witness their astonishment at being offered a cigarette first thing, but such an act, if at all visible across the way, helped encourage others to give themselves up too. And the cigarette lit and a couple of smiles and pats on the back awarded, they were often not unwilling to tell a bit about details on their side of the line. The technique applied by the stout young intelligence officer was significantly different, and I doubt that it worked so well. If he found a prisoner resistant to interrogation, he had him remove boots and socks and stand outside in the snow until he changed his mind. I once passed battalion headquarters and saw one poor wretch, eyes and nose dripping, standing barefoot on a sheet of ice. He had apparently declined to violate his soldierly code requiring him to tell the enemy only his name, rank, and serial number. The safe bellicosity and facile cruelty of that battalion intelligence officer were not unusual in those who stayed well to the rear of the fighting. My memory of the relation of staffs to combat troops, at least in the mediocre units where I gained my experience, stayed with me long enough to color my views about that relation in my subsequent books about both the First and the Second World Wars.

V

So it was as a tiny, insignificant part of the Seventh Army's attack on March 15 that I found myself lying atop a German bunker in the woods next to Sergeant Hudson and Lieutenant Biedrzycki, listening inertly to the shells coming systematically closer and closer until one went off right above us. Its intolerably loud metallic *clang!* did more than deafen me. It sent red-hot metal tearing into my body. One piece went into my right thigh. Another entered my back. When I got my hearing and my senses back, the first thing I did was take a deep breath to see if my lung had been penetrated. When I found it had not, I felt less panicky and, despite the indescribable pain, able to look about me. Hudson, lying a few inches to my left, let out a couple of subdued groans and was silent. I saw his face turn from "flesh color" to white, and then to whitish green as his circulation stopped. One of my men looked down at me with distress and dragged me to the rear. Juan the Medic patched me up, scissoring my trouser leg off and cutting a large hole in my jacket and shirt over the back wound. He shook in the sulfa powder and injected morphine. When I asked him how Hudson and Biedrzycki were, he answered quietly,

"Both dead." I shouted No! and felt a black fury flow over me. It has never entirely dissipated. Juan himself had a bullet through his leg. He received no medal for his cool heroism.

By now efficient new shelling had done us such damage as to put out of the question any continuation of our attack that day. As it began to grow dark, all we could do was to feel profound dismay and to await a counterattack, which never came. The many wounded were gathered in a small nearby dugout, equipped with chicken-wire bunks. On one of these I lay down — keeping my painful right leg draped over the side because I couldn't raise it into the bunk. The wounded in that dugout waiting to be, somehow, evacuated, lay in silence. There was no crying, moaning, or complaining. Except for one man, who had distinguished himself earlier in the day by an obvious attempt to escape the attack by simulating symptoms of appendicitis. Hearing his phony groans and cries, I became furious, shouting in his direction, "Look. There are people here hurt much worse than you are, so SHUT UP!" I think this was well received by the rest.

Conscious that I had a disgrace to overcome and suspecting that others knew why the lieutenant colonel had spoken to me so angrily, I was expiating by affecting extreme nobility. I insisted that I be the last to be removed and conveyed to the aid station. By the time all the others had been taken away, it was completely dark, and I was carried to a spot in the forest where the stretcher bearers promised to return in the morning. During the night, the morphine helped me sleep painlessly on the pine needles, although I was careful to stay on my back and not move so the leg wound wouldn't start bleeding again. To keep the opening in my back closed up, I pressed my left elbow against my left back muscles. (I later found my New Testament bloodstained as a result. The stains are still there, although now white instead of red.) During the night out there, all was quiet except for occasional moans from a very badly wounded German who had been laid a few feet from me. He died during the night.

In the morning, a most welcome sight: four German prisoners, led by a GI I didn't know, arrived with a litter. I was borne shoulder high out of the woods. The long-haired, dirty youth carrying one of my handles at my feet I recognized as one whose ass I had kicked very hard the day before. Overcome with guilt and embarrassment, I managed to unbutton one of the pockets of my field jacket and pull out a K-ration box, which I presented to him. Not recognizing me at all, he was puzzled, and probably imputed my action to lunacy. At the battalion aid station, set up in a nearby house on the road I had hesitated to run across, I was greeted as a hero. In their instinctive generosity, Americans have never understood, God bless them, that the cowardly are wounded as readily as the brave. Shell fragments don't care about the current moral status of the men they penetrate. Thus the Purple Heart remains a misleading and highly popular emblem of noble behavior. The obverse reads, "For Military Merit." No wonder experienced troops consider it a joke.

Fifty-five of us, virtually half our understrength company, were killed or wounded that memorable day in the woods. Before that day, it had been possible for me to imagine that the title of William L. White's popular book of 1942, *They Were Expendable*, about PT boat action in the Pacific, contained some legitimate exaggeration. Now I knew the truth. The fate of Hudson hadn't hit me yet, but it would before long. From the aid station I was taken by litter jeep to regiment, where my tag was checked and more morphine injected. Then, into a four-litter ambulance, with blood dripping down on me from the man above. After a ridiculously bumpy journey, it arrived at a field hospital, established in a large building with a once grand courtyard, now entirely filled with men on stretchers. It was like the scene of the aftermath of the Battle of Atlanta in *Gone with the Wind.* There was no noise but the rustling here and there of medics with syringes and extra pads and bandages and the murmuring of chaplains hearing confessions and counseling courage. Although we didn't know it, triage was going on. The hopeless were being removed to the dying area and the morgue. Those needing immediate operations were hustled into the operating theater. And those like me in no mortal danger were moved aside until the worst of the pressure was off. Because of the magnitude of the Seventh Army attack, which produced an unprecedented number of wounded, the least damaged had to wait their turn. Soon I found myself on an operating table, one of a half dozen under bright lights in a large room. My clothes were now entirely cut off, I was turned over and examined for additional wounds, and my wallet and insignia — someone knew how proud I still was of my gold bar and crossed rifles — were placed in a little cloth bag stuffed into my armpit. From now on a blanket was my only clothing. Before the sodium pentathol began to work its magic ("Count slowly backward from one hundred"), I heard a woman crying as if her heart would break, and I turned my head to behold a nurse weeping uncontrollably over a boy dying with great stertorous gasps a table away.

When I came to, my wounds had been cleaned out, dead flesh had been cut away, and they had been loosely bandaged: it had been found that the way to lessen the risk of gangrene and infection was to leave wounds open for a while instead of suturing them directly. I now hurt, and badly, for the medics were very careful not to overdo the delightful morphine. (Twenty years after the war, in a small

Spanish town I came upon an American morphine junkie addicted during his wartime treatment for a ghastly stomach wound. There were many such.)

Next stop: an evacuation hospital, where "delayed closure," as the medics' term went, occurred. Here I underwent delayed emotional reaction too. Up to now, I'd been able to accommodate the shock of losing Hudson and half my men. But now, realizing intensely what had happened and dwelling on it, I began to cry. In my view, I had failed and disgraced myself. Hudson's death was my fault. The Germans were not to blame, nor the war. I had killed him, and Biedrzycki too. Poor Biedrzycki! He'd been an officer no more than a month, and his reward for the assiduity, skill, and loyalty that had earned him his field commission was to be killed instantly by shell fragments in a meaningless little forest in a trivial little battle in a war already won. It was all my fault, for afraid of giving more evidence of being a confirmed coward, I hadn't run for the entrance of the bunker when the shelling started. They would have followed and would still be living. Turning over and over these convictions and images, I gradually loosened emotionally and bawled like a small boy. For a half hour my noisy sobs echoed through the ward. The other patients, as if accustomed to such embarrassments, and even worse, kindly paid no attention, and I finally stopped and went to sleep.

A day or so later, I was taken by hospital train to the 236th General Hospital in Épinal, a once-charming town on the Moselle River, where I stayed for almost three months. Meanwhile, this telegram had arrived in Pasadena:

THE SECRETARY OF WAR DESIRES ME TO EXPRESS HIS
DEEP REGRET THAT YOUR SON 2LT FUSSELL PAUL JR WAS

SERIOUSLY WOUNDED IN FRANCE 15 MARCH 45 . . .

NEW ADDRESS AND FURTHER INFORMATION FOLLOW

DIRECT FROM HOSPITAL.

J A ULIO THE ADJUTANT GENERAL

Mother and Dad were naturally appalled by the word *seriously*. And they were further distressed after they had sought clarification from my uncle Ed, at the time working in Washington. Consulting the army, he was informed that *seriously* indicated that one or more limbs had been blown off or that a similarly disabling catastrophe had taken place. The situation seemed so unbearable that Mother and Dad sought a comfort they normally wouldn't have had a lot of use for: Pasadena religion. They called the minister of the Presbyterian church, the Reverend Eugene Carson Blake, who came to the house and talked with them. (My rationalist father was later embarrassed by this, and declined to tell me if he'd joined the minister in audible prayer.) I think *seriously* got into the telegram because the condition of all stretcher cases, as opposed to walking wounded, was so understood. If you arrived at the aid station on your own two legs, you were considered to be *slightly* wounded.

To write a letter, I had to sit upright, and at first this was too painful to be thought of, but a week after being wounded, on my twenty-first birthday, actually, I managed to write a letter home:

March 22, 1945

Dear Mother and Dad:

As you may have already learned from the official telegram, I have been slightly wounded. A piece of shrapnel hit my right thigh, between the knee and the hip, but did not break the leg. Another piece hit my back, on the left side, but didn't go in very far. Both have been removed, I am now sewed up, no bones were broken, and I feel OK. [A lie.] They were really very slight wounds, and nothing at all to worry about. . . .

I was hit March 15 at 5:00 PM. The same shell that hit me killed my platoon sergeant and another lieutenant who was with me, so I feel fortunate [serious understatement]. I have felt very little pain, due to morphine and a wonderful new anesthetic the army has. I should be up and walking around shortly, and enjoying these white sheets and nice beds. I'm in a general hospital. . . . It is luxurious, to say the least. Don't worry.

Love, Paul

That's an example of my accustomed act of representing the awful as wonderful, here, less to fool myself than to deliver comfort to the parents. The detail of the white sheets as an emblem of felicity, by the way, needs more attention from folklorists and anthropologists than it's attracted so far. To the muddy, greasy, foul infantryman, white sheets are the ultimate symbol of compensatory delight, safety, and comfort. In the army everything normally white was olive drab, including the toilet paper and the pipe cleaners. And in addition, for soldiers whose business is killing the guiltless and unfortunate, white sheets become the all-time image of innocence. One emotionally high-strung wounded man spoke for all when he said of his arrival at a hospital, "The white innocence of the sheets was more than you could bear." It's no accident that the flag of surrender, bringing relief to fear and agony, is by tradition white.

Actually, for all my insistence that I was feeling no pain, my situation was often very painful. I had to sleep on my back only for almost three months: my leg hurt too much to turn on my side, either way. After a few weeks of inaction, my leg became totally useless, and it took me ten days finally to learn to walk again, with help first from crutches, then a cane. My leg wound remained painful because it proved to be infected — apparently the surgeon who first sewed it up left something in it — and a new operation was necessary. More morphine, then more operating room, then more sodium pentathol while the wound was opened and debrided again, leaving a much deeper gouge out of the leg than formerly. Then, to quell the infection further, penicillin shots every three hours, day and night, for five days. As my arms became too painful from these assaults from the needle, my buttocks were tried. I finally adopted a routine where each arm was penetrated, then each buttock, in careful rotation. All this time, in addition to my regular cheerful misrepresentations home about my smooth recovery, my parents were bombarded (excuse the expression) with printed postcards (WD Form 234) from the hospital, not mentioning infection or the medically embarrassing additional operation but assuring the home folks that I was "making normal improvement."

I was now changing steadily from an innocent to an ironist, and it was circumstances like the following that helped bring about this alteration. One day an orthopedic surgeon was visiting our ward, inspecting patients with damaged bones. My bare feet happened to be sticking out. He stopped suddenly and stared at them, and this conversation took place:

os: Did you ever have polio?
pf: Not to my knowledge.

os: You must have. Can you think of any time you were terribly sick and no one knew why?

pf: Yes, plenty of times.

os: Yes, you had polio. Look at your uniform hammertoes, the way the tendons are all pulled back, pulling your toes up in the air. You definitely had polio, and it affected those tendons. I'm amazed they let you into the army at all, let alone the infantry. If you'd called attention to that condition when you were first medically examined for the army, they'd have rejected you. You can't march with feet like that!

pf: Now you tell me [or words to that effect].

I'd not yet read *A Farewell to Arms*, but in my loneliness of course I enacted a version of Frederic Henry's obsession with Catherine Barkley. I fell in love with a nurse, a delightful small brunette from Boston with a sly sense of humor and an undamaged feeling of wonder at it all. Experienced with the convention of patients falling in love with her, she never divulged her name. My love was entirely nonphysical, except for a bit of hand-holding from time to time. We had our ironic private jokes, like my asking loudly for "a placebo" when she made the bedtime rounds giving out various pills on request. Her freshness, affection, and good cheer helped mitigate the horror she worked in the midst of.

I was in an officers' ward holding about a dozen damaged lieutenants and captains. All of us were so unused to asking subversive questions that it never entered our minds that somewhere in the hospital there must be a luxurious ward, or perhaps private rooms, for the field-grade officers. Our more animal needs were taken care of by a medical-corps ward boy, whose business it was to run constantly from ward to toilets bearing bedpans and "ducks" — male urinals so called because the long spouts into which the penis fitted looked remarkably like ducks' necks. Sometimes, at rush hours like after breakfast, this trade overwhelmed the ward boy and my nurse had to help out, creating spectacles painful for me to see. But the worst my nurse had to bear was dealing with the colostomy of the man in the bed next to mine. He was a distinctly unpleasant second lieutenant who had been machine-gunned in the stomach. The surgeons had given him a temporary colostomy to serve until his intestines were up to their job again. His talk consisted of constant whining: about pain, about the food, about the uncomfortable bed, about every possible thing. This in a room where by silent agreement the officers never, never violated the conventions of military phlegm by suggesting that they were in any condition but sheer happiness at residing for a time between white sheets without frequent mortal noises offstage, and without any need to make decisions affecting the lives and limbs of other people.

But the colostomy victim gave more offense than his mouth alone could provide. By misfortune, the side of his belly containing the little pink artificial anus faced my bed, and we were only inches apart. Frequently and regularly, this little opening would announce with a lifelike gurgle that it was going into action, and before help could arrive, horrible dark brown matter would flow out around the edge of the small bandage. This effluent was the foulest I ever smelled. During the whole war I actually prayed to God only two or three times, but once was after one of my neighbor's most hellish eruptions: "Please God, make it stop." If this had been an institution other than the army, someone might have noticed that this regular performance was nastier than necessary for the man's neighbors and moved my bed, or his. But there was no relief until one day he was evacuated, finally, to England, bitching noisily all the way.

Into this little closed-off world of pain, futility, disgust, and tidied-up horror — the next ward contained thirty soldiers, all with their feet uniformly blown off by Schu-mines — now and then filtered news of other sufferings and sadnesses. We received the *Stars and Stripes* daily, and we had a small radio, tuned to the Armed Forces Network. Normally it brought us continuous popular music, but one day it interrupted that to tell us of the death of Roosevelt. I liked and admired FDR, and enjoyed disagreeing with my father about him, that is, after my pacifist period had been brought to a close by Pearl Harbor. I was sorry the president was gone, but after such deaths as I had seen, and caused, another death, even of so elevated a character, seemed not especially significant. I did feel sad that he'd not lived to see the total victory he'd devoted his last years to. If I'd not been a soldier whose powers of sympathy had already been virtually exhausted, I might have been more moved. In Wilfred Owen's poem "Insensibility," which I came upon much later, I found an understanding of the way combat dulls one's sensitivity to the deaths of others. Speaking of experienced soldiers, he writes:

> *Having seen all things red,*
> *Their eyes are rid*
> *Of the hurt of the color of blood for ever.*
> *And terror's first constriction over,*
> *Their hearts remain small-drawn.*

Infantry soldiers don't make your best sympathizers.

The little radio also brought us news of the German surrender.

To the infantry, that meant not the end of their travail but merely a shift of venue from Germany to the mainland of Japan, and more of the same, but this time with an enemy even more resolute than the one we knew, who should have quit but chose to tear up our bodies instead. As little joyous celebration now as profound grief at the death of the president. When V-E Day was announced, I did celebrate by consuming a can of warm beer I'd been saving. But there was no pleasure in it. The reason is suggested by Kay Summersby, Eisenhower's British girlfriend. She said of the end of the German war: "No one laughed. No one smiled. It was all over. We had won, but victory was not anything like what I had thought it would be. There was a dull bitterness about it. So many deaths. So much destruction. And everybody was very, very tired." One should notice there the absolute absence of anything like the ideological satisfaction noncombatants and promoters of the notion of "the Good War" would expect. No expression of righteous joy that Nazism had been destroyed or that the United States had been glorified in victory, our dead avenged. When the German war ended, a moment one might think an appropriate occasion for wild celebrations, the troops and those intimate with the mess that was now Europe seemed to agree with the British poet John Pudney that "less said the better." The night before V-E Day was proclaimed, another British poet, Patric Dickinson, wondered what the war, after all, had meant, and came up with the lines,

> *There are no words to be said. . .*
> *Tomorrow night a war will end.*

At the hospital I had little to do but write letters.

May 15, 1945

Dear Mother and Dad,

I had my stitches removed yesterday and had my first real look at my wounds, about which I've had considerable curiosity since my last operation. . . . I was a bit amazed when I looked at my leg. I expected to see a small slit a couple of inches long. Instead, the incision . . . is six or seven inches long on the right side of the right leg. . . . That one is going to leave me a rather unlovely scar. . . . Thank God I wasn't hit in the face!

I spent time also trying somehow to avoid the stench of the colostomy and looking up often to see if nursie had entered the ward. And censoring the enlisted men's letters, a task that helped fill in some blank hours each day. It was a help not to know the writers: knowing that their own officers were not reading their most intimate secrets, they permitted themselves more freedom, and some of their productions were entertainingly obscene, praise the Lord. Many hours each day were also consumed in noisy arguments among one's ward mates. A favorite topic was the justice or injustice of the results of the Civil War. This was hashed and rehashed endlessly and with total futility. But my main time killer and entertainment was reading.

In my weeks at this hospital I read scores of the little side-stapled paperback Armed Services Editions, plowing greedily through Mark Twain, Conrad, Faulkner, Thomas Mann's short stories, and the poems of Frost. But in matters of taste I was still the boy I had been a few years earlier, and what I really liked was the amusing and trivial, like the comic writing of Dorothy Parker, Rosten's *The Education of Hyman Kaplan,* Ring Lardner, Robert Benchley, and

Thurber. Despite a mild leaning toward thoughtfulness, the co-editor of *The Sagehen* had somehow survived the carnage.

I could now walk, stiffly, without crutches or cane, and even attend a dance, dating a Red Cross girl of very limited conversational gifts. I was getting much better, and the moment to move from this general hospital was clearly approaching. Saying a sad, loving good-bye to my ideal nurse, I was transported thirty miles to a convalescent hospital at Vittel, once a splendid Victorian spa. Its Grand Hotel, now the hospital, had once catered to people like the characters in Ford Madox Ford's *The Good Soldier* and the fictions of Henry James. Now, the place was filled with hundreds of common people, strolling about in purple corduroy bathrobes bearing the initials

MD

USA

which, if you believed the troops, stood not at all for Medical Department, United States Army, but for Many Die, U Shall Also. At Vittel, we ate elegantly, watched movies, listened to records, played cards, and read, all the time quietly "getting better" and moving inexorably toward rejoining the working army. After a week of this almost civilian life, a further move to a horrible replacement depot ("repple-depple" in the jargon), full of angry officers and mutinous enlisted men. After a few days there, I made a final move, up to the Austrian Tirol, near Innsbruck, where F Company was now installed in the town of Sölden in a breathtakingly beautiful Alpine valley. There was little to do there but play softball and issue passes to disarmed German soldiers trudging through the Brenner Pass on their way home. This valley was an extraordinarily lovely place, but for me it was not a happy one.

My reappearance at F Company was a surprise to everyone and obviously an administrative mistake. I'd been away so long that I should have been reassigned to a new unit, for the company had already replaced me with a strange lieutenant and given him the leadership of what was left of my second platoon. I was entirely superfluous. There was nothing for me to do but perform a make-work duty found for me, supervising the activities (nonexistent) of the company supply room, set up in part of an empty resort hotel. In addition, though officially again an officer of the company, I was obviously not welcome. No one was friendly or comical, and I seemed excluded from intimate group conversations. I had become a pariah, and it hurt.

At first I assumed that this treatment was punishment for my regrettable moment of hesitation crossing the road under machine-gun fire back on March 15, and that made me feel guilty all over again. I didn't stop to consider how many other officers must not have done their best that day, officers now forgiven and welcomed back into the group. (We regarded shows of fear as essentially funny, and joked about them a lot: "Boy, did you see me hiding under the bed when that artillery started to come in!") My exclusion thus seemed mysterious, and I spent many hours considering it, examining it from this side and that. It was a relief — and probably to my fellow officers too — when I was given a week's leave in Paris. It was even more of a relief when, a month later, I found myself removed entirely from this context of embarrassment and transferred to the Forty-fifth Infantry Division, located now in Mering, a town in Western

Germany. The Forty-fifth Division was hungry for replacements, having had close to 65 percent of its men killed or wounded during the fall and winter.

I continued to puzzle unhappily over the mystery of my treatment for almost fifty years. Suddenly, the mystery was solved. And by pure accident. In the early 1990s a friend researching in American military archives came across a document he was kind enough to reproduce and send me:

General Order #157, Hq 103rd Infantry Division

1 June 1945

AWARD, POSTHUMOUS, OF SILVER STAR

Technical Sergeant Edward K. Hudson, 36548772, Infantry, Co. F, 410th Infantry Regiment. For gallantry in action. On 15 March 1945 . . . when Company F . . . was subjected to heavy enemy artillery, mortar, machine gun and small arms fire and his platoon leader was wounded, Sergeant Hudson immediately took command. Despite additional fire from an enemy tank, he ran from man to man, reorganizing and deploying the platoon. Disregarding the heavy enemy fire, he moved forward alone to locate the hostile positions and, although mortally wounded, he succeeded in sending a message informing his commander of the location of the enemy. Sergeant Hudson's actions reflected the highest traditions of the military service.

Pure fiction, all of it, except the specification of the varieties of fire we were being subjected to and the words, "his platoon leader was wounded." It became clear now, a half century later, that a week or so before I surprised the company by showing up, the officers had conspired in devising this fairy tale and perjured themselves in attesting to it. ("*Sanctity of Official Statements.* An officer's official word or statement is ordinarily accepted without question. The knowledge that a false official statement is not only a high crime, but is contrary to the ethics of the military profession, has placed personal and official responsibility for an official statement at a high level. It is punishable under the Articles of War." — *The Officer's Guide*, 1942. More officially, Article 127 of the Military Code of Justice specifies that "anyone who, with intent to deceive, signs any false record, return, regulation, order or other official document, knowing the same to be false, shall be punished as a court martial may direct.") Sergeant Hudson, actually, although no very conspicuous coward, was no more given to this kind of heroic selflessness than the rest of us. With my boy's moral rigor, I'd surely have objected and refused to join this fraud if I'd been present when it was devised. How could the beloved son of the most honorable and incorruptible attorney in Los Angeles, the onetime president of the Los Angeles Bar Association, knowingly sign a false certificate? How could Chickinanna's grandson, taught never even to say "shirttail," compromise his honor by attesting to a lie? How could a young man who had been shown by Mencken that a sense of honor is the main distinction between a gentleman and a poltroon lower himself to the level of his fellow officers? Their silence about Hudson's notable behavior, which might have been thought interesting enough for me to be told about it, for I knew Hudson better than almost anyone, argued something definitely wrong. I have heard from a few of these officers over the years, but none has ever alluded to Hudson's fascinating postmortal performance or its reward.

The effect of this general order, once it came to light, was to augment my already intense skepticism about official utterances of any sort, military, political, ecclesiastical, or academic. It further persuaded me that medal citations, despite the quoting of them in the official multivolume history, *The United States Army in World War II,* are the worst possible documents for historians to invoke for any purpose, except possibly satire, a purpose Joseph Heller honors in *Catch-22* and Thomas Pynchon in *Gravity's Rainbow.* Likewise, in "Lederer's Legacy," a short story by Thomas Aitken about a headquarters clerk in Vietnam whose job it is to "write up" medal citations, we are offered credible news about the conventions of dishonor governing such compositions, with their obligatory clichés, like "lack of regard for his personal safety" and "disregarding the danger involved." "War," says British author Nigel Nicolson, "is the activity of man about which more lies are told than about any other." This is why, like sex, it's not easy to learn much about it except by experience.

I can think of two impulses that might have motivated my fellow officers to commit this act of misrepresentation. One is the desire to bring glory to Company F and to suggest its value as a forcing ground of heroes. The other is the more condonable urge to deliver comfort to Hudson's next of kin, a widow in a remote West Virginia town. But a letter retailing no lies and signed by us all would have done the job better, and more honorably. In a letter we could have said that Hudson was respected by all, that he was an excellent soldier and an effective noncommissioned officer, and that he would be greatly missed. All true, and I would have signed that without reservation. But an unnecessary set of narrative lies, no. Even the other officers must have felt a bit uneasy over these lies, for they all refrained from telling me the happy news that Hudson had been awarded a medal, which would have pleased me.

After V-E Day, the customary distinction between officers and men came to seem less important than a new distinction, that between high-point people and low-point people, describing participants in the scheme devised to bring some fairness into the ultimate orderly return of the troops to civilian life. Points were earned for various things: each month spent in the army earned one point; each month overseas earned one more, and each month actually in combat one more. Each decoration and battle star was worth five points. You got five points for being married and five more for each child. If you had around eighty-five points, you were a high-point man, destined to be discharged very soon. The 103rd Division consisted largely of high-point men. It was going to remain on occupation duty while discharging most of its men. The low-point men — I was one with a mere sixty-four points — were going to divisions slated to fight the Japanese war to a conclusion. The Forty-fifth was one such division. By July 1945, I was installed as a rifle platoon leader again in Company E of its 157th Infantry Regiment. There was little to do but get acquainted and prepare for the move across France to Le Havre and thence to the States for thirty-day leaves before reassembling to train on the West Coast — Fort Lewis, Washington, was the rumored place — for the invasion of the Japanese home islands, said to be planned for November 1. The assault would be mounted from the Philippines and Okinawa, and the Forty-fifth Division was earmarked for the landing on Kyushu.

On the way to this terrifying future we paused at an immense tent camp near Rheims, where we engaged in some desultory training. I was assigned to lecture the officers of the battalion on the flamethrower, which we'd not had to use so far but anticipated shooting into Japanese caves and dugouts with dramatic mortal effect. Morale could not be said to have been very high. Most of us were sick of the war by now. Many of us had been wounded at least once, some more times than that. Angry red scars were visible when we stripped for showers. The way we dealt with the coming hell of further and doubtless much more savage fighting was to ignore its inexorable approach and to solace ourselves with images of the great times (meaning drink and sex) we were going to enjoy on our magical thirty days. I think none of us had the courage to face openly the grave unlikelihood of our survival. Instead, we repressed it below consciousness, where it festered and broke out in nameless angers, quarrels, and fistfights. We spent the hot days of early August bitching, eating, and sleeping. Informed as we were about events on Iwo Jima and Okinawa, we knew the Japanese war couldn't possibly end until we personally ended it with our artillery, mortars, rifles, bayonets, machine guns, and now, flamethrowers.

One day, the normal babble of the camp rises in volume and assumes recognizable forms. "Hot shit!" "Jesus Christ!" "Is it true?" "God damn!" "Holy Jesus!" Unbelievable, such a dramatic reprieve. Equally unbelievable, the news a few days later of a second magical bomb. Then, the negotiations about the Emperor's remaining in place. Finally, the fantastic news about the Jap surrender. Was it a dream? A hoax? There must be a catch. But no, we had won the war. We infantrymen were not going to be killed after all. We were going to see our girls and wives, our parents and children, brothers and sisters again, and live among them happily forever. The sudden reversal of expectation was too much for me to handle phlegmatically.

I was simply speechless, and idea-less as well. The night of the day that brought the news of the total surrender, I repaired to my tent to rejoice in silence and darkness. I avoided talking to anyone, lest I burst into tears in public.

Attended by growing impatience to get home and get out of the detested army, the men of the Forty-fifth Division were finally returned to the United States by ship, from Le Havre. Camp Kilmer in New Jersey was our destination, and from there we went home for thirty days, many to be discharged. But not me. The events of the next year were almost as effective agents in the murder of the former "nice" boy Fussell as anything that had happened so far. My point score was so low that my release from the army was extravagantly delayed, and with nothing for me to do, the army placed me in numerous make-work jobs in a variety of sleazy camps. I became skilled in all the dimensions of frustration and anger, and a new bitterness grew inside me as I endured the army's obedience culture with, now, no pressing reason for it. At Camp Bowie, Texas, I performed as a mess officer. I had been promoted to first lieutenant, but significantly my promotion had come not from officers who knew me and had endured my snotty cantankerousness but direct from Washington, honoring the ruling that after eighteen months of service all second lieutenants were to be promoted, regardless of what their immediate superiors thought of them. Because of this phony promotion, I was then moved to become the executive officer of a company of the Second Division at Camp Swift, Texas, full of disaffected soldiers who wanted out. This company did nothing but lounge in its barracks, concerting disobedience and planning mutinous demonstrations. One day an FBI man visited me and asked me to appoint secretly a sergeant as company stoolie. He was to write weekly to a residence address in Austin, reporting any preparations for mutinous outbreaks in the barracks. It was with deep shame that I complied, for I was growing fully as rebellious as the men. We shared common knowledge and common feelings. We knew that, the war over, German soldiers, if unsuspected of war crimes, were simply allowed to proceed to their homes. Why weren't we? What was the point in keeping us under control needlessly? Was the object, as it might seem, to furnish employment, privileges, and illusions of distinction for a while longer to otherwise unemployable people costumed as generals and colonels?

I wrote home, "The longer I stay here, the more irritated and frustrated I become. If I don't get out soon, I will be a mental case." My Pomona friends were already back in college or advancing their civilian lives. They sometimes sent me cruel ironic letters and telegrams praising my assiduity in serving my country long after the need had vanished. To my parents I wrote:

> *Did I tell you about the Universal Military Training Lecture?*
> *I have never been so angry in my life! Last Saturday, all*
> *officers were herded into one of the large theaters here and*
> *regaled for one and one half hours with a lecture on the subject*
> *of compulsory military training for all. Then, as a climax,*
> *we were ordered to preach the cause among the home folks.*
> *What gall!*

What the troops and I resented was the persistence of compulsion as an institutional principle long after the need for it — to win the war regardless of damage to normal usages — had passed. Perhaps planted here was my later strenuous insistence on intellectual and verbal freedom. Later, I taught Milton's *Areopagitica* with barely controlled emotion, recalling the witless, one-track obedience demanded by the army. Especially when I came upon these words:

> *If every action . . . were to be under pittance and prescription and compulsion, what were virtue but a name, what praise could be then due to well-doing? . . . When God gave [Adam] reason, He gave him freedom to choose, for reason is but choosing. . . . We ourselves esteem not of that obedience, or love, or gift, which is of force.*

To give the restless troops something to do, the division started a school that awarded credit through the high school of the nearby town of Bastrop. Here I taught for a while some forty officers and men, instructing them in the barest rudiments of American Literature, Business English, Public Speaking, and English Grammar. About most of these subjects I knew nothing, but by staying a chapter ahead I managed to get through. In haranguing my platoon, I'd experienced the pleasure of the verbal *libido dominandi*. I now began to refine my technique, learning, for example, to ask a question of the whole group and only after a pause designating one person to answer. But just as I was beginning to feel that I belonged in the front of a classroom, I was whisked to another camp.

This was Camp Chaffee, Arkansas, a reception center for conscripts. My task there for several months was to administer, many times a day, the Army General Classification Test. I was assisted by two privates, who sharpened the No. 2 pencils, and an idle, cynical, and drunken sergeant, who scored the test results by running the IBM sheets through a machine. The test was virtually indistinguishable from an IQ test, and the only interest was in seeing occasionally how high and low the scores ran. Some soldiers made 125 or 130, others 65 or 70. All were assigned work in the army presumably appropriate to their capacities. The thousands of draftees I addressed hadn't yet received their uniforms and knew so little about military procedures that the shout "At ease" would often not shut them up and allow me to begin my mechanical speech: "You are about to take the Army General Classification Test." Since I still looked about sixteen years old, I hoped to awe them into silence and respect by wearing my Combat Infantryman's Badge and the ribbons of the Purple Heart and the Bronze Star — the latter entirely unearned, provided for me by a sympathetic friend back in Forty-fifth Division headquarters to help me raise my point score. But the test takers proved so ignorant that they didn't even know the meaning of these gauds, and keeping them in something like respectful order was never easy.

As if to emphasize how superfluous I was, at Camp Chaffee I also found myself for a time engaged as a lifeguard at the enlisted men's swimming pool. My duties involved sitting on a high wooden platform and blowing the whistle around my neck at the first sign of indiscipline, like men running and whooping happily around the edges of the pool. It was clear that I was supposed to do nothing but repress fun, and this struck me as an entirely typical military duty. Since I couldn't dive, if help had been needed in the pool I would have had to enter by means of a "cannonball" or a belly flop.

All these postwar military experiences acquainted me with the whole dynamic of institutional fraud, boredom, and futility, and I began to understand what service in the peacetime military must be like. My sole recourse was reading, which increasingly dominated my time and my mind. To literature I fled the farthest possible distance from the simplifications and conformity demanded by the military. Compensation for military stupidity and vacuity was the only principle, and I began to use literature as my armor against the army. Of course a lot of pure snobbery was involved: I stopped reading *Time* and turned to the *Saturday Review of Literature,* the *Atlantic Monthly, Harper's,* and the *New Republic,* in those days titillatingly left-wing. My measure of the acceptability of towns in Texas and Arkansas was the availability on newsstands of these magazines, and I was almost never surprised into approval. I am entirely serious when I assert that if I have ever developed into a passable literary scholar, editor, and critic, the credit belongs to the United States Army.

One of my first weapons against military stultification was Henry James. I equipped myself with a volume of James's short stories and another of his short novels. I was delighted, as I wrote my parents in March 1946, to find that "James demands absolute concentration, and absolute concentration is a real pleasure now, after my years of drifting along." Shakespeare was also useful, and I read again and again the plays I'd met first in my freshman year at Pomona, *Henry IV, Part 1* and *King Lear.*

I solaced myself also with the combined edition of *Modern American Poetry* and *Modern British Poetry,* edited by Louis Untermeyer. My copy, now considerably beat up, is of the 1942 edition. On the verso of the title page is a colophon dating it, and me, with some precision. An American eagle, carrying a book in its claws, is depicted diving to the attack (on illiteracy and stupidity, presumably) while bearing in its beak a ribbon reading

BOOKS ARE WEAPONS IN THE WAR OF IDEAS.

It was in Untermeyer that I first encountered the poems of Wilfred Owen and Siegfried Sassoon and Isaac Rosenberg and began to perceive the continuities between infantry fighting in the First and Second World Wars. I remember a violent quarrel with a philistine officer — we were roommates at the time — who sneered at Owen's "Strange Meeting" solely because it was a poem, and the sneerer, like most of the country, I conceived, thought poetry merely effeminate and fairylike.

I made no friends at Camp Chaffee, for by now I had grown unpleasantly sarcastic and snotty. I could tolerate the army when it was engaged in its proper business — killing — but not when it was engaged in make-work and chickenshit. I was willing to accept coercion for a sensible cause — winning the war so we could all go home — but not for a reprehensible one — inviting uniformity of understanding and opinion.

Finally, after I'd been waiting for months, the point score required for discharge dropped to sixty-four, and my ordeal of waste and stupidity was over. I was ordered to proceed to Camp Beale, California, for separation from the service. The process took several days, one of which featured a sly official attempt to entice all young officers into joining the reserve, just as if we cherished the army. We were ushered into an immense hall equipped with hundreds of little tables, on which the printed forms were enticingly spread out. When I saw that genteel pressure was being applied, I asked a major, "Is this obligatory?"

"What?"

"I mean, do we have to sign up for this?"

"No, but we hope you will."

I walked out of the hall and for an hour stood alone outside the door.

The telegram I sent Mother and Father on June 17, 1946, has, in its heartfelt brevity, some eloquence:

GOT OUT

They met me at the train station in Glendale and we drove home.

⇥ VI ⇤

$\mathcal{B}$ Y THIS TIME, the extirpation of Boy Fussell was almost complete. The work of the shell fragments in the Alsation forest was merely one moment in a three-year attenuation of innocence and optimism. Other moments would include my sense of insult at the Camp Roberts shortarm inspections and the tricky attempt to lure me into the reserve at Camp Beale.

Now that there was no longer a need to sustain morale by pretending that the infantry was equal to other branches in honor and status, I could face without self-deception its real ignobility. Experience brought me to the clear-eyed view of military historian Russell Weigley: "The American army of World War II habitually filled the ranks of its combat infantry with its least promising recruits, the uneducated, the unskilled, the unenthusiastic." Those remaining after the Air Corps, the navy, the coast guard, and the marines had exercised their choices "were then expected to bear the main burden of sustained battle." A hell for the men, and a hell for their leaders. I have speculated since why no one at the time seemed to care terribly. Perhaps the reason is that the bulk of those killed by bullets and shells were the ones normally killed in peacetime in mine disasters, industrial and construction accidents, lumbering, and fire and police work. No one we knew, certainly. Wasn't the ground war, for the United States, an unintended form of eugenics, clearing the population of the dumbest, the least skilled, the least promising of all young American males? Killed in their tens of thousands, their disappearance from the pool of future fathers had the effect, welcome or not, of improving the breed. Their fate constituted an unintended but inescapable holocaust.

That was a fairly high-minded cause of my increasingly critical attitude. Another would include my realization of the sheer badness, regardless of advertising and pretense, of the military units I was part of. It was not easy to forget the anguish of the architect's widow or the stupid, clumsy reconnaissance at Nothalten, resulting in the shameful pinning-down of all the officers at once. Although occasionally it occupied foxholes dug by other units, my company almost never dug itself in but lazily made do by lying on top of the ground, the way it did when under artillery fire in the open field on March 15. For anyone with eyes open, it's hard not to share the view of the American ground forces held by British field marshal Sir Harold Alexander, who wrote the chief of the Imperial General Staff after watching U.S. soldiers in action in 1943. The Americans, he said,

> *simply do not know their job as soldiers, and this is the same from the highest to the lowest — from the General to the private soldier. Perhaps the weakest link of all is the junior leadership which just does not lead, with the result that their men don't really fight.*

A few shells and they all stop . . . and . . . call for air support.
They are soft, green, and quite untrained. Unless we can do some-
thing about it, the American army in the European theatre will
be quite useless. They have little hatred of the Germans . . . and
show no eagerness to get in and kill them. . . . Eisenhower and
Patton . . . know pretty well what is wrong — but even they
cannot realize the true extent of their army's weakness.

Even the American leadership came to doubt the usefulness of most of the National Guard divisions. One of the very worst, as Major General Omar Bradley discovered when he commanded it in 1942, was the Twenty-eighth Division from Pennsylvania, shot through with political favoritism leading to merely social promotions and general slackness. Bradley's view seems never to have been acknowledged in Pennsylvania. In the *Philadelphia Inquirer* of May 20, 1995, it is said that Pennsylvania's National Guard Division "has been an outfit of distinction on the battlefield throughout our nation's history." "Hometownism," Bradley called that way of talking. It has to ignore the fact that it was the known weakness of the Twenty-eighth Division that enticed the Germans to attack through it at the outset of the Battle of the Bulge. In the opinion of British military historian Max Hastings, the American forces were so bad (and actually so were most of the British) "that when Allied troops met Germans on anything like equal terms, the Germans almost always prevailed." Thank God the troops, most of them, didn't know how bad we were. It's hard enough to be asked to die in the midst of heroes, but to die in the midst of stumblebums led by fools — intolerable. And I include myself in this indictment.

Like Robert Graves in *Good-Bye to All That*, I swore "on the very day of my demobilization never to be under anyone's orders for the rest of my life." To convince my body as well as my soul that I was finished with coercion and murder forever, I acquired immediately I got home a new wardrobe of a distinctly nonbellicose kind. Instead of tight olive-drab tunics, loose, soft tweed sports jackets in houndstooth checks or herringbone weaves. Instead of heavy boots and leggings or combat boots, loafers. Instead of khaki trousers, gray flannels. Instead of collars displaying metal insignia, oxford-cloth buttondowns. Instead of OD pullovers, bright blue ones. Instead of the army khaki-colored necktie, silk or wool challis numbers with small paisley figures. Here was undeniably dandyism, but of a uniquely Southern California kind, with emphasis on soft comfort, informality, and total freedom from rigor and pressure. Attired in this finery, I would drive to Los Angeles — I'd not driven a private car for three years — and just to show that I was now no one's creature, I'd select a bar I didn't know and have one drink there, pretending to be a confirmed civilian free all the time I had not been. The drink? Always one whose exotic color and taste seemed the farthest distance from 3.2 beer: a sloe gin fizz. One Air Corps flier who'd performed the remarkable feat of surviving fifty bomber missions said when the ordeal was over, "Never did I feel so much alive. Never did the earth and all of the surroundings look so bright and sharp. I had my life." So did I, and I was so happy I could hardly bear it.

From here on, my life would illustrate a theory of antitheses and compensation. What social institutions are the most dramatically opposite to the army? Colleges and universities. Thus my plunging back instantly into my final year of study at Pomona, but now in an entirely different spirit than before. This time, no playful boyisms:

rather, a serious search for answers to overwhelming questions and deep annoyance with intrusions and diversions that might interrupt that process.

Was there meaning in my inches-wide escape from death on March 15? Was there meaning in Hudson's death instead of mine? In his memoir of the Vietnam War, *In Pharaoh's Army*, Tobias Wolff considers the situation of military survivors of frequent close calls:

> *In a world where the most consequential things happen by chance, or from unfathomable causes, you don't look to reason for help. You consort with mysteries. You encourage yourself with charms, omens, rites of propitiation. Without your knowledge or permission the bottom-line caveman belief in blood sacrifice, one life buying another, begins to steal into your bones. How could it not? All around you people are killed . . . but not you. They have been killed instead of you. This observation is unavoidable. So, in time, is the corollary, implicit in the word* instead: *in place of. They have been killed in place of you — in your place. You don't think it out, not at the time, not in those terms, but you can't help but feel it, and go on feeling it. It's the close call you have to keep escaping from, the unending doubt that you have a right to your own life. It's the corruption suffered by everyone who lives on, that henceforth they must wonder at the reason, and probe its justice.*

Now the question pressed on me, How could I justify my life? The only answer I could supply was to try to make it mean something more than jokes, evanescence, waggish remarks, and Menckenisms, to infuse it somehow with what was serious, formal, persisting. The records of my college adviser indicate that when asked my "intended occupation" in 1943, I said journalism. In 1946, I said, "Professor of English." I still conceived my ideal location to be in a world of words, but now the words had to be those aspiring to permanence and universality.

My final year at Pomona confirmed me in a number of attitudes that would remain and intensify. One was the abandonment forever of the high school and collegiate impulse to be "popular" by joining, or at least not offending, the herd. I now became a conspicuous non-joiner, and have never happily joined any group since. I became obsessed with the imagined obligation to go it alone, absolutely, and *teamwork* became for me a dirty word. I became irrationally angry at any attempt to coerce me into group behavior or to treat me as if all human beings are the same. I developed an indignant suspicion of quantitative ways of describing or measuring human talents and values. I was now convinced that my duty was criticism, meaning not carping, but the perpetual obligation of evaluation. I deepened my new empirical understanding of the brevity of life and determined not to waste a second of it in contemptible or silly activity, like sports or gossip or trivia. Before, when I'd noticed ideas, it was for their usefulness for reform or satire. Now, I began to concern myself with them for their own sake. I deepened my anti-Pasadena understanding that anxiety and doubt are indispensable to the makeup of the complete person, and that optimism is an attitude inappropriate to such creatures as human beings. Southern California was simply a metaphor for optimism, or a prop to advance its cause. Fine weather and perpetual blue skies (as in the song) could not sufficiently hint at the idea of evil, so necessary for grown-up understanding. Back in 1872, Clarence King, an early visitor to California, sensed a parallel between the unremitting pleasant weather and the monotonous cheerfulness of the California character. In *Mountaineering in the Sierra Nevada,* he observed of the inhabitants of the Sacramento Valley, "Men and women are dull, unrelieved; they are all alike. . . . The monotony of the endlessly pleasant weather [is] legible in their quiet uninteresting faces." What all this meant for me was a transfer of interest from comedy to irony, and from irony to tragedy and indeed "art" in any form.

My hatred of the army ultimately was diluted by a sense of ironic gratitude for what it had made me. Vietnam veteran William Broyles Jr. articulates what all combat survivors know: "If you come back whole, you bring with you the knowledge that you have explored regions of your soul that in most men will always remain uncharted." Actually, the boredom, misery, and pain aside, what better preparation than a war for a lifetime devoted to the study of people and the language they're enmeshed in?

The intensity of my new opposition to meaninglessness and vagueness, and ultimately dissolution, was perhaps one source of my later passionate concern with "form" in art and expression, as in my book *Poetic Meter and Poetic Form.* Attending these new impulses was a revulsion, almost physical, at fraudulent language, especially patriotic clichés. Furious one day at some newspaper canting, I dashed off a letter to the editor protesting the facile and false formula *gave his life* to suggest the motives of soldiers, who were, after all, for the most part highly unwilling conscripts anxious to give if necessary anything but their lives. Finally, as I reflected for a quiet, studious year on what had happened to me and many others, I came to see the similarity between *infantrymen* and *labor* and to develop some social-justice convictions quite at odds with my upbringing. Wilfred Owen's poem "Miners," in the Untermeyer anthology, struck me powerfully, with its pity for those who sweat anonymously for the comfort of the privileged, so like the predicament of those forced to win the war by dying for the safe and complacent. In Owen's grate can be heard the coals whispering as if they were the pitmen who struggled to dig them out:

> Comforted years will sit soft-chaired
> In rooms of amber;
> The years will stretch their hands, well-cheered
> By our lives' ember.
> The centuries will burn rich loads
> With which we groaned,
> Whose warmth shall lull their dreaming lids
> While songs are crooned.
> But they will not dream of us poor lads
> Lost in the ground.

If this and other things in the Untermeyer anthology affected me powerfully, I was struck even more by another collection, Oscar Williams's *A Little Treasury of Modern Poetry* (1946), produced by Scribner's with such significant attributes of "Treasury" and high values as gilded page tops and a built-in red ribbon placemark, like the Bible. Rereading Williams's introduction now, I'm struck by the postwar tenseness, the air of profound risk and danger, caused by the atom bomb in its early years, and by the way it tended to give "science" a special air of menace, conveniently (for Williams) opposed to the wholly benign effects of "poetry." This simple distinction I bought entirely, being young and fresh, and it helped determine many of my attitudes and decisions for the next couple of decades.

Oscar Williams arranged poems by their themes, which encouraged my early tendency to value a poem solely by the acceptability of the social-satiric position it seemed to be urging. (I hadn't yet encountered Sir Philip Sidney's point that the poet "nothing affirms" nor the New Critical view that a poem is a virtual drama.) Such Williams running heads as "Courage against Chaos," "Idleness," "Brotherhood," and "The Indestructibility of Art" prepared me to look for those themes and to value the poems that most successfully conveyed them. Like many beginners, I valued literature only for what it was saying. An interest in technique and conventions and genre came later. And in responding to what poetry was saying, I treasured any observation critical of the status quo. I was really on the way to becoming a young parlor Leninist, but without the guts to join the Communist Party. Hence my fondness for the poems in Williams's section labeled "Class Struggle," the work of social and political satirists like Cummings ("a salesman is an it that stinks") and John Manifold, together with agit-prop practitioners like Vachel Lindsay, author of

Factory windows are always broken.
Somebody's always throwing bricks,
Somebody's always heaving cinders,
Playing ugly Yahoo tricks.

Factory windows are always broken.
Other windows are let alone.
No one throws through the chapel-window
The bitter, snarling, derisive stone.

Factory windows are always broken.
Something or other is going wrong.

Something is rotten — I think, in Denmark.
End of the factory-window song.

If poems didn't refract my grievances, I lost interest. It would take some time to grow up artistically, to work myself into an appreciation of art's expression value, as opposed to its presumed discursive-truth value. My mind was also being coarsely nourished by two pieces of popular prose polemic, Philip Wylie's *Generation of Vipers* and Frederic Wakeman's *The Hucksters*. The first, some will remember, was a satiric assault on the infantilism of American men, evidenced by the apotheosis of "Mom" and the sentimental childishness of their lifelong devotion to Sport. The second was a facile attack on the American advertising industry. The author was shocked that it required its employees to tell so many lies. Today the reaction would be, What else is new? But in the forties, such revelations were bold and exciting.

There could hardly be found a more effective antidote to the army than the world of moral subtlety delineated in Henry James's *The Ambassadors*. That was one of the works dealt with in the first postwar course I took at Pomona, Frederick Mulhauser's oddly titled Contemporary Novel. (If *contemporary* meant contemporary, what was James's novel of 1903 doing there? Where were really contemporary works like *The Grapes of Wrath* and *All the King's Men?*) Regardless, what better way to purge military crudities than to rise to James's whole concept of art, including his encouragement to total sensitivity, as in, "Try to be one of the people on whom nothing is lost." I found equally telling and useful Strether's Pateresque advice to little Bilham at Gloriani's garden party: "Live all you can; it's a mistake not to. It doesn't so much matter what you do in particular so long as you have your life. . . . Live, Live!" Strether's discovery that the relation between Chad Newsome and Madame de Vionnet, despite its conventional immorality, is really profoundly moral I took as a rebuke to Pasadena's understanding of the appropriate relation between the sexes. The whole French setting did its work on me, making me aware of the paucity and meanness of American social usages, architecture, and general culture. Although I'd been there only once, and under conditions hardly favorable for learning much about it, I now had a connection with Europe and Paris. I perceived that America was not just a bit different but entirely different. It had no antiquity, no Middle Ages, and no Renaissance, and thus lacked, among many other valuable things, a sense of evil and of infinite human complexity. It remained, it seemed to me, mired in the general optimism of the eighteenth century, about which I was to learn more as I went on.

In addition to James, the course in the contemporary novel included other stimulants to intense perception and social subversion: Virginia Woolf's *Mrs. Dalloway,* Joyce's *A Portrait of the Artist as a Young Man,* Huxley's *Point Counter Point,* and Hemingway's *The Sun Also Rises.* Digesting these masterpieces with an enthusiasm as ardent as mine was a girl I was extremely fond of, Margery Cameron, from Portland. She was small, cute, and trim, and the first female I'd known who could be described as an intellectual. Although dressed in the style of the period (Peter Pan collar, soft sweater, wool skirt, bobby socks, and loafers), she declared her individuality by wearing her hair in a bun and refusing to take college, or any, sports seriously. She aspired to be a Writer, and she did write some remarkable if identifiably undergraduate stories in the Virginia Woolf mode. We spent hours quarreling over literature, and I loved her so much that I hated it when she didn't agree with me on one point or another. She had a fine aesthetic instinct, which made her immune to critical fads or any kind of artistic or political theory. Intellectually, she knew at all times exactly what she was doing, and she did it without fear of criticism. As early as 1946 she was ridiculing euphemisms like "that man has a kleptomania problem." After college, she went to New York, married an Asian working for the United Nations, had a little boy by him, and died of a brain tumor. What a loss to the world of wit and honor! Once I went up to Portland on the train to meet her parents and ask her to marry me. She said no.

At the same time, I was getting acquainted with the girl I did marry, Betty Harper. She was a strikingly beautiful blonde with a healthy sense of humor and a powerful social impulse: she liked more people than I did, setting me an example of tolerance that I didn't always imitate. But after Cam's refusal, she became my steady date, and we consumed a great deal of beer together.

Mention of these two women reminds me of the terrible importance to us of good looks, doubtless a California impulse. Both sexes expended hours arguing about who was the most beautiful or handsome person in the vicinity. Cam once studied one of my wrists attentively and finally pronounced, "You are wonderfully made," an observation that did nothing to chill my regard for her. At this point I was in my Tab Hunter period and perhaps too pretty for credibility. My physical vanity was still as strong as when at Hamilton School I mistook the girl's error about the green-ink pen for a tribute to my attractiveness. A standard way of praising someone was to celebrate in public and in their hearing their good looks, and no one seemed embarrassed taking credit for attributes unearned and ultimately, as we learned, irrelevant. What we were doing was embracing

Back at Pomona, 1946.

The Connecticut College Department of English, 1952. Standing left
to right: Billie Hazlewood, Gertrude Noyes, James Baird, Betty Fussell,
Jane Smyser. Sitting: H. M. Smyser, Dorothy Bethurum, Rosemond
Tuve, PF, Catherine Oakes, Pauline Aiken.

Betty at Katoúnia,
Greece, summer
of 1965.

Tucky and PF visiting
Pasadena, 1959.

Tucky, Princeton, spring 1973.

Sam practicing headers,
Princeton, 1970.

Princeton, 1975. Somber publicity
for *The Great War and Modern
Memory (Elaine Miller)*.

Princeton, late 1970s. At lower right, the behind of Dexter-Margaret, named Dexter by Sam until the discovery that she was female *(Mary Cross)*.

WILMA A. DAANE
150 SOUTH MONACO, #610
DENVER, CO 80224

DENVER. CO 802
AUG 18
PM
1986

USA
22

Professor Donald T. Regan
Professor of English
University of Pennsylvania
Philadelphia PA 19104

Mail for Professor Donald T. Regan, his appointment
the result of a misplaced comma.

Sam, Betty, Tucky, PF, in Italy, June 1980.

Harriette's response to
my request for a picture,
October 1982.

Harriette in fall 1943, as she
entered Northwestern.

At a barn dance, 1983.

At the wedding of
Harriette's daughter,
Liese, Washington,
fall 1984.

In Lithuania, 1994.

In Bangkok, 1995.

The Connecticut College Department of English, 1952. Standing left to right: Billie Hazlewood, Gertrude Noyes, James Baird, Betty Fussell, Jane Smyser. Sitting: H. M. Smyser, Dorothy Bethurum, Rosemond Tuve, PF, Catherine Oakes, Pauline Aiken.

Back at Pomona, 1946.

Tucky and PF visiting
Pasadena, 1959.

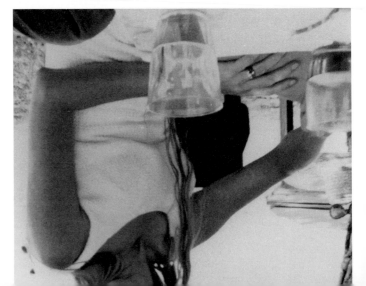

Betty at Katoúnia,
Greece, summer
of 1965.

Princeton, 1975. Somber publicity
for *The Great War and Modern
Memory (Elaine Miller).*

Sam practicing headers,
Princeton, 1970.

Princeton, late 1970s. At lower right, the behind of Dexter-Margaret, named Dexter by Sam until the discovery that she was female *(Mary Cross)*.

Sam, Betty, Tucky, PF, in Italy, June 1980.

Mail for Professor Donald T. Regan, his appointment
the result of a misplaced comma.

Professor Donald J. Regan
Professor of English
University of Pennsylvania
Philadelphia PA 19104

Harriette in fall 1943, as she
entered Northwestern.

Harriette's response to
my request for a picture,
October 1982.

At the wedding of
Harriette's daughter,
Liese, Washington,
fall 1984.

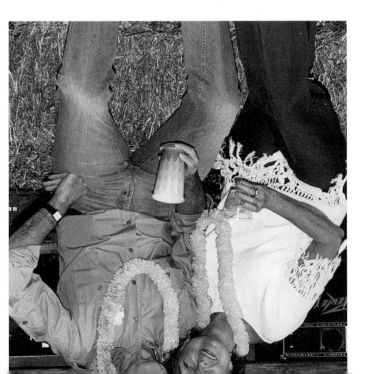

At a barn dance, 1983.

In Bangkok, 1995.

In Lithuania, 1994.

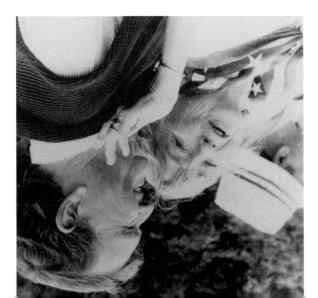

Hollywood's suggestion that only beautiful people are interesting or fit objects of love: Robert Taylor and Tyrone Power were in the ascendant, Walter Matthau and Gene Hackman not yet on the scene.

Asked how combat soldiers survive having been in a war, Audie Murphy said, "I don't think they ever do." No one had heard yet of post-traumatic stress disorder, but for the first couple of years after the war I experienced something close to it. Emotionally, I was very shaky, given to tears at late-night parties, not all attributable to drink. I remember sometimes lying under the furniture crying my eyes out, just as I had at the evacuation hospital. So avid were most Americans to resume without any change their prewar lives that it was assumed that once the war was over, and gloriously and victoriously over, such midnight behavior as mine must be the result of affectation or simple drunkenness. But a few years later, once this phase had passed, I found I could drink all I could hold without any impulse to tears. I have learned that if one does get over the more gross effects of having been an active infantryman, one never gets past certain habits. I still jump at loud noises in the street, and at the machine-gun sound of a compressed-air hammer, I want to throw myself prone regardless of who might think it funny. I button all pocket flaps religiously. I still count silently to accompany such repeated body movements as putting on trousers or walking at the official rate of 120 steps per minute: hut, two, three, four. And when riding in a car or on a train, I still locate in the passing landscape good positions for machine guns, antitank guns, or minefields.

My appetite for literature meant, clearly, that I would have to go on for more study, and safe in the hands of the GI Bill, I began to prepare for graduate school somewhere. Ed, who shared my passion for "English," was already at Harvard and warning me about the stringency with which the language requirements for the Ph.D. were imposed there: one had to pass reading tests in Latin, French, and German, and pass them the first year or else. Latin I thought (erroneously, it turned out) I knew well enough from junior high school, and French I thought I could work up myself. German was the problem, and I added a Pomona course for beginners, reading elementary narratives (most designed for children, like Erich Kästner's *Emil und die Detektive*) and memorizing grammatical paradigms. Encouraged by the three people to whom this book is dedicated, I applied to Harvard, Yale, and Princeton. Yale and Princeton rejected me — until my final year, my Pomona record was appalling — but thanks to Ed's sticking up for me on the spot and perhaps Harvard's greater willingness to take chances on mavericks, I was accepted there.

Why did I always follow my brother to his school instead of choosing my own? The answer is embarrassing. Ed was a real scholar, and I was intellectually insecure, requiring his example and informal guidance to overcome my laziness and shallowness. It was he, not I, who received English Honors at Pomona, and he, not I, was elected to Phi Beta Kappa. When he proclaimed a subject, like Renaissance lyric, worth intense study, I got interested in it, but compared with him and his impeccable scholarship, I was a mere simulacrum. I made up with cleverness and quickness for a notable lack of depth. But I learned to outwit examiners well enough to get by.

For those of us returning to colleges after strenuous or boring or horrible combat years, English studies leading to careers as professors of English seemed much more attractive than at other times. Former soldiers like John Ciardi, Louis Simpson, James Dickey, Karl Shapiro, and Richard Wilbur filled the graduate schools, aiming at the teaching of English literature to a generation unbrutalized by war. We all hoped, secretly if not openly, that our efforts would help restore subtlety, civility, and decency after their wartime disappearance. This seemed almost a religious act, demanding from its devotees their complete emotional and spiritual commitment. The world was now to be saved from its folly, brutality, and coarseness of conscience by the techniques of close reading and disciplined explication. And if some wisdom could be gathered on the way, that would be useful too.

Later, I heard the British scholar Geoffrey Tillotson urge his Harvard graduate students to "live your literature." That's what I was doing, and intensely. It was literary narrative that presided over my move from the West to the East Coast, from the fancied coercion of parents and the persisting infantilism of college all the way to the "European" sophistication of the East. (That Harvard was really no more demanding and exciting than the University of California was a truth I was not prepared to receive at the time.) As a rabidly enthusiastic student of *The Ambassadors,* I easily fancied Pasadena as Strether's Woollett, Massachusetts, unimaginative, puritan, un-idead, and appallingly dull. The "East" was, of course, Strether's and my France. Joyce's *Portrait of the Artist* encouraged me to think of myself somehow as an artist too, obliged by my election to a career of imagination and beauty to flee from philistinism. Besides, it had been clear for some time that my father rather hoped I'd follow him in the law. My disinclination to do so was reinforced as I identified myself with the aesthete Stephen Dedalus, who, just before he flees from Dublin to Paris, observes disdainfully of his father, "Wants me to read law. Says I was cut out for that." Robert Graves encouraged me to say good-bye to all that, meaning Presbyterian church, compulsory optimism and good-fellowship, censorious grandmother, shallow conversation, and empty professional goals, and turn to a new life, as I thought of it, of sensibility and art. Hemingway's short story "Soldier's Home" I embraced as a virtual campaign plan for my impending disjunction from bourgeois life. I identified my cause with that of ex-soldier Harold Krebs, who, returning from the First World War, finds himself alienated from his family and takes off for new pastures. I cast my mother as Krebs's. Urging the unwilling Krebs to get a regular job, she observes that "God has some work for every one to do. . . . There can be no idle hands in His kingdom." Because Krebs's father, who sells real estate, hardly appears in Hemingway's story, finding lively similarities between him and my father proved difficult. But another fictional real estate figure came to my assistance, and I cruelly imagined my father as a nobler version in some ways of George Folansbee Babbitt. Pasadena, after all, was not far from Zenith, as it was not far from Woollett. That these identifications were reductive and grossly unfair did not enter my mind. They were necessary, indeed indispensable, to give my revolt and disgust an irresistible artistic and intellectual sanction.

My final summer in California I spent at Balboa. I loved to shock people when I went swimming with the large pink-and-blue scar on my leg, a disgusting sight that seemed to make the point all by itself that here was a young man with a grievance, or at least an interesting past. During that summer I worked on my French by means of a correspondence course from the University of California. I was lazy and superficial, and my distant instructor often reprimanded me by mail for avoidable errors and stupidities caused by carelessness and inattention. All this time I was sustaining my contempt for what I thought of as the philistine West by frequent recourse to the poems treasured by Oscar Williams and preparing for departure in other ways, like dyeing my OD and pink officers' shirts navy blue and corresponding with Ed about the hazards and joys of learned life in the East. Finally, in early September, I was ready to take off, and together with a rowdy Socialist friend aiming for subversive studies at the New School, set off one bright morning to drive to Cambridge, Massachusetts. The irony of my escaping in my mother's Chevrolet coupé, given to me selflessly and with much love, I didn't notice. Only much later did it cross my mind that at the moment my parents were probably as happy with the removal of this peevish, fault-finding young man as I was at freeing myself from the complacent nest. The adversarial imagery in which I was careful to couch my eastward movement I'm sure caused me later to overemphasize this element of literary and cultural modernism, to see it largely as a melo-dramatic conflict instead of a more gradual, peaceful displacement or natural development.

We are now so used to whipping across the American continent by jet in a few hours that it's easy to forget how immense it used to seem when we crossed by rail or car. It took many days, and instead of looking down at them from a remote, unreal height, we used to be intimate with stopping-places along the way: Barstow, Flagstaff, Gallup, Albuquerque, Amarillo, Tulsa, Joplin, St. Louis, Indianapolis, Columbus, Pittsburgh, Trenton. My friend and I stopped at seedy motels and quarreled constantly. He was much far-ther Left than I, and regarded graduate studies in English as simply a device to bolster the bourgeois order and delay the revolution. Ed had been kindly looking for a place for me to stay in Cambridge, and when we arrived, we carried my stuff up to the third floor of a frame house at 35 Trowbridge Street, three blocks from Harvard. It was owned by three elderly Catholic spinsters, the Misses Smith, who rented rooms to graduate students and lower-middle-class retired men. Smoking was allowed, but absolutely no drink or women. My room, up two flights of stairs, cost seven dollars a week, but before that sounds unbelievable, it should be remembered that seventy-five dollars would buy you a nice gray flannel suit. My bed was made daily and the room thoroughly cleaned weekly. Into this aerie I moved my books, my record player, and my electric fan — in summer it got monstrously hot up there under the roof. In those days there were one or two university dormitories for graduate students, but even if ample space had been available, because of my stubborn principles of individuality and hatred of groups, I would still have chosen to live alone.

For a literary boy from the West — I almost said the Prairies — entering Harvard Yard for the first time was a thrill like my first Strether-like glimpse of Paris. Because my ideas of antiquity were still highly Californian, the eighteenth-century brick buildings of the silent Yard, set off by old elms, struck me as significantly aged and clearly associated with a wisdom that was very uncontemporary, the wisdom the college gate exhorted me to enter and grow in. After all, the Yard was associated with important people whose presence still resonated there. Emerson and Thoreau, of course, and Longfellow. These flagstone walkways had been worn down by men who helped originate and define the United States, people like Increase Mather and Samuel Sewall. Not to mention Oliver Wendell Holmes, Henry Adams, James Russell Lowell, Francis Parkman, George Santayana, Louis Agassiz, Alfred North Whitehead, and William and Henry James. The late FDR had been a C student here, more interested in "activities" than study. John Dos Passos and E. E. Cummings had walked past these very elms, and so had the writer rapidly becoming my personal hero, displacing Mencken, T. S. Eliot. As I wandered reverently around it that first time, the deserted Yard sent me a message: "You are now an advanced student, almost a scholar. This place is serious, and you'd better achieve something. The best of these powerfully willed and strong-minded men didn't come here to horse around but to test themselves against nonprovincial standards and to originate something that might last. See that you do better than your best so far. If you don't come up to the measure this place will impose on you, you're going to have to return home, and in disgrace." I determined to pull up my socks.

Ed, now married and living with Jean out at Fort Devens in a veterans' village hastily made from disused army barracks, provided his usual help. He showed me how to register for my courses and how to cram for the language exams by buying French, German, and Latin flash cards at Schoenhof's Foreign Book Store on Massachusetts Avenue. All over Cambridge you could spot graduate students in the humanities by their devotion, at leisure moments, to their little one-by-two-inch white cards, the foreign words on one side, the English on the other. You worked your way through a pack until you knew them, then you grabbed another bunch and started again.

Harvard in those days being, except for some few classes, totally male, the social transition from the services to the academy was relatively smooth for most of us. Over 70 percent of graduate students were veterans recently demobilized, and rather than by race, color, or creed, you tended to define a man by what he'd done in the war. Because Harvard was not Nebraska State, most of the graduate students, it proved, had been in the navy, and a few had been admirals' aides. I met no one who'd been in the infantry, and few who'd been in any of the ground forces. Although egregious contrast between killing and literary study is required for his 1946 Harvard Phi Beta Kappa poem "Under Which Lyre," Auden lays it on rather thick with his "bloodstains," "battle-line," "sniping," and "slaughter," as in:

Nerves that never flinched at slaughter
Are shot to pieces by the shorter
Poems of Donne,

lines hardly appropriate for the Harvard postwar scene, where former young intelligence, logistics, and staff officers outnumbered ex–German and Jap killers.

We all tended to be military snobs, not about rank but about danger. We quietly rejected as not quite up to standard men who'd been in the service but not in dangerous or romantic branches. The postwar dress conventions required us graduate students to wear whenever possible our suntan trousers, with loafers, tweed jacket, button-down shirt, and necktie. Wearing the tie especially to classes distinguished us from the kid undergraduates, who lived in the costly Houses, dressed any old way, and romped and drank and attended the football games and slavered to get into classy clubs like Hasty Pudding and the Porcellian. They were aiming at business careers, or none at all, but we were quite different, our sights manifestly set on higher things.

My first year at Harvard I was painfully chaste. The girls lived at Radcliffe, across the way, and when especially lonely I'd show up at a Radcliffe "mixer" and look around. I finally found a young creature from Omaha I liked and gradually got to know. She was good-looking and friendly, but seemed already fixed in her upper-middle-class ways and uncritical of anything. She would have done well for

Boy Fussell if he still adhered to Pasadena and its ways, but she didn't at all fit the requirements of his continuing transfiguration. My attempts to persuade her to share my adversarial radical views as well as to permit more intimate physical contact ended in failure and quarrels, and on her part, tears. The climax, in this case so different from a consummation, occurred one night at the opera in Boston. During an intermission in *La Traviata*, overtaken by an impulse to be vaingloriously honest, I foolishly allowed myself to indicate that, devoted as I was to her, I was also seeing as often as possible a girl in New York. (Betty Harper had come East to work in publishing, at Alfred Knopf, and we had resumed, and intensified, our former relationship.) This news caused the Omaha girl to fly into a tearful tantrum, and she fled back to Cambridge, quite alone. I enjoyed the rest of *Traviata* by myself and never saw her again.

The car I'd driven across the country proved a terrible embarrassment and encumbrance in Cambridge. I had no place to drive and no spare time to do it in, and the only place to leave the car proved to be the street. In California, antifreeze was unheard of, and I calmly let the weather turn very cold without thinking of it. Result: a cracked engine block, requiring an expensive welding job. After that, I gave up entirely the idea of ever using the car in the East, but I didn't go so far as to get rid of it. For months it sat upon blocks in storage until I met a married graduate student of English who, having flunked his language exams, was returning, shaken, to California. I sold him the car for a trifling sum and saw the last of it.

The GI Bill was sending all types to graduate school, and not all were committed to the most rigorous of humanistic procedures. One fellow I knew was expelled for lying to a professor about a late paper: he had cleverly thrown it over the top of the professor's locked but roofless library carrel to land on or near a pile of nonbelated and not yet graded papers. Alas, it landed on the floor some distance away, and, interrogated, he tried to argue that it had been on top of the original stack all the time. But earlier, the professor had counted the bona fide papers, and the miscreant was told to vacate Harvard within twenty-four hours.

Draconic punishment of that sort, with no appeal, was a Harvard tradition. Final examinations were given in large rooms to several different classes at the same time, and eagle-eyed proctors, avid to catch wrongdoers, gumshoed up and down constantly. Once I witnessed a proctor rush to one undergraduate, seize his blue book, and ceremoniously tear it in half before his eyes. The student understood instantly that he'd been seen cheating, that he'd been accused and convicted right there, and that he was lost. That's an example of the privileges and the disciplinary style assumed by the higher learning before the 1960s. Today, that young person would be invited to plead his case before a student-faculty-administration committee, and there would be a good chance that the college, not the student, would be found at fault.

Before the year was over, I'd furnished my room with two framed pictures I invested with lots of significance. One was a print of Camille Pissarro's impressionist and unmistakably French *Boulevard des Italiens, Morning, Sunlight,* depicting a bird's-eye view of this busy Parisian street in 1893 with kiosks, horse trams, carriages, and plane trees, the sidewalks busy with knowledgeable and purposeful people. The effect is intensely French-urban and sophisticated. You can almost smell the coffee and the cognac. That print was just what I needed to remind me that I had arrived in my American version of "Paris," and that I had left behind my version of "Woollett." That I was now actually where the original Woollett was, puritan Massachusetts, added complication and irony, which I enjoyed.

At Harvard I was notably hostile and bitter, and made very few friends. "Harvard lets you alone," says David McCord, class of 1921. Accustomed to a flattering gregariousness at Pomona, I soon found myself not enjoying being so excessively left alone. As I became more and more lonely, another picture I'd hung on my wall seemed more and more appropriate as an emblem of my resulting melancholy. (The term *depression* had not yet become chic.) This was an engraving by George Cruikshank, *The Blue Devils*. A poor, solitary man in night-cap and slippers stares into his cold fireplace while all around him appear animated images of poverty, debt, suicide, failure, and cata-strophe. A vicious little imp on his shoulder solicits him with a noose to hang himself. I never reached that stage of melancholy, but some-times I did think of calling the Veterans Administration in Boston to see if I could get some treatment for my sense of alienation and my misery.

At Harvard, in addition to melancholy, I encountered a number of things quite new to me. One was faculty snottiness toward enter-ing graduate students, very like the snottiness with which senior officers in the army habitually treated their juniors. The army term for it was chickenshit. There seemed no analogous Harvard term, but the army one would have served. The implication was that graduate students on the GI Bill had had the impudence to violate the stan-dard relation between a student's rich family and the university. The hated federal government was now in the act, and at Harvard dis-comfort with this new arrangement was unconcealed. Another cause of Harvard snot was the appearance of incoming graduate students who'd been prepared for advanced study in unprecedented ways.

When I underwent my obligatory conference with the medievalist director of English Graduate Studies, Bartlett Jere Whiting, he laughed cruelly when I revealed that I'd worked up my French by correspondence course. He didn't quite openly sneer at Pomona College, or affect not to know what or where it was, but he did manage to suggest that preparation there was a highly uncertain basis for the eventual, if unlikely, earning of a Harvard Ph.D. He made it clear that those unprepared in the three required languages should not expect to survive, and that if that didn't discourage the aspirant interested in mere literature, the requirement in philology — two terms of Old English, one of Middle English — probably would.

Matching the un-California archaism of the immemorial elms and the worn paving stones in the Yard were a number of Harvard usages a critical observer might easily consider nugatory affectations. At Sever Hall, where I had most of my classes, the deeply scored and initialed early-nineteenth-century, twelve-foot-long desks and forms (in modern American, *benches*) had never been replaced by comfortable, practical student chairs with writing arms, as at ordinary universities. The effect, while apparently aiming at an air of antiquity, seemed only self-conscious and bogus. Students and faculty alike carried their books and notes in green baize book bags, clumsy to load and notably absorbent in rainy weather. Not to sport a book bag was to betray a regrettable refusal to play the game. It was by implication to reveal one's unfortunate origin in the intellectual and spiritual sticks. For me, these usages were beginning to complicate my simple West Coast assignment of virtue and value to the East.

Classes began, and disappointment set in immediately. Most of the professors, it seemed to me, conducted classes in the laziest possible way, openly reading from note cards, soliciting no comments or questions, maintaining a needless nervous or supercilious distance from the class. This was not at all true of the best I encountered, but it seemed sufficiently the Harvard style to embarrass that institution's pretenses to educational distinction. The language courses were taught by underpaid hacks, aged, unpromotable assistant professors with stooped shoulders, white hair, and an air of deep boredom. One read the newspaper while we recited in front of him, and all treated their students with something bordering on open contempt. I began to realize that the joy of learning was a meaningful idea only where joyous teachers affectionately encouraged uncynical students, preferably not in crowds but virtually one by one. The contrasting Harvard method seemed distinctly like the army. It was both comically and disastrously distant from all expectation.

My first year I set myself doggedly to pass the language exams, taking undergraduate courses in German and Latin. One had three chances for each exam, and if then one couldn't pass them all, one left. I passed French the first time, because the sight passage to be turned into English came from Legouis and Cazamian's history of English literature for French students and dealt with the quarrel between Samuel Johnson and Lord Chesterfield, a narrative I knew already. German took me two tries, and even as I passed I sensed the closeness of the call and the curious leniency of the graders. Latin was a real impediment. I flunked that test twice, and in the muggy heat of June tried for the final time. Disgrace and an ignominious exposure as a snob and fraud loomed if I failed again and had to return home, or go somewhere else to lick my wounds. To avoid catastrophe, I virtually memorized Ovid in English translation, for I knew Ovid would be on the exam. (Alternate years: Virgil.) There was an anxious week's wait while the Latin exams were read and my fate decided. Each of us had inserted in the blue book a self-addressed postcard, and daily at Trowbridge Street I ran downstairs to see the fatal results. I really didn't expect to pass, for I couldn't imagine real scholars and experts so incompetent as to read my preposterous renderings without laughing aloud. Finally my postcard appeared on the worn silver-plated tray where incoming mail was displayed. I carried it up to my room without examining it, for I didn't want anyone to see my tears. In my room, I turned the card over and found a desultory *P* scrawled in pencil. I had passed. I would become a Ph.D. I would become a university professor. Only a few would ever guess how shaky, if not actually nonexistent, my Latin really was. Passing that test was like surviving Fort Benning, and becoming a real professor seemed as magically desirable as, once, becoming a boy officer had been. Now, if I could only survive the oral exam and produce a passable thesis, and then get a decent academic job, I'd be on my way to a seven-year probationary teaching period, after which, if I behaved myself and paid all my dues (which meant publishing a lot that wasn't entirely silly), I'd be granted tenure, which would guarantee that, like the finally liberated Robert Graves, I'd never be under anyone's orders for the rest of my life. I would finally be released from the life of coercion.

It was at Harvard that I learned how to concentrate and how to finish with delight and even flair intellectual tasks that before would have seemed intolerably boring or would have daunted me entirely. My physical energy was still army energy: on dismal snowy mornings, I could ecstatically leap out of bed and, coffeeless, rush to class to translate aloud the Old English "Dream of the Rood." Then home to hours of flash-card work, with some time spent memorizing the years of the British monarchs from Alfred the Great to George VI.

After that, a chapter or two of the thick volume we all read constantly to steep ourselves in the subjects of the Ph.D. oral examination — even if it wasn't even dimly in the future yet, until we'd finished our two years of course work. The book was *A Literary History of England*, by A. C. Baugh, Tucker Brooke, Samuel C. Chew, Kemp Malone, and Harvard's own George Sherburn. It seemed obvious that if you knew everything in it, you'd have no trouble with your orals, the terrifying ordeal flunked by about a quarter of the candidates, refreshingly fewer than the two thirds that washed out of Benning, but still not a comforting figure. These were days and nights of a literary intensity that can never come again, for verbal culture, in those preelectronic years, was still taken for granted as a permanent and invaluable thing. To excel in it gave one a kind of status unthinkable today. The whole Ph.D. program in English seemed based on the plausible assumption that there would always be significant demand for explicators of Shakespeare and Milton and Johnson and Keats and Melville and Faulkner. TV was not on the scene yet, nor had anyone suggested that "film" might be material for serious study.

But drama certainly was, and at Harvard it seemed to be more important than fiction. One striking exception to the general mediocrity of the teaching was Harry Levin's performance in his yearlong course "English Drama from Its Origin to the Closing of the Theaters." What a delight it was to read three plays a week and to hear Levin comment at length on each. The point that emerged was that Shakespeare, although unique, was not mysterious but was in part the creation of his theatrical context. Thus we read, for example, several revenge plays, and into the middle of them Levin would introduce *Hamlet.* Refreshingly clear now would appear its relation to Thomas Kyd's *The Spanish Tragedy* and Marlowe's *The Jew of*

Malta, and simple ideas of literary originality and "creativity" would suffer a setback. Levin's contextualizing of the Tudor and Stuart drama was typical of the deromanticizing to be met with everywhere at Harvard. The curriculum made it impossible to be simpleminded or sentimental about artistic "inspiration" or unprecedented invention. Every literary genre and technique had an ascertainable cause behind it, which mind could locate, analyze, and contemplate. The result was that literary history and the history of taste became a study as graspable as political or economic history.

Levin was the best lecturer I ever heard, a memorable relief from the normal Harvard standard. His performances — and that is the right word — were notably formal and calculated, which made them seem at one with the plays he illuminated. With his stylish little mustache and three-piece gray suit — impossible to imagine him in gym wear — he arrived on stage and undid his notes. When there was absolute silence, out came the paradoxes and the wit, all delivered with total control and the jokes with a straight face. The sentence structure that was his favorite began with an *if* clause, and it exerted a powerful effect later on many of his students. If he was a bit too fond of designating any change *a sea change,* his words themselves were ennobling and simply lifted one up, made one feel more hopeful about the possibilities of intelligent life for humanity in general. Sometimes his wit was worthy of permanent cherishing; for fifty years I've treasured this observation on classic overreaching: "If Faust wants an infinite number of things at one time, Don Juan wants one thing an infinite number of times." His lectures were so beautifully constructed and their delivery so polished that he delighted to show off by concluding exactly two seconds before the large bell in the tower of Memorial Church tolled to signal the end of the class hour. It was clear, thus, that he saw no reason why a timed segment of intellectual discourse shouldn't exhibit the structure and coherence demanded of any other first-rate literary work.

In a recent memorial essay on Harry Levin, Donald Fanger notes the impossibility of recalling him without invoking the word *elegant.* His learning was prodigious, and in his writings, says Fanger, "mastery of detail complements memorable overviews, and irrepressible high spirits play over an underlying seriousness." In short, an exemplary humanist. And his concerns were broad, extending well past the normal limits of "English Literature." He was a master of Continental culture. His solid comparative literature course, "Proust, Joyce, and Mann," despite his demanding for admission advanced skill in French or German, was popular enough to occasion much secret envy in the Department of English. He had no degree higher than a Harvard B.A., and that seemed to suggest his opinion of the advanced literary learning officially pursued by the English Department and the professionalism for which it prepared its students. He cannot have been so distinguished without awareness of his value, but he seemed the opposite of vainglorious. He was reserved and even shy, and it's likely that he didn't think primarily of himself when he quoted one of his favorite observations from Henry Adams: "A teacher affects eternity; he can never tell where his influence stops."

Also memorable was Walter Jackson Bate, then an intense young man — he was a thirty-year-old assistant professor at the time — whose cheap suit and bright blue satin necktie gave little indication of the subtlety of his tastes in literature and art. He had been one of the beneficiaries of Werner Jaeger and his *Paideia,* and his warm, passionate humanity conferred a unique personality on the "neoclassical," elsewhere conceived of as cold and predictable. He seemed to set himself against two enemies, oversimplification and romanticism, and he was happy to engage both, as he did in courses intellectualizing literary impulses that might seem instinctual, like his course in "The Critical Theory of English Romanticism." Here, his understanding of Coleridge's epistemology burst upon me like a flash and I've never been the same since. For Coleridge, visual perception, and indeed other kinds, is "a repetition in the finite mind of the eternal act of creation" in God's. Art and literature are what result from the conscious management of that power, and thus can be considered in a way divine, an echo of the creative power of the Great I Am. Bate's way with ideas was remarkably clear: he was thinking all the time right in front of you, and without patronizing, letting you in on the process. He had a nice line in irony too, and his students loved the way he found it impossible always to bridle his animal instincts, sidling to the classroom door and, half in the room and half out of it, sneaking a cigarette, while a graduate student was delivering an oral report, not a word of which he missed and on which he commented fully and generously. His memory was extraordinary, and not just for literature. Once, forty years after he'd seen the last of me as a student, I was passing the Harvard Faculty Club, from which he emerged, saying, "Hello, Paul."

Other unforgettable Harvard worthies were less dramatic but almost equally impressive. The Milton presented by Douglas Bush was no less a scholar than a poet, in command of profound classical and Renaissance learning, where Bush himself took no very conspicuous second place. Bush's delivery of Milton's words was heartfelt, even if his odd little voice — very like the actor Victor Moore's — sometimes produced comic effects. A powerful invitation to mimicry was his twangy delivery of the lines in *Paradise Lost* about Eve:

. . . that fair field
Of Enna, where Proserpin gath'ring flowers
Herself a fairer flow'r by gloomy Dis
Was gather'd.

Bush made clear the inseparable alliance between poetry and learning, and that was an antisentimental, ultimately antiegalitarian theme often heard at Harvard. There, one realized what a serious Harvard student T. S. Eliot had betrayed himself to be in the scholarly allusiveness of *The Waste Land*.

My grievances against society made me a natural consumer of satire, and I applied myself very seriously to George Sherburn's course in Swift and Pope. The aged Sherburn was a friendly teacher, especially kind to nice-looking young men, but he was not a very good one. To teach Pope, he simply read from a pack of five-by-eight sheets containing transcripts from Pope's letters, material destined for his monumental edition of Pope's correspondence. This behavior, and students' annoyance with it, illustrated the war between traditional historical scholarship and the New Criticism waged in the late 1940s. I tried to straddle the gap, reading lots of criticism in *Partisan Review, Kenyon, Sewanee, Accent*, and *Poetry*, and later *Hudson Review*, but at the same time keeping up with, and sometimes contributing to, *The Review of English Studies, Notes and Queries, Modern Language Notes*, and even *PMLA*.

My immersion in the critical quarterlies and little magazines, where I encountered lots of contemporary poetry, tempted me to imagine a poetic career for myself. Given the Harvard setting, I decided I was in a fair position to devise learned poems on the Eliot model. Noting that the eruption of Vesuvius in the year 79, which killed Pliny the Elder at Misenum, occurred very near the site of the Allied landing at Salerno in 1943, I tried to bring past and present together in would-be Eliotic fashion in "Misenum," a poem actually accepted and published by the magazine *Perspective*, edited by Mona Van Duyn and other visible literary figures. The poem ended thus:

> *The evil heated breeze blew southward down*
> *To fair Salernum, where the shepherds, watch-*
> *ing their flocks by day, sniffed and went unruffled*
> *Back to gelding sheep. Some helmets were uncovered*
> *By the sand, and they smelled of sulphur.*

So far, not terribly bad, if embarrassingly pretentious. But what follows causes me today active pain:

> *Then an unheard voice of an unknown wrong*
> *Sang with the waves an unsung song:*
>> *Hats of steel like hats of down*
>> *Were later worn at Misenum town.*

(*Hats of down:* Pliny tried to protect his head from falling clinkers by tying on a cushion.) The question the end of the poem naturally invites never occurred to me: the question is, "So what?" Allusions, anyone? Finally understanding that Horace (another allusion?), in observing that nothing is less needed than a mediocre poet, was talking about me, I gave over and henceforth stuck rigorously to the writing of critical prose.

All this while I was living a life for which, if there had been present the slightest religious dimension, the term *monastic* would have been appropriate. I almost never "went out." I saw no movies, paid no attention to sports, and never even listened to the radio, so anxious was I to say good-bye forever to American popular culture. My contempt for anything popular kept me from going to see the famous glass flowers: tourists came to see them, which was a sufficient reason for my disdain. I never even had anything good to eat. Part of my decision to leave the family in California involved eliminating my financial dependence on them, and near the end of each month, when I'd spent my GI Bill maintenance money, I grew very hungry. But the misery was less the more I imagined that I was a martyr to art and learning.

Massachusetts levied a tax on restaurant meals costing a dollar or more. Thus the ninety-nine-cent dinner, popular with restaurateurs and students around Harvard Square. Near the end of the month, I would often eat dinner at a Chinese restaurant where I would limit myself to the ninety-nine-cent fried rice and a glass of water. Such undergraduate places as the Wursthaus were out because they swarmed with loud necktieless undergraduates, with whom most graduate students could not bear to be in any way confused.

It was not until decades later that I realized what a pederastic paradise for some graduate students Harvard had been. Now and then I'd be approached by a male student, whom I turned off with, I hope, courtesy and sympathy. Sexual frustration seemed to dominate the graduate-student scene, except among the married, of whom there were few. Once I attended a compulsory meeting of English graduate students to be informed about some new requirement or other. To give the meeting an air of friendliness and informality, it was held in a nice paneled room with a fireplace. Some students sat in leather easy chairs, the rest, including me, crowded behind.

Suddenly, while intent on the official talk, I felt the hand of the man standing behind me slip around and, unobserved, begin groping me. I delivered my message by quietly stepping to the side. The groper later became a distinguished professor of English at the City University of New York.

I was relieving my frustrations by occasional trysts in New York with Betty Harper. We would meet at some inexpensive hotel, usually on Lexington Avenue, and spend a few days drinking, eating, and sleeping together. One of these occasions was so successful that we agreed to be married as soon as possible. This required the choice of a church, and we selected All Souls Episcopal, a stylish wooden structure on the Cambridge Common dating from the American Revolution. A bullet hole from that war was still exhibited with pride. The rector was Gardner Day, a vigorous anti-Catholic birth-control enthusiast, whose premarital counseling of couples consisted not of theological or even psychological wisdom but of advice about where to have diaphragms fitted despite the local Catholic opposition to such devices. Condoms themselves were not easy to buy and required going to pharmacies well known for winking at the local puritanisms.

Our wedding took place on June 17, 1949. It must have been one of the most meager ever celebrated at All Souls, for I had virtually no friends to invite. The Misses Smith came, apparently with a special dispensation to attend a heretical proceeding, and a few couples I knew, and graduate-student friend Bill Ellis, and Ed and Jean. Jean, very pregnant, as maid of honor positioned her large bouquet to cover the bulge. My mother also came from Pasadena. She grew tipsy at the tiny reception a friendly couple hosted for us, and never forgave me for not inviting her to join us on our honeymoon on Cape Cod, which of course we planned to make a full-time private two-person sex orgy.

When at the end of the summer, we returned to duty — Betty was enrolled at Radcliffe for an M.A. in English — we settled in Boston in a fourth-floor walk-up on Huntington Avenue, off Copley Square, where in the midst of architectural and humanistic pretenses (the library was across the street), the whores plied their trade vigorously. I was "reading for orals," scheduled for eight weeks away, but for recreation we often went back to Cambridge in the evening to the Brattle Street Theater, where Jan Farrand, Jerome Kilty, and Thayer David performed brilliantly in civilized repertory. Except in London, I've never seen better theater continuously. They never put on a bomb, but played the best of Ibsen, Chekhov, Pirandello, Shaw — then still highly regarded — and of course Shakespeare. They produced rarities like *Troilus and Cressida* and the best *Love's Labour's Lost* I ever saw. It left me in tears, just as theater should. The quality was such that one wondered over and over at the learning and taste dominating the proceedings. Did the more sensitive members of the Harvard literature faculty have something to do with it? Harry Levin was often in the audience.

As the date for my oral exam approached, I began to realize the inadequacy of my preparation. In those days, the oral covered everything possible, from Old English to — well, not quite contemporary writing but at least late Victorian literature. Rumor held that a graduate student had once had the temerity to ask Professor George Lyman Kittredge what the oral examination covered. He answered briskly, "It covers the English language and literature and related languages and literatures." I felt gravely unprepared for the ordeal, since I knew virtually no major Victorian poetry or fiction, and in addition was notably weak in Middle English. There would be five examiners, and I hoped for luck in having some who would be lenient.

Sherburn, the examiner in the eighteenth century, probably would be. At one of his rare parties for graduate students, he once asked me to pour the martinis and referred to me affectionately as "our Ganymede." Recalling that, I felt that he, at least, wouldn't sink me.

The toughest assault I received was from Professor James Buell Munn, who normally taught classes in bibliography and similar remote subjects. I had contrived to know as little as possible about the lives of the poets, their verbal structures seeming the only thing about them of consequence. Professor Munn and I conducted the following colloquy:

MUNN: Mr. Fussell, can you tell us where Wordsworth went to school?

PF: I'm afraid not.

MUNN: Then can you tell us where Coleridge went to school?

PF: I don't know.

MUNN: Shelley?

PF: I don't know.

MUNN: Keats?

PF: I don't know.

MUNN: Well, how about Byron?

PF: I don't know.

This consumed some minutes of the two hours allotted for the examination, and when at the end I stepped out of the room to allow the examiners to confer over the result, I was certain I'd failed. You could take the exam twice, if necessary, but your disgrace was widely known. And often the emotional consequences were severe. Bill Ellis failed once, and when I saw him a few hours after the examination, he was still in tears. I was more frightened of failure perhaps than most, for my flight from California had been so weighted with public disgust, so melodramatic and uncompromising, that I could not stand to be revealed, finally, as a phony and an incompetent.

The door of the committee room remained closed for a very long time, and occasionally I heard raised, angry voices:

MUNN:　　　But he didn't answer *one* of my questions!

SHERBURN:　[Incomprehensible, but clearly a spirited defense of the candidate.]

Finally I was invited back in, to be told that I had passed, but barely, and was exhorted most solemnly to master the things I wasn't up on: Old and Middle English, nineteenth-century literature in general, plus Chaucer and Spenser. Even John Gay in my century of specialization, the eighteenth: I'd had to confess to Sherburn that I'd never read Gay's play *Polly*. "Oh yes, you have!" he kept insisting loyally, but I hadn't. It took days of rest and quiet to overcome the emotional shock of having come so close to disaster. The emotion was identical with that of my numerous infantry close calls, and I was aware of an unignorable continuity between those and this.

Only one hurdle now remained, the thesis, which normally ran to about four hundred pages. In one course I'd written a short paper analyzing some playwright's versification, and the professor had suggested that I had some talent for that sort of interpretation. I now saw that I might have a topic and immersed myself in everything ever written about the psychology of verbal rhythm. I decided to consider the theory of prosody in the period I knew best, the eighteenth century. Widener contained about a hundred eighteenth-century treatises on this subject, most of them never checked out or apparently even looked into. Here was virgin territory, and as I read and analyzed and wrote for the next few months, I realized what a boon it was to have a remote, singular, and entirely original thesis topic: no one on the premises could know more about it than I, the local expert.

The carrel in the library where I worked happened to be next to the stacks containing contemporary German periodicals, and when my interest in eighteenth-century prosody and its meaning occasionally flagged, I regaled myself with the bound volumes of the wartime *Illustrierter Beobachter.* This simpleminded Nazi magazine revolted me, and my outrage fastened as well upon the current movement to rearm the Germans and to be nice to them in order to position them to confront our former allies the Russians. I was browsing through the *Illustrierter Beobachter* at the moment West Germany was granted its sovereignty again, and soon the Wehrmacht was revived and renamed the Bundeswehr. Already a thoroughly pissed-off infantryman, to me this rapid, cynical turnaround negated everything officially said a decade earlier about Russia and Germany and disclosed 90 percent of American assertions about other countries to be cunning lies. It seemed I'd been demeaned and all but killed fighting the wrong enemy. These feelings did nothing to alter my self-defined identity as a representative Angry Man.

I finished my thesis in June 1951, giving it the hyperlearned title "Studies in Eighteenth-Century English Prosodic Theory." By this time, all but a few English Ph.D.'s had secured teaching jobs and were now, with wives and children, books, clothes, pots and pans, and rudimentary furniture, on their way to the West Coast and the Middle West, receiving salaries and preparing to conduct their own classes. Ed had been teaching since the fall of 1949 at the University of California at Berkeley. Only I, it seemed, remained unemployed, and the reason was not far to seek. I'd attended a couple of MLA conventions looking for jobs and had seriously busted every interview. I insisted on playing my transfigured self, that is, impudent, insolent, sarcastic, and ostentatiously clever and supercilious. When the chairman of the English Department of Colorado College interviewed me, I carefully told him what was wrong with his department. Later, I recognized myself in Arthur Miller's Biff, in *Death of a Salesman*, who, at the end of a crucial job interview, steals the interviewer's costly pen.

By sheer luck, crossing the Yard one day, I ran into Professor Whiting, who asked where I was going to teach in September. He was appalled to be told that I'd not yet been appointed anywhere. Back in his office, he phoned his friend Hamilton M. Smyser, of Connecticut College for Women in New London, and asked him if he had an opening. I knew Smyser a bit because I'd taken Old English from him. He had been a visiting professor during one summer session, and it was a custom among the more civil graduate students to take the required Old English from Smyser, a kind and easygoing man, rather than from the preposterous Francis Peabody Magoun, an absentminded, witless pedant said by some to have been the model for the cartoon character Mister Magoo.

It chanced that Smyser had an opening. One of his instructors had failed to achieve his Ph.D. from Columbia, and had just been "let out," as we used to say. The Old-Boy network proved to be working fine, and after a visit to New London, I signed a one-year contract paying me $3,200 per year (the most I'd ever earned, and the beginning of my lifetime relations with the Social Security system).

I was granted the title Instructor in English. In July Betty and I moved to New London and settled into a fifty-dollar-a-month apartment on the second floor of a house owned by the college. Built uniformly of gray stone, the college sat on a treeless hill a quarter mile away. Its resemblance to a maximum-security prison was augmented by a tall gray smokestack.

⊹ VII ⊹

CONNECTICUT COLLEGE, it proved, had hired a dangerously angry
young man. To survive in the infantry, I had mastered the technique
of productive anger, the impulse required for effective close-combat
killing. I knew the sheer fun of destruction and how to cause it with
a few blocks of TNT and a detonator. The war accustomed me to
strong emotions, especially when enlisted in the service of antagonism, contempt, and the urge to succeed any possible way. I was used
to the role of unyielding adversary.

From the 1950s on, my presiding emotion was annoyance, often
intensifying to virtually disabling anger. Anger at my accepting invitations to make too many changes of identity too fast: from college
to professional killer, and then to benign professor. I was angry at
myself for my inability to make sense of this process, to infer from it
some general enlightenment instead of cynicism and nihilism. I was
angry at the whole postwar atmosphere of public misrepresentation
and fatuous optimism, the widespread feeling that the war had produced good for the United States, with good defined as people's ability to buy new cars and refrigerators. So what if 85 million people had

been killed, most of them civilians? Here, no one had been bombed, eviscerated, burned to death, raped, or torn apart. Here, the war was now largely represented almost as a source of fun, for which act national euphemism became necessary: the War Department was euphemized into the Department of Defense, the armaments and war budget became the defense budget, and soon air strikes — later, surgical air strikes — would replace the bombing of women and children. Public rhetoric was growing indistinguishable from commercial advertising, and I came to regard both as the cynical manipulation of the weak of mind by the cunning and the avaricious. Increasingly the country seemed managed not by an elected government but by the National Association of Manufacturers, abetted by the Central Intelligence Agency, forcing anyone of energetic conscience to embrace the role of enemy. And how could I avoid indignation at the local bragging habit, America's proud pointing to its three thousand colleges and universities without noticing their failure to produce more than a handful of first-rate minds? I was bitterly conscious that the central thinkers of the modern world — Freud, Marx, Darwin, Jung — had all arisen elsewhere.

I became wildly opposed to any manifestation of censorship, which had been responsible for shielding Americans from the adult facts of the terrible war they'd been presumably engaged in. I even began to consider the causes of the hammertoe oversight, not to mention the business of the foreign matter left in my leg wound, and my anger grew at what I took to be a tradition of widespread professional carelessness and insensitivity. All these occasions of my anger seemed attended by a new phony language aiming at gentility and fraud. The all-but-universal worship of science, social science, and analytic philosophy would soon encourage the half-educated to pepper their discourse with terms like narratology, disciplinarity, engendering, and interface. It was impossible not to notice America's rapid rehabilitating of German and Austrian Nazis, its tacit encouragement of leniency in the few remaining war-crimes trials, and its designation of anything vaguely socialistic as dangerous and disloyal. How could I not be angry perceiving that the anti-Nazi "cause" for which I'd almost lost my leg and which had devastated so many of my young men and their families was actually worth so little that it could be easily discarded and forgotten after a few short years? I was at white heat over McCarthyism's fastening traitorous intent upon heterodox opinion. The term *un-American* was echoed from all sides, and the blacklists of the disaffected and the angry flourished and multiplied.

And I was bitterly angry at men of my age who had managed to survive the war in comfort and cleanliness. I was especially furious at those given to bragging about their cleverness in avoiding the combat their social inferiors had had to perform, and many dinner parties were ruined by my coarse antagonism. From now on most of what I said became protests, and most of what I wrote, even if disguised as critical essays or pleasant nonfiction books, was really Protest Literature.

One underlying cause of my rage I seldom specified in public: I was rusticated to a mere girls' school, while my friends enjoyed their first teaching jobs at Amherst and Williams and solid Midwestern state universities like Michigan. By contrast, I was condemned to an atmosphere of insignificance and ineffectiveness. The girls I taught seemed content to abjure public service, muckracking journalism, or the life of justice and even administration for a lifetime of cooking, interior decorating, niceness, and child rearing. In short, I was not at all the right person to guide young women along a path marked out by their rich fathers. As if in revenge, I elevated my intellectual requirements until they produced in the helpless student victims tears and tantrums, and I learned always to keep a box of tissues in my desk drawer.

I taught, of course, mainly freshman composition, which required the sort of strenuous duty I'd not performed since the army. Classes began at 8:00 A.M. and met six days a week, until noon on Saturday. Roll was taken assiduously, and no cuts were permitted on days adjacent to official holidays. I had to mark and comment on fifty themes a week, and on each hold a half hour's scheduled conference with the student. There was no cushion, no leeway, no escape from this relentless duty. When once the college president, Rosemary Park, insisted on my presence at commencement, effectively quashing our plans for an escape to Europe for the summer on a vessel sailing in early June, I realized anew that colleges as well as battalions and regiments had their own forms of chickenshit. The faculty's resemblance to troops was emphasized by the precise roll-taking at the monthly faculty meetings, with no absences permitted. How could I help equating the college administration with the military staff I'd been hating for years? Both seemed to me to consist of parasites, sequestered safely in offices and orderly rooms while others performed the real strenuous work in the field. I was not an easy subordinate.

A tone of puritanism prevailed at the college. There was no drinking on the campus, parietal rules were strictly enforced, student social events were tightly chaperoned, and it was assumed that members of the faculty agreed wholeheartedly with the administration that one of their duties was safeguarding the students' purity. Smyser, who liked a drink and who lived in a college apartment, felt obliged to convey his numerous empty bottles to the town dump by night, lest they be discovered by the college trash remover and commented on by the administration. None of the rest of us went so far, but we were careful to pull down the shades when we drank. Despite the intent of the college, a flaccid courtesy and gentility dominated instead of intellectual rigor. One carried an argument only so far and then stopped. The prevailing sweetness was violated only occasionally, when a temporary faculty person arrived for a year or so. Then Richard Stern or John Hollander would bring to the Aryan, Anglophile English Department a style more suggestive of the Sorbonne or of a really first-rate yeshiva than of a girls' finishing school. Stern endeared himself to me by the way he shouted out his favorite critical remark, "Unreadable!" when confronted with such respectable, canonical works as *Sir Gawain and the Green Knight* or Goldsmith's *The Vicar of Wakefield*. The department had never before been the stage for such forthright, and not always courteous, critique.

To the prevailing puritanism and teetotalism was added a tone of shallow postwar high-mindedness. The light blue flag of the United Nations flew on its own pole next to the U.S. flag, and one week in the school year was designated United Nations Week, when discussions were compulsory on the new world of international cooperation and peace and general niceness. All in aid of "international understanding," which to my satiric mind implied understanding and thus forgiving the German lower-middle-class attitude toward the Jews. I felt that I was being hauled bodily into a world where the idea of evil would be unthinkable, a notion belonging only to the history of dead ideas. In such a world, intercourse with real literature would be impossible, and attempts to teach it frivolous and innocuous. A corollary of United Nations Week was Religious Emphasis Week (was Conn College really a high school?), focusing on the hoped-for elimination of sectarian differences and the new world of religious agreeableness. My attempts in the classroom to locate and emphasize adversarial moments in the literature we read didn't get very far.

Although at the time I thought I was a superb teacher, I was actually a very bad one. I had no talent for leading discussion, only for lecturing, and I aimed to cram into student heads all relevant information about authors and works, as if I were preparing them for a Harvard oral exam, junior grade. Not having served as a teaching assistant in graduate school, the last group I'd addressed — harangued would be a better word — had been my infantry platoon, and it was rather in military style that I laid down the grammatical laws applying to student writing, as well as the permissible approaches to the interpretation of *The Great Gatsby* and *Heart of Darkness*. My severe style of presentation, as well as my rigorous grading, were both consistent with my lifetime practice of exercising the *libido dominandi*.

The English Department taught one novel in common, selected after portentous discussion and voting. During my first two years it was Forster's *A Passage to India*, fashionable those days because it opened up the One World topic and seemed to suggest the sensibleness of the United Nations. Then, we had two years of James's *The Portrait of a Lady*. Although by this time I was able pretty well to bury the war beneath a myriad of newer impressions, now and then it would come back, and in full color. James begins *The Portrait of a Lady* with a discourse upon British teatime, all too typical, haters of James will say. On this occasion tea is being served on "the lawn of an Old English country house," and the bright green of the lawn is complemented by the red brick of the house facade. I could never read that passage without suddenly confronting an ironically similar image, the image of Sergeant Engle's brilliant red blood pouring from his ruined mouth onto the green forest floor. My students must have wondered why, when I read aloud from the early paragraphs of James's novel, I paused for a moment to recover myself, lest my voice break.

Clearly, I couldn't stand the idea of spending the rest of my life correcting the comma faults of these girl-children. The only way out was publication, and I set to work revising my Harvard thesis, producing finally an actual book, *Theory of Prosody in Eighteenth-Century England*, which Connecticut College published in its monograph series. Because this first book was produced by a local job printer, I had to design it myself, and I already knew enough about typography from that junior-high print shop to stand unafraid before the mysteries of ten-point Garamond and to understand the difference between body and display type.

Betty meanwhile was working, first as an editor and writer at the college alumnae office, then as an assistant in the English Department, where, as a Radcliffe M.A., she taught freshmen in a much more likable, and I'm sure more effective, personal style than mine. A typical evening would find us seated side by side at a long table in our apartment, marking piles of themes with red pencils and relieving the tedium by reading out, now and then, student gaffes of an especially comic sort, like "What this college needs is more pubic entertainment." That was certainly true, for the students were in a state of constant deprivation. With me some were pleasantly flirtatious, and I enjoyed their fancying me an occasion of erotic delight. One group devised a song, which they recorded and presented to us:

We want to tussle
With Mr. Fussell
Out on some balcony.
We want to fall
In love with Paul, etc.

What erotic satisfaction the students were permitted came largely from the nearby coast guard cadets, generally scorned as hicks and boobs, or from Yale students, admired for their money, Ivy style, and conventionality. Many marriages took place between the college beauties and the Yalies, and many safe, placid lives resulted.

At one point, oppressed by the weight of theme reading and gentility, Betty and I engineered an escape to Europe for the summer, this time leaving at a date that did not conflict with commencement. We sailed on the *Liberté*, formerly the German *Europa*, awarded the French as postwar reparations. It was an immense eighty-thousand-ton liner of the old-fashioned type, with a tourist-class bar at the stern that almost vibrated itself off the vessel when the screws were turning at top speed. We spent a lot of time there, chinning with friends from Harvard and the like.

The *Liberté*'s first port of call was, for some reason, Plymouth, and we chose to alight there, close as it was to Exeter, the first of the cathedrals we'd been enjoined by colleagues to wonder at. From there, we went by train all over England. After England, hurried tours through France, Austria, Italy, and Greece. Before Italy and Greece, I'd known nothing of antiquity, and what I saw in Rome and Athens charged me up for a lifetime. I would never forget the thrill of seeing, at the Theater of Dionysus, in Athens, the marble seat in the front row reserved for, as the still-legible words proclaimed, the Priest of Dionysus. It was all real, I now understood, not just figments of literary and cultural history. I saw now that as Americans, we would ourselves disappear into remoteness and finally invisibility just like these people, and our god of Sincerity would some day become as distant and finally unknowable as the ancients' god of Irony.

Even on this first crude tour, I learned a vast amount about America. It was clear now that having experienced no antiquity, Middle Ages, or Renaissance, America was missing a lot that was necessary for a civilized culture. The architecture of Rome alone delivered a clear signal about what modern America lost when, pursuing efficiency and utility, it replaced the architectural curve with the architectural straight line, thus forfeiting many things associated with the Baroque — paradox, intellectual sinuousness, double vision, even metaphor and irony. It was dawning on me that there were a lot of other admirable attitudes than forthrightness and that ancient writing and behavior provided a useful gauge for measuring American habits of self-pity and moral canting. Presentimental: that's what antiquity was, and that tone, available in, say, Suetonius's *Lives of the Twelve Caesars,* I found as refreshing as the water from the Castalian Spring, which I drank from my cupped hand as I climbed up to Delphi. I told myself that drinking those waters couldn't help but improve my prose style.

Although I didn't teach well, my first four years in the classroom introduced me to a life only professors know, at least at the outset of their careers before seniority and perquisites have softened their duties somewhat. For one thing, the concept *weekend,* so significant elsewhere, does not suggest a spacious time for play or unwinding. It means two full days of marking themes, followed by a full Sunday evening working up the eight o'clock class for Monday. People who have not taught college English may be surprised to hear that one must reread a work every time one teaches it, at least for the first few years. Until one has taught for some time and amassed folders of old notes, as well as accumulated many texts annotated in their margins with things to say, class preparation is a nightmare of pressure and rushing. It's not generally known that to talk well in a classroom for fifty minutes, you must devote about three hours to preparing.

Again, one learns that for a professor the year begins in September, not January. The resolutions most people make at New Year's the professor makes at the beginning of a new college year, and they may go like this: I will be nicer to the students, trying harder to conceal my boredom as they tell me things I've heard hundreds of times before and affecting belief as they retail their phony excuses for late papers; I will get that article finished and send it out; I will be more careful not to ridicule my colleagues' preposterous theories or raise my eyebrows at their stupid remarks; and I will quit dropping comments suggesting dissatisfaction at working all my life in a female seminary and implying the mediocrity of those satisfied with such a life.

Both Betty and I taught, with delight, Joyce's *Portrait of the Artist*, and Betty combined studying Joyce with attention to Grantly Dick-Read, for she was pregnant and determined to have the child through natural childbirth. When our little girl was born, on March 4, 1955, we betook ourselves to a list of women's names in Shakespeare and settled on Rosalind, from *As You Like It*. This was fine for formal purposes, but for domestic use we turned to Joyce's *Portrait* and came away with one of our favorite locutions, "baby tuckoo," in his first paragraph. Tuckoo soon contracted to Tucky, and Tucky her name has remained.

Betty and I at first lived in New London with no automobile: the cracked-block episode in Cambridge had persuaded me that motoring in the East was so different from motoring in the West that I'd better leave it alone. But when the Volkswagen began to appear in the U.S.A., with its air-cooled, if noisy, engine, I saw that it would come through freezing weather undamaged if I did nothing. I bought a metallic brown one with bright red fake leather upholstery. A friend declared that the interior smelled "like a doll's purse," and she was right. During the 1952 presidential campaign, I registered my hatred of militarism and everything connected with it by opposing Eisenhower and driving around New London in this ugly midget vehicle with a large STEVENSON sticker plastered on the front of the roof. I didn't despise Eisenhower, for he'd been the only general my troops and I respected — for his kindness, his understanding of the soldiers' needs and fears, his distance from the vainglory and love of violence manifested by General Patton. My feelings about Ike the General coincided with Lincoln Kirstein's. He names Ike at the head of his heroes in his poem "Hymn," a contemporary demotic song of praise:

First: our Supreme Commander, Ike Eisenhower,
Painter of sorts in pleasant times, our
Daddy-O in the unpleasing times,
Whose decent manner, common sense, justice, stump weak
  rhymes;
Who endured stupendous waiting,
Winning worst wars with least hating.

No, I didn't despise him, I just thought a longtime civilian would be a relief, and I recalled that General Grant hadn't brought a lot of glory to the Republic. Best of all would be a witty civilian like Adlai, after the years of cant and solemnity.

In 1955 *Theory of Prosody in Eighteenth-Century England* paid off. That is, someone noticed it and regarded its young author as a minor authority on its subject. I had a letter from Rutgers University in New Brunswick, New Jersey, asking if I'd like to be considered for a place teaching the literature of the eighteenth century, and not just to undergraduates but to graduate students as well. I'd have preferred a nibble from a better place, but Rutgers, with its graduate programs and professional schools and proximity to New York, was sufficiently attractive. I accepted the offer when it finally came — it involved a nice salary increase — and left Conn College with no regrets. I was moving from a small all-female institution to a large all-male one, although I expected some tough work dragging engineers, aggies, and champion lacrosse players into the world of the heroic couplet and *The Beggar's Opera*. But in July, crammed into the VW with baby and cat, we set off happily for New Jersey.

When I arrived at Rutgers in the summer of 1955 I felt little but delight. I was not at a girls' school anymore but a real university of over forty thousand students, whose catalog with scarlet covers and map of the extensive campus seemed suggestive even of Harvard's usages. Teaching young men would be a welcome novelty: no longer, I felt, would I have to pussyfoot around certain subjects or watch my army-coarsened diction carefully.

On several summer afternoons I strolled around the deserted campus, scarcely able to control my excitement as one "university" feature after another disclosed itself. Even the football stadium, which professionally I of course deplored, assured me that I was now in a mainline institution, even if, unlike Harvard and Princeton, it had fraternity houses.

Even as over the years my first raptures wore out, I never entirely got over the feeling that I was connected to a well-known institution founded in the eighteenth century after the model of the University of Utrecht. It was not, of course, Princeton, seventeen miles away. Princeton was a national and international institution, Rutgers merely a New Jersey one. Occasionally a student would be admitted from a neighboring state, but not often. The result was that over 90 percent of the students came from the public high schools of such places as Collingswood, Asbury Park, Toms River, Browntown, Union City, and Murray Hill, no very trustworthy guarantees of sophistication or extraordinary secondary-school preparation.

But happy as I was at the outset, my feeling that this was where I belonged was dealt some cruel blows during the first weeks of classes. A student interviewed recently for a guide to colleges found the Rutgers student body ranging from "positively moronic to absolutely brilliant." Teaching the required introductory courses, I seemed to encounter only the first group. All entering students had to take the infamous Davis Test, a test of grammar and middle-class usage devised by a colleague, Rexford Guy Davis. Its function was to divide the freshmen into two groups, the hopeless and the possible. The younger English faculty was assigned the task of taking the hopeless, sports-obsessed, often unshaven young men in their McGregor jackets through such courses — one bright colleague designated them "punitive" — as "Remedial Grammar" and "Remedial Spelling," where the word *millinery* was used to trap the unwary into errors. A student's triumphal entry into a regular composition section depended on his passing the Davis Test and mastering the use of the objective case, allowing him to abjure such socially disastrous locutions as "He gave it to she and I." Some never passed the test and after the first year returned, shaken, to Mantoloking. Sometimes we younger faculty, just out of Harvard and Yale, felt that everyone in New Jersey needed to pass the Davis Test, especially when we heard the prim university telephone operator ask, "Whom shall I say is calling?" Engaged in supervising operations like coaching for the Davis Test, I sometimes could hardly believe I was a professor and not a junior officer again, urging the backward on and encouraging the unready with, always, the handy threat of punishment.

In addition to having to deal with such stultifying material, we young English teachers carried a 25 percent heavier teaching load than was customary at Connecticut College. Now and then, one was allowed the relief of replacing a section of "Remedial Something" with a section of "Technical Writing," required of students in engineering and agriculture. This was tedious work for the unlucky teacher and riotous fun for the students, who were fond of cynically submitting annually a hoary term paper titled "The Agriculture of the Delmarva Peninsula," a classic from the fraternity files.

The English faculty, with a couple of exceptions, seemed as little energetic as the students. Once one attained tenure — easy to do if you published your revised Ph.D. thesis, wrote a half-dozen articles, taught not too irresponsibly, and served without complaint on a few college committees — one virtually gave up what resembled an intellectual life and settled down to await retirement, teaching the same stuff every year (simply changing the dates on the syllabus) and in the summer driving to the national parks.

Two young instructors joined the department when I did. One

was a flaming Stalinist who later spent his career at Humboldt University in East Germany, teaching the youngsters there to scorn the artistic elements in literature in favor of its social-reform potential. Once I put on a final examination for all freshmen Robert Frost's sonnet "Meeting and Passing," a poem quite devoid of any social or political implications. "That poem," he declared loudly, heard by several hundred students, "is shit, pure shit!" The other newcomer to the department disappeared after a couple of weeks and was finally located by the chairman in a low Manhattan hotel surrounded by empty bottles.

The senior members of the department were more orthodox, but few had minds interesting in any way. Some openly suspected T. S. Eliot of fraud because his poems seemed more obscure than Carl Sandburg's. One professor was so enamored of James Branch Cabell's mildly naughty romance *Jurgen* that he pressed for its inclusion in the required readings for the Ph.D. oral exam. Another thought James Gould Cozzens's heavy middlebrow novel *By Love Possessed* a masterpiece and urged us to make it part of the freshman course. Another, a hobbyist of William Dean Howells, succeeded — because he was director of graduate studies — in establishing his own permanent course in Howells for graduate students. Yet another, a rabid, socially insecure Catholic, could never understand the wickedness of his colleagues in pursuing their cheerful atheism. When I arrived, the English Department was totally *Judenfrei,* as if we were teaching in Germany about 1937. When the department hired its first Jew ever, in 1959, the Howells man courteously invited him to join the local Episcopal church. A shining exception to such dolts was John Ciardi, recently of Harvard, whose coarse, satiric presence was what the department desperately needed, but he was around only a few days a week and resigned finally to deal in real estate. Except for the Byron scholar Leslie Marchand, mediocrity reigned, registering itself in vigorous expressions of contempt for the Department of Comparative Literature, which attracted away our brightest students.

In some ways Rutgers was like the army. A vast gulf of privilege separated the faculty from the scorned enlisted men, and student morale was always a problem. Demoralized by the conviction that they were quite a different species from the students at Princeton, our tough young clients had to be reassured of their value by certain innovations brought about by President Louis Webster Jones, who'd arrived from Bennington. It was he who commanded that a new logo be devised, one with "royal," classy overtones. The result was a Caslon capital Q with, on one side, 17, and on the other, 66. (When the college was founded in 1766, it was called Queen's College.) Above the Q, a crown, like the one on Columbia's logo. To match, Caslon italics, traditionally a "colonial" typeface, were now used on all the campus signs. Two of those signs, reading DEPARTMENT OF ENGLISH, hung from the front of two adjacent wood-frame family houses on College Avenue. The houses had been reconstructed inside into class and seminar rooms, with "offices" upstairs. But the transformation seemed not yet really definitive, what with the tatty, dirty shower curtain still hanging disconsolately in one of the bathrooms.

As I suspect is true of all state universities but the very best, the top administration was generally admirable while the echelons below ranged from the adequate to the execrable. Doubtless some civil-service convention, de jure or de facto, is responsible. Whatever, at Rutgers it seemed that an incompetent department secretary couldn't be fired. She or he could only be moved elsewhere to damage another department. The students were the frequent victims of lower-administration bumbling, and they devised the term "the Rutgers screw" in reaction to the numerous fuckups, in registration, record keeping, and programming, they had to endure. The finer sensibilities among the faculty had occasion often to wince at some new vulgarism or gaucherie, like renaming the Department of Physical Education the Department of Human Kinetics. There was everywhere a marked drift toward simpleminded literalism, which prompted the university to jettison its century-old term for its athletic teams, the Scarlet — cf. Harvard's the Crimson — and flesh it out in an adolescent direction as the Scarlet Knights, with its childish Prince Valiant overtones. The Rutgers style of mistakes and getting it slightly wrong seemed to pervade everything. At the only commencement I attended, inattention to the appropriate symbolism of hierarchy and respect for learning resulted in the faculty's tediously standing while the students entered. The reverse practice is, of course, customary in sophisticated institutions, and even in courtrooms. The state of the university library was disgraceful, largely because its management had been entrusted to an amiable but lazy and uneducated old professor of English. The result was that damaged books were seldom repaired, and that books often overflowed the shelves and piled up on the floor. Attempts to install a checker at the entrance to stem the epidemic of stolen books were rebuffed as an insult to the students. When I left in 1983, closing out twenty-eight years at Rutgers, I no longer expected anything to be done right. I was thus not surprised to be presented with a would-be elegant certificate ("suitable for framing," I'm sure someone said) conveying the right sentiments but with my name meticulously misspelled. More anger. And the Rutgers sloppiness could be moral and intellectual as well as administrative. I was once approached by the chairman of the

English Department and asked to sign a palpably false certificate attesting to graduate students' teaching hours so that the federal government could be cheated. My refusal to play the game occasioned profound surprise.

While I was toiling away six days a week at Rutgers, Betty was taking care of Tucky. Since I was using our only car, she was developing cabin fever, confined in our house in Middlebush. At Pomona she had done quite a bit of acting, and she now discovered that in Princeton there was an intelligent theatrical group performing such classics, still known in the 1950s, as Shaw, Ibsen, and Chekhov. In the evenings when I brought the VW back home, she drove to Princeton to work with this group as director and actress while I agonized with boredom over student themes. We were delighted to find her pregnant again, and in the spring of 1957 I sped her down to the Princeton Hospital for the birth. Joy lasted only until the doctor came with sad face out of the delivery room.

"Well, we were able to save Betty, but we couldn't save the baby. It was born dead, and we could never get it to breathe." It was a little girl, and since she had never lived, we never even named her. The whole experience dramatized the abridgment of hope and the delusions of optimism that were to become my most familiar intellectual and emotional themes, and the death of this little girl, when life and delight were expected, pushed me further toward my identity as an ironist. Betty, made of firmer fiber than I and more sanguine by nature, recovered from the disappointment sooner. For weeks I had to endure the well-meant questions of kind colleagues, "Baby here yet?" and answer, "Yes, it was born dead." This stillbirth reinforced our feeling that a bit of relief from our accustomed setting and duties might do us some good. Besides, I was beginning to despise the

United States with a cold passion and felt an irresistible impulse to distance myself from it. A culture that in 1954 had felt it appropriate to add the canting words "under God" to the infantine Pledge of Allegiance to the flag was, I felt more and more strongly, not for me.

Indeed, in 1957 the United States, trapped in ideological rigidity by the Cold War, was the sort of place any decent person would want to leave. There was the civil defense foolishness, the assumption that a nuclear war could be survived quite handily, with attendant follies of home air-raid bunkers and home defense exercises. There was the constant public avoidance of any idea that might seem remotely socialistic, or even contemporary. The South was resisting integration with the same sort of insane vigor with which the cigarette companies were denying that tobacco had any connection with lung cancer. The new toy, television, was rapidly revealing that it would constitute a national disaster, creating a new race of zombies to be sold worthless things by conscienceless advertisers. The swinish, mendacious Richard Nixon had been chosen by the people to be their vice president. A further assault on decency was a new strain of compulsory religiosity. Congress managed to suggest that agnosticism was little short of treason. A year after the "under God" business it determined that IN GOD WE TRUST, a lie that before had defaced only the coinage, must now adorn the paper currency as well. In addition, the cancellation stamp PRAY FOR PEACE began appearing on our letters. (A witty friend had an adversarial rubber stamp made reading, "Pray for Separation of Church and State," which she applied to her letters.) American culture seemed more than ever bellicose, ignorant, selfish, and greedy, shot through with quasi-religious fraud and hypocrisy. It was time to seek relief, or at least variety, elsewhere.

In the evenings, exhausted from explaining Comma Fault and Grammatical Agreement to bored classrooms, I pored over lists of teaching posts and research fellowships abroad. The Fulbright Lectureships, paid for with American funds left in Europe after the war, looked especially attractive. Professors selected for this duty were supposed to be fluent in the language of the country they applied for, but their lectures could be in English. They were to teach American materials, which for me would mean American literature, about which I didn't know a whole lot, having focused on and taught British. There were many university positions in West Germany, and assuming that I could work up to standard my conversational German, I applied for the University of Munich, with a safety application to Heidelberg. It turned out that R. W. B. Lewis, better qualified than I, won the Munich job, but I got Heidelberg, and suddenly we were sprung, at least for a year. June found us aboard the *Mauretania* — the last time we ever took a British ship, what with the bloody white gloves of the artless roast carver and the needlessly snobbish distinctions between the classes. Tucky was outfitted winningly in her red riding hood, a tiny bright red hooded sweatshirt with RUTGERS on the front. In this she scampered about the decks, barely staying aboard the vessel and occasioning loving anxiety in all she ran past.

A new Volkswagen was waiting for us on the Southampton docks, and we drove to London, where we spent the summer, Betty and Tucky enjoying Kensington Gardens and I enjoying the reading room of the British Museum, preparing to avoid disgrace when I taught American literature. I read Emerson, Thoreau, and Whitman, Frost, Pound, and Stevens, and the novelists (most of them satirists of the American condition) I proposed to teach in a course in the modern American novel, which I assumed would be popular among the German young. Finally, in September we crammed everything — Tucky, linens, kitchenware, clothes, books, toys — into the car and set off for Heidelberg.

I should have known that it was the headquarters of the American army in West Germany. It simply teemed with uniformed Yanks and their wives and children. It contained more Americans than New Brunswick, but they at least had places to live. We had none, and houses and flats to rent seemed entirely nonexistent. But after a few days of growing despair and aided by the *Auslandsamt* of the university, we found something. It was awful, but at least it was a place, three rooms on the top floor of a three-story house where a U.S. sergeant and his family also had rooms. One of our rooms was devoted to all functions requiring water — the toilet, the bathtub, and the kitchen sink, all together. Another room, some distance away, was our bedroom. Still another, also separated, was a living room, dining room, and "study." Escaping the United States was clearly going to involve sacrifices, but at least we were abroad, and we had a car, and we were young and springy.

I found teaching at Heidelberg wonderful, because the classes involved no discussion, only lecturing in the archaic style. I would enter the lecture hall to the knuckle-rapped greeting of a hundred enthusiastic students and would harangue them for an hour about Hemingway, Sinclair Lewis, or Dos Passos, and would then leave. It was not required that I keep office hours or set the students papers to write or exams to take. For them, as for me, the class was sheer entertainment — the comprehensive state examinations they were preparing for didn't even deal with modern American literature but with such philological arcana as the behavior of vowels in Old Norse. In addition, I gave a seminar on Whitman and Frost, where I did try to get discussion going, but the students, not being acquainted with the tradition, declined to play, and I ended up doing all the talking myself. Although silent in class, the students I did talk to, in the halls or on the sidewalk, delighted me with their intelligence, seriousness, and humanity — not a few hated their fathers for what they knew they'd done in the war.

Despite its war guilt, in many ways postwar Germany exhibited welcome signs of an ideal new republic. The old nation had been obliterated, and the American occupiers, many of liberal mind, had made a new one, which showed what America might be if it could start over, with European assumptions. German cities now displayed a rare community consciousness, manifesting itself in new municipal theaters and opera houses and public swimming pools and sports grounds. The highways were unmarred by billboards, and advertising on the radio was rare. We hoped to enjoy the theater but found that our German wasn't good enough. We went to the opera instead, driving a few miles to Mannheim, where excellent state companies performed. There, women wore long dresses, men dark suits with white shirts and white-on-white ties. I wore that outfit too.

Even if we could have understood more, theater would have proved less satisfying, for producers sought banal and trivial plays that avoided insights into contemporary actuality, so much of which was suggestive of shame. The German search for the theatrically harmless and optimistic led automatically to the plays of Thornton Wilder, especially *Our Town,* presented everywhere in West Germany. While the less cheerful works of Arthur Miller and Tennessee Williams were unknown, Wilder was performed somewhere every night and celebrated in the press as a distinguished American man of letters, author of important novels as well as plays. I found myself deeply angered by this cunning whitewashing of the human capacity for evil. It had the implicit effect of persuading German theatergoers and readers that their country and they couldn't have done anything wrong in the war, all people by nature being as innocent and sweet as Wilder depicted them. If you are an ordinary person, and if Thornton Wilder has shown you that ordinary people are moved by only the most virtuous impulses, then all that recent rumored misbehavior by ordinary people in the *Einsatzgrüppen* and extermination camps can't have taken place, *nicht wahr?* All that stuff must be only rumors started by — shhhh! — the Jews. These views I registered as satirically as possible in an article I published in the *Nation,* "Thornton Wilder and the German Psyche," and it was similar impatience, annoyance, or outright anger that propelled most of my writing and book-making over the next thirty-five years, beginning with a new anthology of eighteenth-century British writing I edited with two colleagues. It was designed to drive into oblivion the standard textbook, which riled me every time I taught from it. That book presented a largely sentimental view of the material, printing long, harmless bucolic poems and giving ample space to the effusions of the un-bright and the unsharp. I wanted quite a different selection, emphasizing acerbic writings, with plenty of satire, that might suggest an appropriately ironic response to actuality, especially to the international horrors we had just concluded. I wanted that dark, ironic vision to form a part of anyone's experience of the future. In a sense, this college textbook constituted a weapon in my war against euphemism and baseless optimism. Making this subversive anthology, *Eighteenth-Century English Literature,* took longer than I expected. At first I'd thought I could finish my share of the editing in two or three years. It took twelve.

At Heidelberg, even when I was totally taken up by my teaching, I could never entirely shake off a wartime feeling of oddity, of being "behind the Kraut lines." My imagination furnished the streets with all the sinister bustle of their wartime years, with German soldiers, Red Cross workers, party members, and air-raid wardens busy at their ill-begotten and increasingly depressing work. The war was constantly in the background, and one still came across newspaper classified ads reading, "Who knows what happened to Obergefreiter Hans Liebe, last heard from on the Eastern Front in December, 1944?" But the war was not mentioned in Heidelberg, except by a few young people, and its invisibility and virtual nonexistence (Heidelberg had not been bombed) stiffened all my social encounters with Germans my age or older. Never did I ask a middle-aged person, "What did you do in the war?"

This year in Germany, with travel during the long vacations to Sicily and Spain, inaugurated for me a serious European period, which has never come to a close. I can trace back to 1957 my lifetime fondness for European reality, involving careful attention to wine and food, productive cynicism, sexual freedom, sun and water, the fun of languages, and enthusiasm for beneficent socialism, as in bike paths, the absence of private universities tied to the views of private money, and enthusiastic state support of theater and music. My half-European orientation is hard to slough off. Finishing a crossword the other day, I was confronted with the clue *Georgian Capital,* in seven letters. Of course I wrote TBILISI, but soon saw that it didn't fit and that the right answer was merely ATLANTA.

Experience at Heidelberg with a very un-American understanding of what a university is also produced a profound impression. As the year went on, I became increasingly disenchanted with the

American university, with its nervous concern about student well-being (in every aspect except the intellectual) and its hypertrophied and needless administration, constructed, presumably, on "business" lines. I began to see American colleges as little more than overgrown and pretentious high schools, where genuine education seemed increasingly unlikely. It was hard to forget Mencken's satire of the American "proliferation of colleges." "They are even spattered," he notes, "over such barbaric States as Mississippi and North Dakota, where it would be dangerous to be educated in any real sense."

The University of Heidelberg allowed the students to live where they pleased in town. There were no "dormitories." Their social and sexual lives were regarded as their own business, the university having no deans, counselors, or "relationship advisers." The university assumed that students, being adults, could have their misbehavior, if any, attended to by the police, not the university, which had a quite different mission, the development of intellect, a mission performed by no other social institution. At Heidelberg there were only three "administrative officers." There was a president, elected from the faculty each year. He (never she — this was the 1950s) occupied the presidial office for a year and, while continuing his scholarship, performed the few ceremonial duties attaching to the office. There was a bursar, who took in the students' and the state's money and made it over, in appropriate shares, to the faculty. And there was a housing officer, who helped the students find lodgings with the town's many landladies and adjudicated the inevitable disputes with them. There was no provost, no alumni officer, no vice president in charge of development, no head of the division of athletics, no coaches, no head of academic advising (the students were assumed to be bright enough to find in the catalog what they were interested in), no Office of Alcohol and Drug Education, no Budget Office, no Career Planning and Placement Office, no university chaplain, and no "bookstore" selling more T-shirts and condoms than books. The students attended the lectures and seminars they considered useful adjuncts to their continuous reading. The point was to pass the examinations at the end of their university years, and any way they prepared themselves was fine.

But finally our Fulbright year was over. The Heidelberg students gave us a farewell party, featuring much beer and wine and a hilarious mimic of my self-satisfied teaching style. Soon we were westbound on the *Flandre,* a small new French Line vessel. The monumental Atlantic storm it endured on this voyage caused much damage and fractured many limbs, and the management decided to employ it in the future in Mediterranean service only. Resuming stateside usages proved to be not entirely gratifying. It will be easy to imagine my seldom-concealed new disgust with the American university, its central and simple mission clouded by the hordes of administrative parasites clinging to its body. I returned also with an augmented sense of the dignity of the professor. This I manifested immediately by having a graduate assistant perform the humble task of taking attendance in my lecture classes and consulting with students about all nonintellectual matters — overdue papers and the like. I returned also with a new understanding of how tiny and parochial a part of literature the American portion was. When before I would have taught freshmen *The Great Gatsby,* now I taught them *Crime and Punishment.*

To our delight, Betty was pregnant again, and this time the hurried nighttime drive to the Princeton Hospital ended happily, in the birth of a son. We named him Martin, after Luther. Before Martin's birth I had joked that this time if the baby was a boy we were going to name him Samuel Johnson Fussell after my most intense — next to Mencken — literary enthusiasm. We didn't, but we called Martin "Sam" so long in boyhood that when adolescent he went down to the courthouse in Trenton and had his name legally changed to Samuel. He had always hated Martin, he explained, and was delighted to have his long-standing nickname become his real one.

Now an associate professor on tenure, I felt secure enough to go my own way without much regard to any social envies and anxieties from my Rutgers colleagues. I was using the university library in Princeton so much that it seemed logical to live there and commute to New Brunswick. This I did for the next twenty-three years. On the drive back to Princeton, there was a long stretch of absolutely straight two-lane road, with, at the end before it turned, a small hill covered with shrubbery. I never saw it without thinking it a perfect position for an antitank gun, should Princeton ever be attacked by an envious New Brunswick, which sometimes seemed a not unlikely possibility. As the years passed, almost all our social and cultural life was in Princeton, doubtless to the annoyance of people at Rutgers, even though almost no one lived near the university. Our social crime was not living at a distance but living in Princeton, suggesting snobbish dissatisfaction with the state university's social and intellectual ambience.

Late one Friday afternoon I was working on the third floor of the English Department building. I was tired and looking forward to returning home. Suddenly, rapid steps on the stairway. A colleague, just arrived, had been listening to his car radio. It had brought him the news that the president had been shot, and badly, perhaps mortally. The first thing I thought of was a right-wing coup, organized by the American military bothered by Kennedy's apparent willingness to have the Bay of Pigs invasion of Cuba fail, his lack of evident enthusiasm for the whole reactionary, truculent business. Driving home, I half expected tanks and troops at every crossroads.

In Princeton Betty and I quickly collected the children from school, locked doors and windows, and settled down, TV and radio on, to try to understand what was happening. In this we were joined by Maggie Roth, the separated wife of Philip. She normally devoted herself to vague quasi-literary operations and to phoning abuse at Philip, in which the words "my attorneys" figured prominently. We spent the night watching TV and drinking cognac and crying, wondering what all this meant for the United States. For me, the assassination augmented my sense that there was something radically wrong with the country, its emphasis on mere freedom gone wildly awry to embrace owning lots of guns and discharging them at will when angry. W. C. Williams once noted in "To Elsie" that "the pure products of America go crazy." It was not just Lee Harvey Oswald, with his paranoia and self-righteousness and monomania, who seemed so pure a product of America. It was his pathetic mother as well, convinced that by his murderous action Lee had achieved what every good American lusts for, celebrity, and had become, thus, "a world historical figure." And one should add the bizarre Jack Ruby, anxious to become a heroic object of national admiration for killing the killer. It was beginning to look as if the practice of insensate violence was becoming a firm element of American national uniqueness. It was beginning to look as if a pronounced leaning toward the psychopathic would have to be included in any future list of national characteristics.

There was still a lingering bit of my innocence to be destroyed, namely, the belief that widespread experience of literature and the ideas enacted by it would serve as an antidote to the fatuous and menacing collection of American folk attitudes and behaviors perhaps appropriate once to the frontier but well out of date now. If the John F. Kennedy murder did not wholly destroy that optimistic belief, it suffered all-but-terminal damage five years later, when first Martin Luther King was killed, and then, two months later, Robert Kennedy. What were we witnessing? Was it true that now the bottom dogs were wreaking their revenge against distinction, whether black or white, and that therefore a similarity could be discerned between these assaults on exceptional people and such apparently remote phenomena as the Cultural Revolution in China, the actions of the Khmer Rouge in Cambodia, and — to stretch the point just a bit — the annoyance of American students at being confronted with ideas, and even literary and cultural forms, identifiable with "elitism" or marked by a notable elevation above the styles and capacities of the folk? Distinction itself was becoming a stigma. The boy who had been instructed by James Truslow Adams's "The Mucker Pose" and had been impressed by Mencken's awareness of the dangers of the American lust for intellectual equality could be expected, now, to become a man who sensed threats to excellence lurking everywhere.

Although Lyndon Johnson soothed us by promising no change in the social direction of the Kennedy administration ("Let us continya"), no one knew what was going to happen now. R. W. B. Lewis reported Ralph Ellison as saying, "As a Negro, as a Liberal, and as a writer, I say — let's wait and see." For all of us whose lives were invested in universities, resuming the placid regularities of the schedule and performing the well-known exercises provided a comforting sense that nothing basic had been destroyed. But some distance below consciousness we seemed to know differently. Without specific insight, we now felt that anything could happen. And indeed, the Vietnam fiasco was waiting in the wings.

My pedagogic reaction to the assassinations was to increase the emphasis in my classes on Americans criticizing America. I think I was trying to suggest to students the responsibility of the educated, and even those aspiring to be educated, for actively seeking out America's most loathsome faults and then — an imperative obligation — correcting them. Later, in 1979, I was impressed by this message to youth in *The Official Boy Scout Handbook*: "Take a two-hour walk where you live. Make a list of things that please you, another of things that should be improved." Then the crucial injunction: "Set out to improve them." Thus, I rummaged my library for useful naysayers and exposers of the rottenness of America. In Whitman's *Democratic Vistas* (1871) I found his usefully unoptimistic critique of These States, especially telling because so much at odds with his usual, better-known uncritical celebrations:

> *Society, in these States, is cankered, crude, superstitious, and rotten. . . . The element of moral conscience . . . seems to me either entirely lacking or seriously enfeebled or ungrown.*
>
> *I say we had best look our time and lands searchingly in the face, like a physician diagnosing some deep disease. Never was there, perhaps, more hollowness at heart than at present. . . . The spectacle is appalling. . . . A lot of churches, sects, etc., the most dismal phantasms I know, usurp the name of religion. Conversation is a mass of badinage. . . . The depravity of the business classes of our country is not less than has been supposed, but infinitely greater. The official services of America . . . are*

saturated in corruption, bribery, falsehood, maladministration.
. . . The great cities reek with respectable as much as non-
respectable robbery and scoundrelism. In fashionable life,
flippancy, tepid amours, weak infidelism, small aims, or no aims
at all, only to kill time. . . . The best class we show is but a mob
of fashionably dressed speculators and vulgarians. . . . I say that
our New World democracy, however great a success . . . in a cer-
tain highly deceptive superficial popular intellectuality, is, so far,
an almost complete failure in its social aspects, and in really grand
religious, moral, literary, and aesthetic results.

Looking about him, especially in Manhattan, what Whitman sees
is a world of "petty grotesques, malformations, phantoms, playing
meaningless antics." Everywhere, "low cunning," "an abnormal li-
bidinousness, . . . with a range of manners, or rather lack of manners . . . , probably the meanest to be seen in the world." (And all
this well before the age of television, porno VCRs, blockbusting
adolescent films, and the capture of a passive upper middle class by
the cynicisms of the rag trade. "Are you still using last year's work-
out wear?")

The solution Whitman proposes is one bound to recommend itself to every university teacher of literature. What is desperately
needed, Whitman insists, is a new rich, subtle, difficulty poetry, which
"seldomer tells a thing than suggests or necessitates it. In fact," he
says, as he warms to his work, "a new theory of literary composition
. . . is the sole course open to these States":

Books are to be called for, and supplied, on the assumption that
the process of reading is not a half-sleep, but, in highest sense, an

exercise, a gymnast's struggle; that the reader is to do something for himself, must be on the alert, must himself or herself construct indeed the poem, argument, history, metaphysical essay — the text furnishing the hints, the clue, the start or framework.

And then the climax. Such a new understanding of books and reading would help supply what Americans need most, self-respect earned by individual effort:

That were to make a nation of supple and athletic minds, well-trained, intuitive, used to depend on themselves and not on a few coteries of writers.

That is, literature can save the world, just as we veterans of mass murder and stupidity, who went into serious careers of teaching it, always assumed.

If Whitman in *Democratic Vistas* was a critic of America providing useful stiffening to the otherwise flaccid mind of the ordinary college student, I found Ezra Pound to be another. Excited by critic Hugh Kenner's vigorous interpretative books *The Poetry of Ezra Pound* and *The Pound Era,* I discovered that Kenner's Pound could serve as handy personal ammunition against the genteel and the received, an illustration of criticism functioning as useful adversary proceedings. What young professor of English in the Eisenhower era could resist calling students' attention to "The Rest":

O helpless few in my country,
O remnant enslaved!

Artists broken against her,
A-stray, lost in the villages,
Mistrusted, spoken against.

Lovers of beauty, starved,
Thwarted with systems,
Helpless against the control,

and so on? What impatient young despiser of middlebrow American culture and the insensitivity of his thick senior colleagues could fail to find his views registered in part 3 of "Salvationists":

Come, my songs,
Let us take arms against this sea of stupidities —
Beginning with Mumpodorus;
And against this sea of vulgarities —
Beginning with Nimmim;
And against this sea of imbeciles —
All the Bulmenian literati?

And what young devotee of *Democratic Vistas* could fail to feel his understanding of the American problem enriched by a stanza like this, from Pound's *Hugh Selwyn Mauberley?*

Faun's flesh is not to us,
Nor the saint's vision.
We have the press for wafer;
Franchise for circumcision.

(The "rest" and syncopation at the beginning of the second line also recommended this stanza to the young prosodic theorist.)

If I'd honed my instinct for irony in the army, I joined with it my pleasure in the mystery of coherence, developed by repeated consideration of Aristotle, as extended and deepened by Coleridge, with flashes of insight contributed by Walter Jackson Bate. One kind of poem I grew fond of seemed to appeal to me by exhibiting both the straight-faced irony I valued, and the understated absolute unity that delighted me. Examples? Poems whose motivation is not clear until the end, when the speaker's initial urge to utter becomes apparent. Thus "Zonas," in this little effort from the *Greek Anthology:*

> *Pass me the sweet earthenware jug,*
> *Made of the earth that bore me,*
> *The earth that someday I shall bear.*

Similarly, William Drummond's "Madrigal," where the reader wonders about the cause of the speaker's misery until the end of the poem reveals the secret:

> *My thoughts hold mortal strife,*
> *I do detest my life,*
> *And with lamenting cries,*
> *Peace to my soul to bring,*
> *Oft call that Prince which here doth monarchize;*
> *But he, grim-grinning King,*
> *Who caitiffs scorns and doth the blest surprise,*
> *Late having decked with beauty's rose his tomb,*
> *Disdains to crop a weed, and will not come.*

Irony is not necessarily critical or moralistic: Robert Herrick is a master of this kind of irony, sprung only at the end of the poem, as in "Upon a Child":

> *Here a pretty baby lies*
> *Sung asleep with lullabies:*
> *Pray be silent, and not stir*
> *The easy earth that covers her.*

Irony and elegy: the two coincide effectively there, and as I grew older irony and elegy attracted me increasingly until they seemed to merge into a single intense feeling. That feeling I sought to evoke in my essays and books, especially, finally, *The Great War and Modern Memory* and *Wartime.*

⇌ VIII ⇌

$\mathcal{T}$HE ARCHAIC TERM *Haight-Ashbury* alone is enough to suggest the atmosphere of the sixties, the rebellion against restraints, the anti-rationalism, the lust to evade reality through pot and LSD — one student of mine ended up in a state mental institution after blowing his mind in quest of the "psychedelic." It was the Age of not just Aquarius, but of Esalin, mysticism, "meditation," encounter therapy, self-actualizing and self-transcendence, any sort of ego-stroking exercise charlatans could dream up to exploit the credulous and the infantile. To the young and untutored, the loose and formless acquired value, while the structured, completed, organized, suggested oppression at best, "Fascism" at worst. Thus the widespread sixties assumption that poetry is a therapeutic outflow of individualism best unrestrained by publicly known forms. In poems as in personal behavior, letting it all hang out was obligatory. I thought this preposterous, for it relegated most of the poems of the past to the garbage can — probably the wildly egalitarian point of the naive young, most of whom had never encountered an actual "poem." Real poetry posed a threat to the popular, sentimental, antihierarchical impulses of late-twentieth-century America. Hence the effort to replace it with something named the same but posing no danger. Poems not recitable to guitar accompaniment in bars and coffeehouses didn't seem, now, to be poems at all — too hard, requiring an antisocial, silent, individual effort to experience them.

Naturally appalled by these notions, I devised a graduate course titled "Technique in English Poetry," dealing with poetic meters and stanza forms as adjuncts to meaning, and emphasizing the indispensable elements of convention and control in all the arts. The definition of a "poem" I pounded into students was "a delightfully coherent verbal construct occurring against a significant grid." The *coherent* was a tribute to Aristotle, the *grid* (an obvious steal from technology), a suggestion that without a metrical scheme to vary from, variation, and hence rhythmic meaning, was not likely. I also invoked the idea of syncopation, by which I hoped to make sense to those fond of jazz. Pound supplied the essential theme: "Rhythm must have meaning. It can't be merely a careless dash-off with no grip and no real hold to the words and sense." Asking why the opposition between flux and form, time and the timeless, was so overwhelmingly the subject of short poems, I concluded that the very act of writing in a relatively fixed stanzaic form focused the mind on stability and fixity, as opposed to accident or the ordinary unshaped flow of thought and language. I was still obsessed with that topic many years later in a lecture at the University of London, "Poetic Forms and the Lyric Subject," where *the lyric subject* meant mutability and the pathos of the transient, as in Herrick's

> *Fair daffodils, we weep to see*
> *You haste away so soon.*

You have to read a lot of English lyric poetry to observe that the poems, thousands of them, are all really about the same thing. And I did read thousands of them, searching constantly for poems sharp and brief enough to serve as teaching examples.

As I found it easy to do with courses I was deeply involved in, I decided to turn the course into a book. At the time, I had unwisely agreed to be the editor of a series of literary studies issued by Random House, and I offered to write one of them. It was the summer of 1963. Betty and Tucky and Sam took off for Cape Cod, where I joined them each weekend, flying from Newark to Hyannis. Alone in a quiet house in Princeton and with nothing else to attract me, I found writing easy, and by September I'd produced, after one writing and one rewriting, the two hundred pages of *Poetic Meter and Poetic Form.* My relations with Random House became strained when I discovered that as editor of the series, I was not just supposed to find authors for the books and persuade them to write them, but to copyedit the manuscripts as well and prepare them in every respect for the press. I quit, and my annoyance then was similar to my annoyance much later at my own innocence when I discovered that I had carelessly signed a revision clause in the contract. This obliged me to produce a revised version of my book upon commercial command, regardless of the lack of significant changes in the subject. The revised version, which appeared in 1979, made a considerable concession to the contemporary by adding a chapter on free verse, but as I explained in the foreword, "I have not altered the generally traditional point of view, believing that the great classic majority of English and American poems deserve a fair shake on their own terms." The book is still being used by elderly English teachers in remote parts of the country, although its implicit antirevolutionary tendency has not recommended it to the young. (Once during a break in one of my graduate seminars, when the students had all briefly left the room, I strolled idly about the table, glancing at their open notebooks, curious to see what they were regarding as important in our proceedings. In one boy's, there was a comment reacting to the attitude I was gradually developing toward the fashionable political and "social-justice" movement in literary interpretation. The student had written, "Has Fussell ever *heard* of Marx?")

Another graduate course I liked to give during the ethically radical sixties was "The Eighteenth-Century Humanists." People who'd read literature at Harvard in the forties developed a special acquaintance with the words *humanism* and *humanists,* for Douglas Bush in particular talked endlessly about the tradition of Greek and Latin learning, including its strain of secular skepticism, practiced during the Renaissance by those called humanists. When such scholars and artists sought to harmonize Christian belief with their worldly, fleshly humanism, you got Christian Humanism, the mainstay of Harvard's understanding of Renaissance writing and art. Harvard's enthusiasm for Christian Humanism seemed to betray its persisting proximity to nineteenth-century Boston, where Christian high-mindedness managed to accommodate the most blatant pursuit of worldly success.

The eighteenth-century writers I chose to call humanists were Swift, Pope, Johnson, Sir Joshua Reynolds, Gibbon, and Burke. They shared something definable that became clear as I read them again and again for the eighteenth-century anthology and that I tried to define in the first chapter of the book I made out of this course, *The Rhetorical World of Augustan Humanism,* published in 1965. More clear even today than when I wrote is my intense objection to the quasi-utopian tone and assumptions of the American 1960s, which have persisted and deepened despite the illusion of significant shifts in public attitudes. "What is Humanism?" I asked, and to answer, I devised a composite eighteenth-century humanist, a mind still close enough to the fading humanism of the Renaissance to echo its convictions — for one thing, its suspicion of moral progress and its skepticism about ever-renewed solutions to timeless, unsolvable human problems. The humanist, I said, assumes that the individual human consciousness is a construction of humanity's own imaginative making, and that thus the power to think in signs and symbols is the quintessential human attribute. The humanist regards himself as best employed in acts of evaluation, and insists on the close alliance of ethics and expression. To the humanist, the world of external nature is morally neutral and irrelevant to humanity's real — that is, moral — existence. Even if not registered in overtly religious terms, man's nature is somehow "fallen" (because the imagination can always imagine improvements). It is fallen as *Paradise Lost* and *King Lear* imply, and thus in need of some ceremonies of "redemption." For the twentieth-century humanist, literature provides the redemptive experience. It was in my perception of the essential evil of people acting without the constraints suggested by high culture that the infantry veteran and the scholar coincided.

The publication of these two "protest" books at virtually the same moment in 1965 was one of my most exciting experiences, for these were real books, not college-published monographs or textbooks. *Poetic Meter and Poetic Form* began its public life as a paperbound text, but Random House soon decided it would do as a trade book as well and issued a snappy clothbound edition, with my initials on the cover. The *Rhetorical World* was so much a real book, and one to be proud of, that it was published by the Clarendon Press, the branch of the Oxford University Press specializing in contributions to serious thought in history and literature. I had sent in the manuscript without any query or preparation, and I was as astonished as delighted when it was accepted with enthusiasm and no suggestions for changes. For years, Oxford remained my publisher for books with some ambitions of seriousness.

From the fate of these two books I learned something crucial. I learned that I loved writing, even writing against deadlines, and that I enjoyed as almost nothing else watching the pile of first-draft yellow paper, augmented daily, grow gradually from a fraction of an inch to a full four inches, representing one hundred thousand words. I loved every part of the process, and I think my early delight in the school print shop has kept me close to the old-fashioned method of making books — that is, typing them myself, not word processing or dictating or any of that sort of thing. I like correcting my yellow pages with a No. 1 soft pencil. I like to count words and make up chapter and section titles. I even like to make indexes — no stranger or hack has ever indexed books of mine except anthologies. I like what many authors affect to hate, the whole publicity process once the book has been produced. I love being flown at publishers' expense to San Francisco or Seattle and installed in a good hotel (lest the news get about that the publisher is stingy or close to folding) with ample free food and drink, whence I issue forth to be driven to local bookstores and radio and TV stations to affect the momentary style, very momentary, of a celebrity. I love being interviewed. I love mail generated by my books, and I answer every letter, except now and then one so abusive — these seem to come largely from prisons — that conversation with its author seems a waste of energy. I delight not just in making books and publicizing them but in observing their progress through the world, and that includes pleasure in even the most hostile reviews. At least someone is paying attention, and the *libido dominandi* operates pleasurably even when one fails to dominate. And if one book is widely pronounced a disaster, there's always the ream of yellow paper begging to be turned into the next one.

Thus in 1964 I signed a contract to deliver a book about Samuel Johnson as a writer. Since not much profit was expected from this, I received a minuscule advance on minimal royalties. But I didn't care a lot because I was going to research this book not in New Brunswick or Princeton or even New York but somewhere abroad. Those were the days when it was heady excitement to be an academic. Every year, it seemed, one was vouchsafed a promotion and a salary increase. Every year one's teaching load seemed to diminish, while one's position in the faculty parking lot improved. As colleges and universities multiplied, so did students, and now very many arrived at colleges without any understanding of what they were supposed to be doing there. The general lack of intellectual curiosity among them meant that professors' scheduled conference hours tended to be largely unused. The result for me was two or three hours a week when I could read and take notes in my office undisturbed. By spring I would have a whole stack of five-by-eight cards covered with notes, and sometimes complete paragraphs waiting to be fitted into their proper places in a book. I would write it during the summer, producing first six pages a day of draft, and finally eight pages a day of finished text, ready for the printer. This brought one out a winner by September 1. The army had taught me to endure duty with pleasure, and I actually enjoyed getting up at five-thirty and starting to write at seven. I seldom had to continue past noon. My rule was that when I'd finished my daily word length, I could quit, spending the afternoon on something different, like a movie, or a long walk. Next morning, back to duty.

As professors' lives grew gradually easier, finally some were paid for not teaching at all, at least for a year now and then. Among the largesse showered on Rutgers in the sixties was a dramatic increase in research funds. In 1965 I was granted a research year to work on my book tentatively titled *Samuel Johnson, Writer,* and we all set off again, this time in a Peugeot with a luggage rack on top to hold the two large black fiber cases I'd had made to contain my eighteenth-century library. I knew that, having lived for a year in Germany, this time it would be someplace else. "The world was all before them, where to choose." We decided on France, but because Paris struck us as too overpowering for young children, we began considering various smaller provincial cities, like Dijon and Lyons. An older friend, the journalist David Dodge, had just come out with a humorous book about the French Riviera, and he persuaded us that Nice was just the place we wanted: the winter weather would be tolerable, he maintained, and the city was a convenient center for exploring all Southern France as well as Northern Italy. Persuaded, in July we aimed the car at the French Line pier on the Hudson and supervised its storage in the hold of the *France,* then gloriously new and very romantic. Arriving in Le Havre, we drove to Marseilles and transferred the car to the deck of a small vessel heading for Greece. We ended at the large Greek island of Euboea for the summer.

While there in the bright sunlight, reduced to the simplicities of stone, light, and water, I started to write a short book about Whitman's *Song of Myself.* For all my enthusiasm over Whitman's brave plain speaking in *Democratic Vistas* and my excitement over his joy at noting the precise features of actuality, I didn't seem able to celebrate plausibly his urge toward metaphysical unity and his abdication of the human task of qualitative discrimination. I found that I loved

> *. . . limitless are leaves stiff or drooping in the fields,*
> *And brown ants in the little wells beneath them,*
> *And mossy scabs of the worm fence, heap'd stones, elder,*
>   *mullein and poke-weed,*

but knew that I wasn't the type to do unaffected justice to "Showing the best and dividing it from the worst age vexes age," an act that seemed exactly my proper business. After weeks of trying, I gave up and threw the manuscript out and devoted the rest of the summer to swimming and retsina, keftedes and melons.

At the end of the summer I flew to Nice to find us a place to live, while Betty drove the children up through Italy to join me. Like most Americans, I had imagined my French adequate for practical tasks, but at a number of real estate offices I learned with profound humiliation how mistaken I was. Nice was rapidly demolishing the houses and villas like the one I'd fantasized leasing for a year and was turning itself into an all-high-rise condo center, with no place to live but *Appartements de Grand Standing,* blinding white and as ugly and antihuman as any in Miami Beach. We had imagined a Riviera villa like the ones frequented by the Hemingways and the Fitzgeralds and the Gerald Murphys, but even ordinary detached houses were vanishing fast.

Indeed, there seemed to be only one villa left to be rented, in Cimiez, in the hills above the city but within walking distance of the center of town. It was called Villa les Marguerites, located on the winding Chemin des Pins, a few hundred yards below the hotel where

Queen Victoria used to summer and Henri Matisse to paint. Our nineteenth-century villa was heavy and roomy — each child had a room, and there was an extra bedroom for visitors. I unloaded all my books about Johnson in the small study and set to work reading and note taking. The anomaly of the whole enterprise appealed to me — reading one of the greatest English moralists on a site that, with Monte Carlo on one side and Cannes on the other, was a byword for hedonism, rampant sexuality, and flagrant irresponsibility.

The children we enrolled in a nearby private school populated by a rich variety of small Europeans, where children were referred to less often by their names than by their countries of origin. Tucky and Sam were friendly with Les Españols, and were themselves designated Les Anglais, meaning less natives of England than speakers of English. By the end of the year their French was marvelous, their accents touching to hear. Since Betty and I spoke French only in restaurants and at the wine shop, our spoken command of that language remained pitiable, although we could read well enough to enjoy thoroughly the daily *Nice-Matin,* with its never-failing narratives of auto crashes and local burglaries and murders, imputed always to the Corsicans, offshore. Living in France did teach us something valuable about not just French but other languages: you don't have to ask a grammatically complete question to get a satisfactory answer. To the bartender, *toilette?* is sufficient, just as in Turkey *tuvalet?* will do, and in Italy *gabinetto?*

For the fleshly, Nice was a paradise: on the beach at nearby Juan-les-Pins, we sunned and swam and ate picnics and drank the wine, all the while ignoring the disaster shaping up in Southeast Asia that would change the United States drastically. Later, Robert McNamara declared that the main American errors in Vietnam — specifically, the decision to magnify the conflict and to try to "win" it — were made in the late spring and summer of 1965. While we devoted ourselves to swimming and gourmandizing and sporting our espadrilles in Greece and France, fancying ourselves the heirs of the writers and artists of the twenties, on the other side of the world working-class American youths were, uselessly, dying in agony, and by their thousands. If you thought about it, it seemed gravely unfair, and it was. How unfair I didn't wholly appreciate until, returning to Rutgers, I learned that attending college, any college, for any purpose, was a sufficient reason for draft deferment. The class system was doing its dirty little work quite openly, and nobody seemed to care. Nor were the rest of us morally clean. Early in the war, I had written disingenuous letters testifying to the deep religious convictions of sons of middle-class friends of mine to keep them out of the army, and later I was perfectly happy to see many of my students flee to Canada, leaving the less-fortunate boys, those emanating from Trenton and Camden instead of Bernardsville, the job of pursuing America's misbegotten course in Southeast Asia. I never knew anyone whose son had been killed, wounded, or even badly inconvenienced by the war. It now seems hard to believe that any of us emerged from the years of the Vietnam debacle entirely guiltless. I think that my objections to the Vietnam War stemmed less from humanitarian impulses, as I pretended, than from my simple hatred of the army and all its works.

The new easy, expansive academic era of the sixties and seventies offered more than richer salaries, light teaching, and more generous research handouts. It seemed to inaugurate the age of something little known before, at least to academic nonscientists. I mean the foreign-delegation boondoggle, sponsored by the federal government.

I was lucky enough to be on several. Each was a lovely free vacation and tour abroad and each was, intellectually, a laughable farce. I still smile when I hear the well-intentioned term "cultural exchange."

One of these luxurious trips was a cultural delegation to the Soviet Union. The Helsinki accords had been signed in 1975, presumably opening wide the intellectual doors between the United States and the USSR. The rumor reached the United States that after years of intransigence, the official intellectuals of the Soviet Union, historians especially, had decided to quit dumping on the czarist era and to begin recognizing its continuity, in many hitherto unmentionable respects, with the "revolutionary" years that followed. What these historians, it was said, were interested in producing was a continuous cultural history of Russia, one that would bridge the gulf between the wicked past and the rosy present. To assist them in this enterprise, and to provide models of standard cultural (especially literary) history, a group of cultural historians from the United States was assembled to be shipped to Moscow for a conference on this subject. Each of us was to produce a paper (reading time, one hour) on a national cultural historiography. These we were to present at a huge, highly publicized conference in Moscow, fully equipped with simultaneous translators and all the trappings of a serious international congress. It was to be attended by Russian professors and students, historians, linguists, and, as it turned out, scores of government hacks and not a few KGB men.

I had spent weeks preparing a paper titled "Empiricism and Theory in British Literary Historiography." My main point was that literary history, as an enterprise pursued by serious intellectuals, seemed largely done for. What I was really talking about, it became clear, was the decline and fall of literary history as an intellectually respectable and publicly useful pursuit. Perhaps it was this suggestion of hopelessness in the very activity where the Soviets hoped to make a triumphant entry into the civilized world that explains what happened next. I delivered my paper with due seriousness — it was clear that levity was as unwelcome as irony — and when I finished, the chairman slowly rose and announced to the audience, "We will have no discussion of Professor Fussell's paper. It deviates too far from Leninist norms."

That's what the USSR was like then, and that's an attitude it seems unlikely to shake off overnight or by a simple change of administration. One of the older party functionaries we met on this junket — he had something to do with the preposterously named Writers' Union — was a rough, portly, clearly unliterary man named Boris Vladimir Rodionovich Shcherbina. When the Chernobyl disaster erupted twenty years later, it was no surprise to find that event openly lied about on Soviet television. The speaker, grown older and fatter but no more self-respecting, still performing his boss's will, was Comrade Shcherbina. One splendid thing about English literature is the way it can supply appropriate comments for all occasions. In 1736 Alexander Pope presented Frederick, Prince of Wales, with a puppy. On its collar, Pope, a supremely self-respecting and toady-hating man, had engraved,

I am his Highness's Dog at Kew.
Pray tell me, Sir, whose Dog are You?

Connoisseurs of both poetic justice and black humor will want to know Shcherbina's destiny. In 1988, now risen to deputy prime minister, he issued a secret order forbidding physicians to designate radiation as a cause of death. To show everyone how safe Chernobyl was, he visited it himself. When he died soon after, the cause of his death was duly unspecified.

But no amount of fear of the authorities and low proletarian cunning and bugging of hotel rooms and official rudeness could spoil the beauty of the czarist architecture of Leningrad, where we were transported by night train after the Moscow conference. Leningrad's Palace Square and the Catherine Palace in Pushkin remain for me permanent models of ideal human settings. Grand but not without dignity, distant from any smallness or meanness, places where you could imagine life mysteriously glorified by architecture and architectural space.

A few years later another boondoggle offered further opportunities for contact with Russia. As the Cold War began to show signs of thawing, someone at the Smithsonian had the bright idea of assembling a number of Russians and Americans to plan a portable museum of folly, the folly of the long-continued and fatuous Russian-American cultural hostility. The museum would be open for a time in Moscow, then in Washington, and then it would travel in both countries. It was hoped that it would humiliate its visitors into sense and prepare them for a new start in U.S.-Soviet relations. Twenty of us, ten on each side, met for several days of talks at a resort outside Moscow. The talk was wonderful, for the group included Stanley Cavell, Dore Shary, Gunther Schuller, Ihab Hassan, Robert Hughes, and similar worthies from art, contemporary music, and history, and their Soviet counterparts. But, as so often happens with such well-intentioned group efforts, finally nothing came of it.

Nor were there any visible results from another overseas conference, this one involving ten American literary scholars touring China and meeting their counterparts. From the agenda one could have predicted that this enterprise would vapor away in well-meaning vagueness, for both Americans and Chinese agreed to read each other papers on the general topic "Lyric Narrative." There being no such definable thing, I was puzzled about what to do, but I finally decided that "pastoral" might sort of fit the assignment and produced an essay on "The Persistence of Pastoral" and went with that. We Americans did our act in colleges and universities all over China, where mutual incomprehension — all assumptions were, as could have been prophesied, too far apart — pleasantly reminded me of the mad transactions of the Grand Academy of Lagado in Swift's *Gulliver's Travels*. The main thing I remember from this two-week exercise, besides the excellence of the food and our hosts' desire to please, was the scarcity of toilets and the unwillingness of our benefactors to demean the grandeur of the learned occasion or sully their own modesty — Toilet Shame being a well-known Asian feature — by indicating unambiguously where relief might be found.

But from these meetings we did learn something worthwhile. We learned about the savagery of the recently concluded Cultural Revolution, and the more pessimistic among us wondered how long it would take to arrive in our country. We met one victim among tens of thousands, a mild professor whose intellectual subtlety and integrity had riled the proletarians. This harmless pedagogue had first been beaten almost to death with two-by-fours wielded by the envious young and then consigned to work for years shoveling pig shit out in the country. He seemed to me preternaturally patient, almost forgiving, and I told him something hard for him to understand, namely, that if the young and ignorant had ever treated me that way, I'd spend the rest of my life not attending literary conferences but tracking them down and achieving my revenge, perhaps with my own two-by-four. I'm afraid that there you have the West versus the East, another indication, perhaps, of the futility of bridging valuable cultural differences by means of academic conferences. These communal cultural efforts had the effect of persuading me that intellectual and artistic work worthy the designation could never be generated or conducted by organized groups. It could be achieved only in conditions of lonely self-solicited silence by largely eccentric and antisocial individuals. If the term *discussion* has always seemed to me to imply mild warnings of wasted time, *workshop* sets off a clangorous alarm.

As late as the 1970s, running up stairs was for me a positive delight, and I still looked and felt young. But soon I became aware as never before of my mortality, of the way each day and week shortened my time here. The deaths of my mother and father, in 1971 and 1973, made it unmistakably clear that, after Ed, I must, actuarily speaking, be next. My sensitivity to mutability and transcience, which I'd registered already in *Poetic Meter and Poetic Form*, became a leading motif in *Samuel Johnson and the Life of Writing*. The conclusion, where I talked about Johnson's fondness for elegy and irony in *The Lives of the Poets*, was really about myself. Johnson's poets, I wrote, all have enough in common "to merge into something like a species. Johnson's species . . . is the writer as representative man, obliged by his frailty to imitate and to adhere to genres and conventions which he has not devised; tormented by the hunger of imagination only to be always defeated of his hopes; and finally carried away by the very stream of time it has been his ironic ambition to shape, and by shaping, to arrest."

Ever since my return to civilian life in 1946 I'd been recalling my experiences in the war and considering their relation to everything else I knew. Did service as a young infantry officer in whatever time and place bring some special knowledge of humanity in relation to oneself? Was my war unique or quite commonplace and hardly worth special notice? To see how widespread my experience had been, I sought out narratives by young literary-minded infantry officers with whom I could in some way identify myself. I didn't want fiction. I wanted testimony. There was little, those days, from Americans. I found what I wanted (fiction, most of it, but I didn't understand that until later) in a number of British autobiographies from the First World War. Three especially attracted me, and I read them over and over, imagining myself into the minds and bodies of three young officers who'd waited for ten years after their war before inviting literary form and the device of plot to furnish meaning to their raw memories. They were Edmund Blunden, the shy Oxford poet and poison-gas victim who wrote the ironically quiet, well-mannered *Undertones of War* in 1928; the rowdy Robert Graves, who said *Good-Bye to All That* in 1929; and the privileged countryman, horse-lover, and poet Siegfried Sassoon, who in 1930 published *Memoirs of an Infantry Officer*. Reading these books, I found in them the sort of sensibility I'd looked for in vain among my fellow officers in the recent Army of the United States. I immersed myself in First World War infantry poetry too, preeminently that of Owen and Isaac Rosenberg. Sassoon's less subtle antiwar poetry (actually anti-upper-class and anti-staff poetry) I was also drawn to, for its Menckenlike, muckraking features. In the first few years after my war, it was easy for me to identify Sassoon's "staff," the bloated, stupid, self-satisfied senior officers, with types I'd known in Pasadena and was now encountering among the deans and such of the colleges and universities where I found myself laboring in the trenches. Without knowing exactly what I was doing, I was becoming interested in the relation between physical violence and terror, on the one hand, and the conventions and limits of language, especially published language, on the other. The sophisticated memoirists had their way of dealing with this matter, but how about all the others, the thousands of "ordinary" men who'd not been the beneficiaries of a literary education and who kept diaries or made notes or wrote unpublished — and largely unpublishable — memoirs when they returned home? To what degree was acute and compelling memory of traumatic occasions a dividend of a literary education?

I knew that I could find a lot of these folk memoirs in the archives of the Imperial War Museum in London. In 1971 I inquired of the keeper of documents, a young historian named Roderick Suddaby, about reading through this archive, and a summer later I lived in London for the express purpose of learning this material. Most of it was unread before, except perhaps by family members cleaning out drawers and closets and then sending masses of papers to the War Museum for safekeeping. Every morning except Sunday for three months I presented myself with my pass at the front door of the museum and was led by a warder past the tanks and artillery pieces installed on the ground floor up stairways and elevators to the top story. There I was assigned a large room and a large rectangular table. Suddaby, an experienced researcher, heard calmly my wish to read through the Great War archive that summer, and agreed that each morning the left end of the table would be filled with material which, by late afternoon, I was to move to the right end for return to the vaults. All summer I was the only person reading there. It was a perfect environment for concentration.

The stuff Suddaby supplied me was in beat-up cartons, mostly, and its authenticity and variety took my breath away. There were little notebooks still stiff with the mud of the Somme or Ypres. There were field orders, platoon rosters, copies of letters from young lieutenants to the parents of the dead, mangled identity disks, the string still dark with the sweat of some hopeful boy violently killed over fifty years ago. The material hadn't yet been sorted, let alone classified and cataloged, and going through it daily was one of the most emotional adventures of my life. In the face of such a plethora of material, I decided that I'd have to impose strict limits on my curiosity: I stayed with the ground forces, largely infantry, ignoring artifacts, no matter how compelling, from the Royal Flying Corps and the navy, as well as stuff from the home front. What I wanted was displays of language that would define the similarity of infantry experience, and the difficulty of containing it within words, in the two land wars against Germany.

And for the Allied infantry, the two wars were very similar. If the Great War soldiers lived in trenches, we lived (theoretically) in foxholes, and our tactics of infantry warfare were hardly more refined than thirty years before, consisting of mass attacks in skirmish lines, ambushes, patrols, and defense while dug in. The infantry weapons, with the exception of the bazooka and the antitank mine, had undergone little change. For the Americans, indeed, the heavy machine gun and the automatic rifle and the hand grenade were the very same. The bayonet was shorter, but it was still a bayonet, to be affixed to the rifle before an attack in a thoroughly nineteenth-century way.

Thus for three months I lived in the trenches with the British infantry, accompanying them on their raids, drinking their rum, searching for lice in my trouser seams, and affecting British phlegm as they prepared to jump the bags and charge directly into machine-gun fire. How did they do it? What did they think about it? How did they control their fear, or at least prevent it from showing? These were questions an ex–infantry officer from another war, but a notably similar one, seemed uniquely prepared to ask.

If in one way the resulting book, *The Great War and Modern Memory,* was an act of implicit autobiography, in another it was a refraction of current events. During the Vietnam War I had grown sick of hearing phrases like "body count" from otherwise fairly civilized people. I had listened with silent revulsion to most of the talk about the war, with speakers' utter failure to imagine what, regardless of which "side" or ideology it was attached to, the suffering of infantry was like. One of my objects in writing this book was to reawaken the reader's imagination and power of sympathy in a world too far gone in the complacencies of mechanism, scientism, and abstraction. The wounded hurt terribly. The dying go out in bewilderment and agonizing wonder, and they call upon Mother, even if they are German or Vietcong. Not far from my mind as I wrote were Wilfred Owen's words in "Insensibility":

> . . . *cursed are dullards whom no cannon stuns,*
> *That they should be as stones.*
> *Wretched are they, and mean*
> *With paucity that never was simplicity.*
> *By choice they made themselves immune*
> *To pity and whatever mourns in man*
> *Before the last sea and the hapless stars;*
> *Whatever mourns when many leave these shores;*
> *Whatever shares*
> *The eternal reciprocity of tears.*

To my mind, Owen's *many* did not exclude the youth of Southeast Asia torn in half by our machine guns or shriveled by napalm into small, smelly black objects.

Was my book classifiable as "History"? Doubtless not, and historians noted that it exaggerated, neglected important data, and generally behaved irresponsibly — significant, if a quasi-scientific account of trench life in the Great War had been my aim. But it was not. I was writing like an essayist, for whom only a small part of his material was the facts and public imagery of European history. Like Dickens's fat boy, I wanted to make the reader's flesh creep. I wanted my readers to weep as they sensed the despair of people like themselves, torn and obliterated for a cause beyond their understanding. I had cried so often while writing the book that to steady myself I often had to take a long walk and breathe deeply after writing some heartrending passage. And sometimes I compressed my lips tightly so that those close to me wouldn't know what I was feeling. But as I worked I grew unashamed of my tears and regarded them as part of what I was doing — reanimating in myself an appropriate memorial pity. Beside me as I wrote were Matt Rose and Sergeant Hudson and the uniformed German children with their brains oozing out, all alike cheated by the twentieth century. To hint at one thing the book was about, I dedicated it to the memory of Hudson, and to give the proceedings empirical authenticity, to remind readers that I was alluding to a man who was once real and alive, like themselves, not an idea but an actual person, I wrote the army and asked for Hudson's army serial number, which I placed after his name.

And when the book was published, the mail I received suggested that I'd achieved some emotional if not intellectual success. Indeed, some of the mail was positively spooky. One elderly British reader was moved to a sort of clairvoyance, enabling him to describe very accurately our street, our house, my study, and even to note that in our living room "the drums of peace" had displaced "the drums of war." How could he have known that Tucky's jazz drum set stood in one corner?

On the other hand, some of my literary relations with the British have produced highly comic results. When in 1984 I moved from Rutgers to the University of Pennsylvania, it was to occupy the new Donald T. Regan chair of English Literature. Regan, just retired from Merrill Lynch, had been chairman of the Penn board of trustees, and his business associates had raised money to honor him with an academic chair in his name, which went to the Department of English. Simultaneously, I was writing *Class: A Guide through the American Status System,* which grew from an article in the *New Republic.* This was hardly a serious book, for often the presentation was conducted in the comical voice of an excessively earnest, pedantic professor of sociology, accustomed to rigid classifications and pseudo-scientific method. Among other things, the book was a satire on academic solemnity. In due course, it appeared as a mass-market paperback, in England as well as the United States. To suggest my awareness that a book like this might seem not quite the thing from a writer who before had dealt with humanism and war, I supplied an author's note modeled on those cunning paragraphs amateur actors provide for playbills. They read like this: "In real life, Angela Markham is a dental technician." Mine began likewise with "In real life": "In real life, Paul Fussell is Donald T. Regan Professor of English Literature at the University of Pennsylvania." In the United Kingdom professorships named after people, especially living people, are not as common as in the U.S.A. The editor of the British paperback couldn't resist clarifying my presumed meaning by inserting a comma, thus: "In real life, Paul Fussell is Donald T. Regan, Professor of English, etc." Thus for months, and it's still happening, I would receive anti–fan mail from England beginning as follows:

> *Dear Professor Regan,*
>
> *Your book is so offensive that I quite understand why you feel it necessary to hide your actual identity behind such a ludicrous pseudonym as "Paul Fussell."*

Letters still arrive at Penn addressed to Professor Regan, and by now the staff there says nothing but quietly sends them on to me.

One night Betty and I sat down and addressed the question, What should I write next? I had learned that in making a book, there was no substitute for a passionate obsession with the subject and all its vibrations. That may seem obvious, but many writers get stuck in projects they're really not insanely devoted to. I had been thoroughly possessed by the Great War and its culture. What next? After talking half the night, Betty and I concluded that next to war, travel and everything connected with it, especially its relation to narrative, was one of my passions sufficiently intense to animate a book. Thus I got a Guggenheim Fellowship in 1977 for "a study of the literary status of travel writing," and we set off again, basing ourselves this time in London and preparing to go to Eastern Turkey and Iran to learn something about the Middle East and Islam. Iran happened to be in the final throes of disencumbering itself of the Shah, but he was still in charge when we set off, and we assumed travel there would be safe enough. (We had already had some hairy experiences, notably in

Egypt during the Six-Day War, when the hotels were empty: tourists, hearing, quite accurately, of Israeli planes strafing the Cairo airport and of Egyptian soldiers roaming the streets with fixed bayonets, canceled bookings by the thousands.)

Before we left London, someone had told me about Robert Byron's book about traveling in Iran, *The Road to Oxiana*, published in 1937. I found a copy at Hatchard's and was captured immediately. On the spot I decided that anything I wrote about travel and its literary dimensions would have to dwell extensively on Byron. There was something about his brave contempt of normal "educated" opinion, as well as his talent for passionately seizing a subject and educating himself in it without assistance, that delighted me. When he was at Oxford, most people were going sentimentally gaga over Greek sculpture and similar fleshly idealisms, "those inert stone bodies," as Byron says, "which already bar persons of artistic sensibility from entering half the museums of Europe." Appalled by the general tribute being paid to such "vacuous perfection," Byron decided to dash in the opposite direction, toward stylization and nonrepresentation. In Byzantine art he found what he wanted, and he wrote extensively about it. Since I had experienced, especially in Greece, something of Byron's mystique of travel, I loved his insistence that travel — real travel, not group tourism — is "a spiritual necessity" and an indispensable element of liberal learning.

If *The Great War and Modern Memory* was oblique autobiography, as much about my war as its ostensible subject, *Abroad: British Literary Traveling Between the Wars* was similarly autobiographical, memorializing those ecstatic transatlantic and Mediterranean voyages Betty and I had taken before jet aircraft consigned the ships to the wreckers. As I wrote, nostalgically and surely sentimentally,

When you entered Manhattan by the Lincoln Tunnel twenty years ago, you saw from the high west bank of the Hudson a vision that lifted your heart. . . . You saw the magic row of transatlantic liners nuzzling the island, their classy, frivolous red and black and white and green uttering their critique of the utility beige-gray of the buildings. In the row might be the Queen Mary *or the* Queen Elizabeth *or the* Mauretania, *the* United States *or the* America *or the* Independence, *the* Rafaello *or the* Michelangelo *or the* Liberté. *These were the last attendants of the age of travel, soon to fall victim to the jet plane and the cost of oil and the cost of skilled labor.*

To exhibit what travel once had been before our age of rampant utilitarianism, in *Abroad* I went on to celebrate the travel writings of, among others, Graham Greene, Peter Fleming, Christopher Isherwood, and Norman Douglas (actually more a resider-abroad than a traveler). Although not myself a pederast, I was drawn to Douglas in part because his frequent flights across national borders to escape the outraged parents of children he'd been attracted to couldn't help seeming a bit like my own flight from the respectability of Pasadena. One of my chapters was about the Mediterranean as a treasured venue where the British could see their school learning realized — especially their Horace and Virgil — but actually that chapter was an autobiographical registration of the delights Betty and I and the children had known on French and Italian beaches and our shared belief that, as the character Cyril Fielding puts it in Forster's *A Passage to India,* "The Mediterranean is the human norm."

In Evelyn Waugh's *The Ordeal of Gilbert Pinfold,* Gilbert (that is, Waugh) rhapsodizes about the Mediterranean Sea in terms that speak to me uncannily: "The sea might have been any sea by the look of it, but . . . it was the Mediterranean, that splendid enclosure which held all the world's history and half the happiest moments of his own life; of work and rest and battle, of aesthetic adventure and young love." Waugh's Mediterranean "battle" was Crete, mine began with going ashore at Marseilles. His "work" was writing novels in Mediterranean seaside cities and towns, mine was sketching out my book on Johnson in Nice. My aesthetic adventures began in Florence and Rome in the early 1950s, when my young love was intense and steady, itself hardly separable from the aesthetic adventures available at the Uffizi and the Pitti and the Vatican. I ended *Abroad* with elegiac exaggeration, dwelling on the way the war put an end to travel in the old sense, not just during the war but ever after it, as the liners were replaced by cruise ships looking less like ships than squat hotels in anomalous motion, and travel, as a mode of active liberal learning, was replaced by passive tourism. What I was really saying was that it was more fun to be twenty-eight years old, when I first wandered around Europe, than fifty-five, when I couldn't help feeling that something had been lost.

⇥ IX ⇤

LONG FAMOUS, like other rich suburbs, as a locus of alcoholism, in the 1970s and 1980s Princeton became a divorce center as well, and as usual, alcoholism and divorce seemed closely linked. The marriages of many old friends came apart, and as the 1970s ended, Betty's and my marriage began to end too.

Betty rented a New York studio apartment, noting that she found it hard to do her writing in Princeton. Her gradual disaffection with the pomposities and provincialisms of an academic environment played a part too. She now spent the middle of each week in New York, returning to Princeton for Saturdays and Sundays. Before we were entirely aware of it and its implications, she was spending virtually all her time away from Princeton, and we agreed that a legal separation would formalize a situation that had already become a matter of fact. We sold our house, I moved into a two-room Princeton apartment, and Betty bought a condo in Greenwich Village. But this makes it all sound too rational and orderly. Actually the separation was as messy and emotional as such things customarily are, with terrible feelings of anger and guilt. The only certainty for both of us during this period was that we were both miserable.

One of my few bright moments was the publication in 1982 of *The Boy Scout Handbook and Other Observations,* a collection of essays and reviews from American and British periodicals. Knowing that the word *essays* was, in New York publishing, virtually a guarantee that a book would sink without trace, I substituted *observations,* a detail picked up by painter Jim Aplin, who contributed a distinguished illustration for the jacket. It depicted a somewhat old-fashioned Boy Scout observing through binoculars a city whose tall buildings were reflected in the large lenses. My book used for its title that of its lead essay, my celebratory review of the 1979 edition of *The Official Boy Scout Handbook,* in which I had praised its uncompromising ethical vision. Was the ghost of Boy Fussell tugging at the sleeve of the satirist and skeptic?

Looking back on them now, I see that several essays in this book share a concern with other people's deficient sense of honor or honesty. In "The Purging of *Penrod,*" for example, I registered my anger at the publishers of the paperback Tempo Books for their cowardice in cleansing the text of Booth Tarkington's entirely innocent *Penrod* (1914) of references to race that contemporary Political Correctness might find offensive. And even worse: lying about what they had done to this irreplaceable American classic by asserting, "This Tempo Books edition contains the complete text of the original hard-cover edition." What bothered me was not just the lie but the insult to the bookish reader, who is assumed to be so ignorant and tasteless as not to recall that one of the best chapters is titled "Coloured Troops in Action," not, as in the PC text, "Troops in Action." I concluded, perhaps needlessly: "The past is not the present: pretending it is corrupts art and thus both rots the mind and shrivels the imagination and conscience."

A similar contempt for ordinary people and their capacity to make up their own minds about difficult questions was visible in the literary and artistic censorship then being practiced in South Africa. Armed with a "credential" from the *New Republic,* I went to Johannesburg to consult with Nadine Gordimer about this situation and to research in a public library the infamous official *Jacobsen's Index of Objectionable Literature,* a veritable display case of lower-middle-class Dutch sexual anxieties. Playing nanny to the presumably child-like citizens, the state was forbidding the sale of works by such as Gore Vidal, Norman Mailer, Mary McCarthy, Edmund Wilson, John Updike, Philip Roth, Martin Amis, James Baldwin, and Tennessee Williams, as well as works implicitly recommending opposition to militarism as a civilized ethical position. I registered my objections in a satiric essay titled "Smut-Hunting in Pretoria."

Here's another example of my annoyance with offensive literary actions. Finding that Graham Green's publishers had so little self-respect as to designate their author "the most distinguished living writer in the English language," I couldn't resist grasping the publisher's invitation to attend to Greene's use of language. The result was the review-essay "Can Graham Greene Write English?" which ridiculed this wholly dishonorable blurb by presenting instances of Greene's schoolboy difficulties with grammar (the distinction between *who* and *whom* caused him lots of trouble) and sentence structure, not to mention his clichés, clumsiness, and wordiness. My attack was aimed less at Greene, who was doing as well as his equipment would allow, than at the institution of advertising and its ability to corrupt everything, literature included.

The topic of the ethics of authorship and of the book trade solicited me once again as I made an essay out of the contents of a bulging folder I'd been building up over the years. It held examples of self-pitying and self-celebratory letters to the editor dashed off in fury by hypersensitive authors smarting from unfavorable reviews. In a mock-analytic display of the inviolable conventions of these letters — I considered them a well-established literary genre, highly characteristic of our own bizarre age — I satirized their authors' juvenile vanity and ignorance — ignorance of such wisdom as Johnson's: "An author places himself uncalled before the tribunal of criticism, and solicits fame at the hazard of disgrace." I was particularly hard on writers claiming to be "misunderstood" by a reviewer. If a writer's been misunderstood, I asserted, "it's his fault . . . because he's supposed to be adept in matters of lucid address and explanation, and if he's failed there, he's failed everywhere." In any case, even the coarsest conception of honor requires that when hurt, one keep it to oneself. It was hard not to recall the complaints of the colostomy kid in the hospital at Épinal.

Not all the essays concerned what I took to be the subject of honorable behavior. Some were aesthetic-social, like "A Place to Recuperate." I was growing so sick of America's lucrative urban and highway ugliness, its general lack of public beauty and amenity, that sooner or later I knew I'd have to discharge my annoyance. This I did by imagining an ideal place of a vaguely French-Swiss-Italian kind, a small provincial city by a large lake, with a Romance language spoken and architecture dating from no later than the middle of the nineteenth century. I furnished this city with ideal restaurants served by elderly male waiters in black and white, band concerts in the central *place*, shops selling things made desirable by tradition, not advertising, sophisticated bookstores with highly educated salespeople, and an old-fashioned hotel by the lake. At the end of this fantasy I released my imagination to an almost erotic degree: "When you look across the lake you look not upon emptiness but at boats, and, far away, the dim outlines of the distant other shore with light-blue mountains rising behind. While you're here the weather is bright and clear, warm in the daytime but at night cool enough for good sleeping." When I'd finished, I felt satisfied to have invented so artistically and believably a fictional place, and I was thus distressed by a conviction of my artistic failure when I found that some readers believed that I was "describing" a real place without invention or art. One man in Canada assured me that if I'd disclose where this place was to him alone, he'd promise never to divulge the secret lest tourists rush to desecrate this idyll.

In several concluding essays on the Second World War, I emphasized the dishonorable, cowardly, unimaginative, and ultimately childish practice of heroizing and cheerfulizing that egregious disaster that killed and maimed millions and ruined Europe and set back civilization several centuries. I was still doing what I would always do, suggesting what the war was like for people the stylish don't run into at cocktail parties. Already I was meditating a fuller treatment of this theme, which finally emerged in 1989 as *Wartime: Understanding and Behavior in the Second World War.*

Some readers were beginning to sense that by contemporary American standards my essays were betraying something like a serious, even archaic, ethical concern, as well as an unacademic breadth of focus and insolence of manner. A bright young Washington journalist, Curt Suplee, was struck by these phenomena and, sending a photographer in advance, arrived in Princeton for a daylong scrutiny. The result was an extensive profile, headed "A Class Critic Takes Aim at America," in the *Washington Post* for September 28, 1982.

Coming upon this article in the *Post*, a widow in her fifties living in Virginia came alight and wrote me at Rutgers:

Dear Dr. Fusillade:

    I just read the Washington Post *interview of September 28. I think I am in love with you. I am a liberal snob. A career woman, which is to say I spend little time scooping out watermelon balls, or making lampshades out of corrugated paper. . . . Sometimes use incomplete sentences.*

She signed her name Harriette Behringer and invited me for a meal whenever I was near Washington. Of course the guts and wit of this letter delighted me, but anxious about such unacknowledged menaces as obesity and buck teeth, I wrote back,

Dear Harriette Behringer,

    Thanks for the fascinating letter. You sound like a pretty frisky kid. [And then the crucial point:] How about a photograph?

She responded with a recent snapshot taken at a swimming pool in Peru. She was slender and eminently attractive. I phoned her immediately, and soon we were deluging each other with affectionate letters and phone calls.

We simply had to meet. We decided that the fairest way was to meet halfway between Princeton and Washington, say, Wilmington, Delaware. On the appointed day in December, I went to keep our lunch date at the Hotel DuPont. The Christmas decorations were in place, and behind the large Christmas tree I spotted a pair of neat black pumps. As I went forward, my heart leaping, she came to me, and I said, "You're Harriette. I'd know you anywhere." Before long we were weekending at each other's premises. I learned what she did as director of public and community relations at the Xerox International Center in Leesburg, Virginia. She learned what I did by sitting in on my classes and seminars. We wanted to travel together, but I was afraid of my tendency to dominate and lecture if we went anywhere I already knew. Thus we selected Morocco, where I'd never been. When later I moved to Philadelphia, she sold her house and did the same, but we lived in separate apartment houses a couple of blocks apart. After a few years, we decided to marry. I transformed my separation into a divorce, and Harriette and I were married in April 1987. We were in our sixties, but in all ways we might have been ecstatic twenty-year-olds.

Wanting to devote all my time to writing, I'd retired early from Rutgers in 1983, and my hope that I could live well on royalties and fees was sustained for a while by the publication that year of *Class*, which garnered lots of publicity and some hostility. (An author once complained in Johnson's presence about attacks on one of his books. Johnson replied: "Nay, Sir, do not complain. It is advantageous to an author that his book should be attacked as well as praised. Fame is a shuttlecock. If it be struck only at one end of the room, it will soon fall to the ground. To keep it up, it must be struck at both ends.")

Writing *Class* involved reading everything I could find on the subject, observing attentively the social implications of familiar objects, and taking expert advice: from a veterinarian about the social-class aspects of owning various types of dogs, from a woman who knew a lot about both flowers and people — she assured me that red geraniums outranked pink ones socially — and from a professor of music, who submitted observations about the social-class import of various musical instruments. A lot of my data about domestic house facades came from the week I'd spent in Indianapolis "covering" the five-hundred-mile auto race for *Harper's*. I stayed in a hotel on the edge of an upper-working-class area some distance from the Speedway, and took different routes during my walks there, observing front-yard Snow Whites and Seven Dwarfs and flower beds outlined in defunct lightbulbs and old truck tires painted white. Except for a page or two, the book is unrelentingly facetious, packed with exaggerations and palpably irresponsible assertions, and I was astonished to find how many readers took it seriously. In chain bookstores I found it classified under Self-Help instead of Humor. In Japan it was regarded humorlessly as a sincere, trustworthy guide to American actualities, and tourists were seen deplaning in San Francisco with the book pressed to their bosoms.

Another of my books appearing in 1983 was a landmark in my long career of discovering that books and television don't mix. The reason, if unwelcome to strict egalitarians, may seem obvious to the more hardheaded: the two audiences are different. The book audience at its best is active, intellectually self-propelled. The TV audience is passive, happy to be filled up and told what to do and think by entrepreneurs of clichés.

I have been involved in several efforts to pretend that this gulf between grown-up readers and the TV audience doesn't exist, and every one, without exception, has aborted, occasioning for the producers waste of money and for me waste of time. Back in 1981 I was approached by a New York book packager (although *cooperative publisher* was the term he preferred), who informed me that he'd just pulled off a coup. He'd managed to secure the rights to the semifictional autobiography of Siegfried Sassoon, and he was negotiating with a British film producer to create for Thames Television a thirteen-part dramatization. I agreed to furnish a severely cut version of Sassoon's text and to provide copious illustrations. *Publishers Weekly* was fed the story:

> *While not designed as a tie-in with the programs [a lie], a volume edited by Paul Fussell and drawing upon various Sassoon writings, including excerpts from the novels, will be seeing the light this year [a vain hope]. . . . Oxford University Press is to be the U.S. publisher, Faber & Faber the English. Approximately 100 contemporary photos, drawings, and paintings, some in color [no: too expensive], will complement the text.*

Animated by a quite decent advance, I set to work. The first thing to do was to return to Sassoon's *The Complete Memoirs of George Sherston* and to note excerptable passages visual enough to be "illustrated." At the same time I had to maintain the continuity of the narrative. Once I'd made and typed up the abridged text, I went to London to search for the pictures. I worked with Michael Willis, of the Still-Photograph Archive of the Imperial War Museum. His knowledge of the collection was astounding.

One of the passages I wanted to illustrate was this, indispensable if Sassoon's homosexual-aesthetic bent was to be understood:

> *As I stepped over one of the [dead] Germans an impulse made me lift him up from the miserable ditch. Propped against the bank, his blond face was undisfigured, except by the mud which I wiped from his eyes and mouth with my coat sleeve. . . . He didn't look*

to be more than eighteen. Hoisting him a little higher, I thought what a gentle face he had, and remembered that this was the first time I'd ever touched one of our enemies with my hands. Perhaps I had some dim sense of the futility which had put an end to this good-looking youth. Anyhow I hadn't expected the Battle of the Somme to be quite like this.

PF: "Mr. Willis, I wonder if you could find — I know it's a difficult request — a photograph showing a dead young German soldier whose face could strike an observer as 'good-looking'?"

Mr. Willis: "Yes, I think there's one like that in Book Number F-161."

And he took down one of the large heavy volumes containing contact prints of every picture in the collection. There, as he pointed, I saw exactly the picture I needed.

At first, the hope was that the TV series and the tie-in book would burst on an astonished world at the same time. There was talk about engaging Michael York to play the young Sassoon, and we saw that he could be made to look rather like him. But negotiations with all parties dragged on and on, and before we knew it, Michael York had become forty years old, and looked it. Of course the TV plans collapsed, and we were left with a warehouse bulging with copies of *Siegfried Sassoon's Long Journey,* a book that now had no real rationale, as British reviewers acutely, if snottily, observed when Faber & Faber published it in the United Kingdom.

Another time, approached by a filmmaker from California, literary scholar Samuel Hynes and I agreed to serve as consultants on a TV special about British literary life between the two World Wars. The filmmaker was young and seemed quite rich and lived in

Pasadena, a fact that seemed to acquire ominous significance as we went along. Hynes and I contributed a substantial essay designed to persuade the National Endowment for the Humanities to support the project. As we drafted this and sent it back and forth for revision, we began to perceive not just that we and the filmmaker had quite different ideas about what the film should be, but also that the filmmaker's conception of the subject was hopelessly shallow and sentimental, when not grossly snobbish. He had apparently been unduly ravished by the TV film version of Waugh's *Brideshead Revisited*, whose account of between-the-wars life he mistook for significant actuality.

He conceived that in Britain literary life was practically the same as upper-class social life, with *social* carrying all the connotations of High Society. Inherited money and property seemed a requisite for the life of writing. Orwell, Joyce, and Lawrence were ignored, while Harold Acton, the Sitwells, Nancy Mitford, Duff and Diana Cooper, and Anthony Powell were presented as the mainstream. It seemed almost as if the production of literature implied a houseful of servants, holidays abroad, constant champagne, and an endless verbal stream of social cleverness and wit. The pilot program the filmmaker hoped would wring money from the National Endowment he titled "A Question of Class: English Literary Life, 1918–1945." It should have been titled "A Question of Classiness." The film, based on interviews with surviving elderly remnants of the British upper class, enlivened by tunes from showbiz hits of the period, was never completed. Hynes and I were paid little or nothing for our embarrassing complicity (I was filmed in a deeply shaming interview with Anthony Powell), and the world was spared a further exhibition of the gulf between responsible thought and piquant show business. The pilot antedated by some years *Lifestyles of the Rich and Famous*, but its mode was roughly the same. As if by secret agreement, Sam Hynes and I seldom allude to our degradation, in which, as usual with the TV exploitation of intellectuals, vanity played a considerable part.

Meanwhile, I was continuing to read for my book on the Second World War, and as my savings gradually diminished, I became interested in the offers of further teaching jobs the mail brought from time to time. I was in my late fifties, and, God willing, had a good ten years of teaching left in me. Stanford solicited me, but a visit out there persuaded me that the only place to live would be an undistinguished little cedar-shakes bungalow costing $1 million. Besides, I thought there would be something ignominious in returning to a California I'd made such a to-do about despising, and the place seemed now in many ways worse than when I'd left, having in the meantime produced both Richard Nixon and Ronald Reagan and their rabid fans. Finally, an offer from the University of Pennsylvania allowed me to remain happily in the East.

Before I left the New Brunswick–Princeton area for good, I felt the need for some sort of private ceremony recognizing the twenty-eight years I'd spent happily teaching at Rutgers. One Saturday, when I knew the classrooms would be unused and the campus largely deserted, I paid a sentimental visit to the places I'd taught in, pausing in each classroom to recall favorite students and moments of intellectual and psychological pleasure. The satirist smiled at the impulse of colleges to dignify buildings, no matter how ordinary, as "halls," but the sentimentalist indulged the melancholy thought that when deserted by students, classrooms are dead in a way no other public spaces are. What ecstasies and shames have been experienced in these neutral rooms, with their characterless fixed-arm chairs, blackboards, and teachers' desks. What intellectual beauty has had its moments there in the midst of such depressing plainness and utility. What spirits have soared at the A on the returned paper, and what tears have gathered to greet the D. College students are so fresh, so noisy, and so beautiful that their absence from empty classrooms is unignorably melodramatic and touching. They and their charming loquacity pass, but the room is silent, and it remains, in its permanence and anonymity making its ironic comment: "You young people will grow old; your hopes and certainties alike will fade away; your vigor and beauty will vanish; you will be replaced by others like you, equally self-certain and self-concerned." Every empty classroom echoes the substance of Ecclesiastes, warning the happy, careless young that the days are coming "when the keepers of the house shall tremble, and the strong men shall bow themselves, and the grinders cease because they are few, and those that look out of the windows be darkened." And warning that one should acquire wisdom (not, notice, information, cunning, or technique) before the inevitable, before "the silver cord be loosed, or the golden bowl be broken, or the pitcher be broken at the fountain, or the wheel broken at the cistern." That is, Many Die, You Shall Also.

The gulf pointed to there, the gulf between youth and age, innocence and experience, levity and seriousness, was obsessing me as never before, and I now realized that it had been my only subject all along, manifested now as a focus on metaphor, now as irony, and now as the attention of the satirist to the vast distance between the ideal and the actual. And after a few years at Penn, a new gulf presented itself.

Penn was a splendid place. The faculty was serious, learned, and productive, and the students were bright and willing, although in most respects no more impressive than the best students at Rutgers. What was different was that they weren't, by and large, gathered from merely one American state, and that not a large one, but came from all over the United States, and from Asia and Europe as well. Morale, among both students and staff, was high, in part because of Ivy League vanity, in part because the country seemed to take the place seriously, sending, for example, presidents' wives and cabinet officers to decorate commencements and plucking off teachers and administrators for elevated government jobs in "culture," science, and economics.

Economics: the very word is like a bell, signaling for me a vivid awareness of another abyss, the one separating liberal learning from vocational, the disinterested from the self-interested. I'd never taught before at an institution where the studies aiming to stretch the intellect and make real the whole course of human history seemed to take second place to those designed to help students make lots of money. Many American universities, alas, had business schools, but Penn seemed unique in offering degrees in business not just to university graduates hankering after master's degrees but to undergraduates as well, who as freshmen could enroll in the Wharton School of Business and take commercial and managerial courses from the beginning. This struck me as a terrible sellout to money, like the habit at Penn of giving buildings ("halls") brand names to gratify corporate donors skilled less in the decencies of learning than in advertising and merchandising. The Revlon Center at Penn is an example, named after a brand of nail polish and lipstick. It's a question how much of the parlor Marxism and emphasis on Political Correctness that brought ridicule to the university during the eighties and nineties were simply a reaction on the part of the humanely educated to the shameless capitalistic vocationalism being vended at the Wharton School.

And worse: illiberal censorship amounting to outright fraud, on the advertising model. Over the years, the *Daily Pennsylvanian,* the independent student newspaper, has honored in action the axiom of all respectable journalists: what someone doesn't want you to publish is journalism. All else is publicity. On Alumni Day, May 15, 1987, thousands of Penn graduates, including hundreds from the Wharton School, assembled for old times' sake. That day's *Daily Pennsylvanian* observed the occasion with a story headed "Alumni Return for Graduation Weekend." The headline went on to the heart of the matter: "Record Gifts Expected." But regrettably, on the front page some unpleasant facts greeted the alumni: "Four Students Arrested for Dealing Drugs: Report Names Senior [University] VP in Police Cover-Up." But there was worse. An article in the most conspicuous place on the front page, the upper-right-hand position, delivered this news: "Wharton Prof Charged with Raping Child." It sounded like something you might find in a college paper's April Fools' Day edition, but it wasn't. The story revealed that a forty-seven-year-old professor of accounting had been arrested, charged, and released on $10,000 bail for allegedly committing offenses against his four-year-old step-granddaughter, including rape, statutory rape, involuntary deviate sexual intercourse, indecent assault, and corruption of a minor. As usual, copies of the *Daily Pennsylvanian* were available in stacks around the campus.

From the reaction of some professors and administrators at the Wharton School, the editors of the paper, confident of the facts in this sad story, facts that have never been disputed, could infer with some pride that they were performing real journalism, not cover-up, publicity, or institutional advertising. Apparently despairing of rebutting the unpleasant facts or asserting their falsity, the Wharton authorities simply began removing and hiding the newspapers so that the well-heeled alumni wouldn't see them.

If this attempt to cover up unwelcome facts was unseemly, not just at a university devoted, presumably, to the free play of the mind over all subjects, but anywhere the First Amendment might be conceived as a guide to civilized behavior, worse was the statement of justification emanating from the office of the dean of the Wharton School once the Alumni Day scandal had become well known:

> *The Wharton School confirms that on Friday, May 15, copies of the* Daily Pennsylvanian *were removed from two buildings at the school, and it is regrettable that this has caused concern within the university community.*
>
> *The Wharton School strongly believes in freedom of speech and of the press, but it also believes in news reporting that reflects all facets — the positive as well as the negative — of the University. Friday's edition of the* Daily Pennsylvanian, *which focused on allegations of rape, drug use, and administrative cover-ups, was most inappropriate and not balanced reporting when 3,000 alumni were returning to their alma mater. Many who saw the front page felt that the overall negative impression conveyed to alumni was not reflective of the current state of a great University that has much to be proud of.*

It may not be necessary to point to the more swinish elements of that statement: the evasive passive voice *(copies . . . were removed)* and pompus waffle *(it is regrettable),* cunningly avoiding mention of the agents of action so that the misdemeanor can be pinned on no one specific;

the notion that some facts are most inappropriate because they are unpleasant, despite their being published in a privileged setting devoted to little more (it was once thought) than free inquiry and the development of bold intellect and fearless utterance; the phrase *balanced reporting,* designed to conceal the meaning, *reporting I like because it makes me and my school look good.* And finally, the assumption that the function of independent news reporting is to publicize "the current state of a great University" rather than to deliver accurate data, regardless of its ultimate use or implications.

In addition, how could the newspaper in this case convey positive as well as negative "facts"? It tried to give the accused a chance to reveal the silver lining in his indictment, but when phoned he declined to indicate a positive side — indeed, to comment at all on the charges. Nor did his lawyer consent to suggest a positive side. Writing an angry essay about this scandal and wanting to be certain of the facts, I sent a prepublication copy to the dean of the Wharton School, informing him that I was going to publish it and asking him to please correct facts he thought wrong. In his reply, he wrote, "Relative to the inquiry you made, the facts in your account are not correct because . . . significant facts have been left out." And then, an attempt to frighten me off by mention of *an attorney:* "We received an attorney's opinion at the time of the incident that might indicate that your conclusions are incorrect as well." I answered, "I am as anxious as you are that the facts in my essay be correct, but I can't correct any errors unless you tell me which facts are incorrect. Can you indicate specifically where my facts are wrong? Then I'll be happy to make corrections." There was no reply. Three years later the dean of the Wharton School resigned. Did my agitation hasten his departure? I'd like to think so, and to think it also exposed the quality of moral reasoning and behavior to be found among the administrators of a high-class university school of business. After all, it's not easy to shake off advertising and publicity habits after a lifetime. Lest anyone feel unambiguous pleasure at the outcome of this affair, it's essential to know that the poor accused professor was convicted, sentenced to a considerable term in prison, and after a few weeks there, hanged himself in his cell.

"A bit of a troublemaker" — so I was designated by the president of the University of Pennsylvania after I'd published the view that intellectually pretentious universities would do well to scale down, if not abandon entirely, their high-powered athletic programs, which seem, when you think about it, to have little to do with their proper (their only?) business, the development of intellect, so sorely needed in the United States. It was certainly as a troublemaker that I ruined one social evening at the president's house. His wife's mother was an honored guest. She sat next to me at the table. Desiring to make some high-class literary conversation with the nice professor of English, she asked me, "What do you think of Lillian Hellman?" At the moment Hellman and Mary McCarthy were embroiled in their famous lawsuit arising from McCarthy's public assault on Hellman's honesty. I was very much on McCarthy's side, and I answered, "I think she's a liar," mindful of Hellman's twists and turns during her Stalinist period. My harmless neighbor said nothing in reply. She quietly folded her napkin, placed it gently on the table, and left the room.

The essay about the shame of the Wharton School appeared in *Thank God for the Atom Bomb and Other Essays,* and the title essay, published first in the *New Republic,* was also not innocent of a desire to make trouble. There, I argued autobiographically that to the ground troops about to invade Japan, the atom bombing of Hiroshima and Nagasaki was hardly an occasion for guilt. Just the opposite — rejoicing and relief so overwhelming that it was hard to hold back tears, and gratitude so genuine that even those who had spent the preceding months violating many of the Commandments, especially "Thou shalt not kill," assumed that their standing with the Almighty was still so unimpaired that they could without anomaly thank Him most fervently.

I knew that the "Thank God" essay, although gratifying to the aging ex-infantrymen, would annoy pacifists, certain social scientists, international reformers, and others ignorant of the ugly physical and psychological details of the war they had little intimate knowledge of. Letters poured into the *New Republic*, celebratory ones from combat veterans, and expressions of outrage and rebuke, virtually all from obvious noncombatants. One letter writer called my arguments on behalf of the soon-to-be-immolated invasion troops "monstrous mitigations"; another stigmatized Harry Truman's decision to drop the bombs as "a very grave *moral* mistake," ignoring the embarrassment that war itself, the very quintessence of immoral activity with its mass murders of the innocent, seems not an appropriate context for invoking moral criteria. One of my intentions was to strike back at the high-minded and unimaginative and thus achieve an infantryman's small revenge against remote, insulated observers of the war laboring under something close to Owen's "insensibility." One such I singled out by name in the essay. He was J. Glenn Gray, author after the war of *The Warriors: Reflections on Men in Battle* (1959). Curiously, I'd encountered him one afternoon in 1944, behind the line. F Company was resting and recuperating in an Alsation town. Gray was in the Counterintelligence Corps, ferreting out evidence of German espionage against American forces. In pursuit of their duties, CIC men could assume the insignia of any military rank they needed for plausibility or deception. J. Glenn Gray approached me as a young lieutenant colonel and ordered me to deploy my platoon to assist him as he burst into a nearby house in search of a spy. My men were to cover all side and rear doors and windows to prevent the spy's escape. Gray entered the house by the front door, pistol in hand, but there proved to be no spy in the house, and after a few minutes my people were released to return to their billets and their bitching, sock mending, rifle cleaning, and coffee heating. I never saw Glenn Gray again, but I was aware that normally he resided at division or even corps headquarters, where I presume he returned after his visit to the front and his little exercise with my platoon.

In most ways Gray was an admirable man, and his outlook on everything was noble, elevated, and responsible. After the war he became a much-admired professor of philosophy at Colorado College and an esteemed editor of Heidegger. But *The Warriors,* his meditation on the moral and psychological dimensions of modern soldiering, betrays his remoteness from experience. Division headquarters is miles — *miles* — behind the places where soldiers suffer abject terror and madness and relieve the pressure by crazy brutality and sadism. Indeed, unless they actually encountered the enemy during the war, and encountered him face to face, most "soldiers" have little idea what war is like. Despite his sensitivity and intelligence, Gray's optimistic and congratulatory view of human nature never underwent testing on the line. He never witnessed things like the Great Turkey Shoot. Thus he was able to write, "When news of the atomic bombing of Hiroshima and Nagasaki came, many an American soldier felt shocked and ashamed." Shocked, yes, but why ashamed? Because we'd killed civilians? We'd been doing that for years, and as a matter of policy, in raids on Hamburg and Cologne and Frankfurt and Mannheim and Dresden and Tokyo, and besides, the two A-bombs wiped out ten thousand Japanese troops. If in the rear some of the soldiers Gray talked to felt ashamed, down in the rifle companies no one did, for the bombs saved those soldiers' young lives, and they had learned from close combat how much they loved those lives. But, writes Gray, "The combat soldier knew better than did Americans at home what those bombs meant in suffering and injustice. The man of conscience realized intuitively that the vast majority of Japanese in both cities were no more, if no less guilty of the war than were his own parents, sisters, or brothers." As I commented, perhaps a bit too rudely, "I find this canting nonsense," reminding readers that the purpose of the atom bombs was not to "punish" people but to stop the war. I went on to observe that the pity is not that the bombs were dropped on the Japanese but that they weren't ready in time to be dropped on the Germans, thus stopping their suicidal resistance. If only the bombs could have been produced faster and dropped at the right moment on Hitler's headquarters (where Colonel Von Stauffenberg's July 20, 1944, bomb didn't do the job because it wasn't big enough), much of the Nazi hierarchy could have been pulverized immediately, saving the lives of around four million Jews, Poles, Slavs, and Gypsies, not to mention the lives and limbs of millions of Allied — and German — soldiers. If the bombs had only been ready in time, the boys in my platoon would not have been so cruelly killed and wounded.

The future intellectual historian who will write *The History of American Canting in the Twentieth Century* will find much to study and interpret in the utterances of those who dilate on the special wickedness of the A-bomb droppers. Such a position can perform for the speaker a valuable double function. First, it can display the fineness of his moral weave. And second, by implication it can also inform the audience that during the war he was not so socially unfortunate as to find himself down there with the ground forces, where he might have had to compromise the purity and clarity of his moral system in the interest of survival. Down there, which is where you find the people you and I don't normally know (just as we probably don't know anyone who was killed in Vietnam), down there is the place where coarse self-interest is the rule. When the hysterical young enemy soldier comes running toward you with wild eyes, firing, do you shoot him in the foot, hoping he'll be hurt badly enough to drop or misaim the gun he's going to kill you with, or do you shoot him in the chest (or if you're a prime shot, in the head) to make sure that you, not he, will survive that mortal moment?

As a result of my differing so strongly and satirically from the views of the late Glenn Gray, which I regarded as shamefully unearned, I heard from his relatives, annoyed that I'd besmirched the memory of a good man. That he was a good man I did not deny, but his being so conspicuously a good man was, I answered, part of the trouble. War is no place to practice his kind of goodness, and allowing it to color one's vision is to get things seriously wrong, to mislead oneself and others.

In *Wartime: Understanding and Behavior in the Second World War*, I continued campaigning against the ignorant notion that the war wasn't really so bad. My adversaries were all those who would see nothing significant in the elimination of the ironic quotation marks around Studs Terkel's title *"The Good War."* In some letters and diaries from the war edited by Ronald Blythe, we find a London air-raid warden describing a little boy fetched out of a fire who kept saying, "My little widdle, my little widdle," as he searched for it with his hands. But it had been burnt off. Blythe ends his anthology with a famous letter of farewell written by a flight officer to his mother. He says, "For all that can be said against it, I still maintain that this war is a very good thing; every individual is having his chance to give and dare all for his principle like the martyrs of old." Tell that to the boy who lost his widdle.

In *Wartime* I focused so vigorously on military misapprehensions and errors, on all the army cruelties and fatuities I could find, that the book could be read as a satire on human nature in general. Nearing the end, I began to look for some memorable counterbalancing evidence of human decency. I found it in the behavior of Dwight D. Eisenhower as he waited for the Normandy invasion to succeed — or fail. On a torn-out notebook page he wrote out in pencil a statement to release if the operation should abort and if he had to withdraw the troops — with what losses and shame can only be imagined. At the end of his short statement, he added, "If any blame or fault attaches to this attempt, it is mine alone." The word "noble" isn't heard much today, but that moment deserves it, constituting, as I wrote, "a bright signal in a dark time." Eisenhower's words suggest a general moral principle for all administrators and executive officers: when you succeed, give all the credit to others; when you fail, take all the blame yourself. *Wartime* derives as much from a nineteen-year-old's immersion in Mencken as from a seventy-year-old's residual anger. It's amazing how the events of a life sometimes give an illusion of coherence, of things coming full circle. In 1990 *Wartime* was lucky enough to receive a prize from the Free Press Association, and the name of the prize was the Mencken Award.

Increasingly as I've grown older, I find myself brought close to tears by evidence of such nobility as Eisenhower's on that desperate occasion. And I know I'm not the only elderly person who finds it hard to remain unmoved at church services (any denomination), weddings, and commencements — much harder on me than funerals. It's hope ritualized that gets to me, or evanescent beauty and youth in any form. And despite some of my critical views about America, the very idea of the Constitution moves me, for there's an implication in it of the essential decency of ordinary people who make up the electorate, crazily as they may behave on occasion. That implication, however false, does honor to human nature and to the admirable hope that people will act justly and wisely if given the chance. I can't stroll through any military cemetery without choking up — not so much for the dead boys, who are, thank God, now out of it, but for their families, who can never be wholly happy again.

During my final years of teaching, I had to be very careful what I talked about, and quoted, in front of a class, for I found I could not navigate unmoved through certain things. The heroic, noble ending of Christopher Smart's *A Song to David* always broke me up, like Matthew Arnold's *The Scholar Gypsy,* both of them tributes to human courage and intense focus enlisted for valuable ends. Years ago I found I could no longer read aloud in front of a class Eliot's "New Hampshire," from *Landscapes.* The lines suggesting children's outdoor play,

> *To-day grieves, to-morrow grieves,*
> *Cover me over, light in leaves . . . ,*

came too close to commenting on the innocence about their forthcoming deaths and burials of the happy young people before me. I can no longer read dry-eyed Emerson's "Concord Hymn," nor hear the hymn "Abide with Me." Even the words of my boyish letter to my parents about returning from the bivouac at Camp Roberts, my saying that despite our pains and exhaustion, we were marching "tall and proud," can trigger tears.

"Did Professor Fussell stop teaching the poems of Robert Herrick because he found reactionary and wicked Herrick's adhesions to a rigorously hierarchical society that places women in a lowly position?

"Not at all. He stopped teaching Herrick because he found it hard not to cry in public when he came upon lines from 'To Daffodils' like

We have short time to stay as you,
We have as short a spring;
As quick a growth to meet decay
As you, or anything."

If you don't want to see me go all to water, don't perform in my vicinity "Amazing Grace" — the slow bagpipe version is the most potent — taps, or, for some reason, "O Canada," although I can listen quite unmoved to "The Star-Spangled Banner." Is this vulnerability to sentimental emotion the result of simple aging, with attendant self-pity, or has it something to do with the war?

Any wounded veteran will assure you that for him the war has never ended. It's impossible for me to affect forgetfulness when each month the government check awarded for my 40 percent disability arrives, and when each winter the wet cold awakens pain in my leg wound. I still think of the faculty men's room as the officers' latrine. I still let angry, disgusted army rhetoric burst forth, as when I refer to a dim colleague as "that dumb fuck" or silently urge some slowpoke in line to *move your ass.* I still have army dreams, although now they're likely to be more technical than terrifying. In a recent one, I was somehow in charge of a case of neatly packed, wax-shined mortar shells, painted olive drab with yellow markings, and looking beautiful, like distinguished works of sculpture. Instead of the standard sixty or eighty-one millimeters in diameter, they were six inches across. In the dream scene, there were no clear orders about what I should do with them. Were they to be dropped into tubes? If so, where were the tubes, and what were we aiming at? Regardless, I was ravished by the shells' inert, passive beauty, while slightly scared of the menace they represented. Again, sometimes I waste time devising wild schemes of revenge against the Germans. Like even today resettling them all in Madagascar and making over the former "Germany" to the Jews, to be renamed "Israel North." All this serves to flesh out Martha Gellhorn's observation about those of us who grew up in the 1940s: "War was our condition and our history, the place we had to live in." And the end of the war was not the end of the disaster, as Howard Nemerov understands in "Redeployment":

> *They say the war is over. But water still*
> *Comes bloody from the taps, and my pet cat*
> *In his disorder vomits worms which crawl*
> *Swiftly away. Maybe they leave the house.*
> *These worms are white, and flecked with the cat's blood.*

The war may be over. I know a man
Who keeps a pleasant souvenir, he keeps
A soldier's dead blue eyeballs that he found
Somewhere — hard as chalk, and blue as slate.
He clicks them in his pocket while he talks.

And it's not just ex-soldiers for whom the war will never be over. In the late forties I was having lunch alone in a Cambridge restaurant. A middle-aged woman was watching me so closely that I felt uncomfortable. Did I know her? Had we met somewhere? Suddenly, without warning, she burst into uncontrollable tears.

Did I remind her of her dead son?

Had she been angry for a long time too?

COPYRIGHT ACKNOWLEDGMENTS

INDEX

ABOUT THE AUTHOR

PAUL FUSSELL was born in Pasadena, California, and educated at Pomona College. In the Second World War he was a twenty-year-old army lieutenant, the leader of a rifle platoon in the 103rd Infantry Division in France. He was severely wounded in the spring of 1945. After the war he earned a Ph.D. at Harvard and has since pursued a career as a literary scholar and critic, writing and editing many books on eighteenth-century British literature, poetic technique, travel writing, and military culture, together with two volumes of social and cultural criticism. His book *The Great War and Modern Memory* won the National Book Award for Arts and Letters in 1976 as well as the National Book Critics Circle Award for Criticism and the Ralph Waldo Emerson Award of Phi Beta Kappa. He has held fellowships from the Guggenheim Foundation, the National Endowment for the Humanities, and the Rockefeller Foundation and taught at Connecticut College, Rutgers University, the University of Heidelberg, King's College London, and the University of Pennsylvania. He lives in Philadelphia with his wife, journalist Harriette Behringer.